The Chief Security Officer's Handbook

The Chief Security Officer's Handbook
Leading Your Team into the Future

Michael Allen

Chief Security Officer, Financial Services, Toronto, Canada

ACADEMIC PRESS

An imprint of Elsevier

ELSEVIER

Academic Press is an imprint of Elsevier
125 London Wall, London EC2Y 5AS, United Kingdom
525 B Street, Suite 1650, San Diego, CA 92101, United States
50 Hampshire Street, 5th Floor, Cambridge, MA 02139, United States
The Boulevard, Langford Lane, Kidlington, Oxford OX5 1GB, United Kingdom

Notices
Knowledge and best practice in this field are constantly changing. As new research and experience
broaden our understanding, changes in research methods, professional practices, or medical treatment
may become necessary.

Practitioners and researchers must always rely on their own experience and knowledge in evaluating
and using any information, methods, compounds, or experiments described herein. In using such
information or methods they should be mindful of their own safety and the safety of others, including
parties for whom they have a professional responsibility.

To the fullest extent of the law, neither the Publisher nor the authors, contributors, or editors, assume
any liability for any injury and/or damage to persons or property as a matter of products liability,
negligence or otherwise, or from any use or operation of any methods, products, instructions, or ideas
contained in the material herein.

Library of Congress Cataloging-in-Publication Data
A catalog record for this book is available from the Library of Congress

British Library Cataloguing-in-Publication Data
A catalogue record for this book is available from the British Library

ISBN: 978-0-12-818384-7

For information on all Academic Press publications
visit our website at https://www.elsevier.com/books-and-journals

Publisher: Stacy Masucci
Acquisition Editor: Elizabeth Brown
Editorial Project Manager: Isabella C. Silva
Production Project Manager: Paul Prasad Chandramohan
Cover Designer: Matthew Limbert

Typeset by SPi Global, India

To Janine my inspiration
A special thanks to the hardworking and patient team at Elsevier and to those who believed I could get through this Mike Hurst, CPP, MSyI, FIRP, Jonathon Harris, PSP, CPP, Eddie Sorrells, CPP, PSP, PCI, and of course Lawrence (Larry) J. Fennelly a living legend and great mentor!

Contents

About the Author

Mike (Michael) Allen is a Canadian security executive specializing in enterprise security, premises protection, and risk assessment. Mike has years of experience in security metrics, facilities emergency response, international security operations, and leadership. Mike has held security management roles for hotels, commercial office towers, and a major Canadian bank.

Mike has more than 20 years of progressive experience in the security field, most of which have been in premises and financial institution security management. Mike is an advocate of public and private partnerships, the convergence of related practices, and elevating the security profession. He has earned numerous professional designations including the Certified Protection Professional (CPP), Physical Security Professional (PSP), and the Professional Certified Investigator (PCI) from ASIS International. He has also earned the Certified Fraud Examiner (CFE) designation from the Association of Certified Fraud Examiners, the Certified Anti-Terrorism Officer (cATO) from the International Association for Counterterrorism and Security Professionals, he is a Certified Protection Officer (CPO) from the International Foundation for Protection Officers (IFPO); and has the Certified Lodging Security Director (CLSD) designation from the American Hotel and Lodging Educational Institute. Mike completed a certificate in Security Management from New Buckinghamshire University in the UK. Mike is currently the Chief Security Officer for a premier Canadian financial institution.

Mike has lectured for the ASIS International Toronto Chapter certification program sessions for several years. Mike has served as the secretary and treasurer for the Overseas Security Advisory Council (OSAC) in Toronto. Mike has written articles, provided interviews, presentations, and commentary on various topics with Canadian Security Magazine. Mike is an occasional guest speaker at local colleges and various associations on travel security, personal security, cybersecurity, and risk management. In 2009, Mike was named among a few upcoming security professionals in Security Director News' 20 Under 40.

Introduction

The Chief Security Officer's Handbook is intended to draw critical thinking from the reader about how they operate today, where enterprise security risk management is headed, and how to seamlessly align their programs with the goals of their enterprises.

As security professionals progress from security specialist to expert and finally as a leader, they need to align the security program with the enterprise. The time of trying to create a separate mission and brand for Corporate Security is gone. Security executives must adopt the goals, missions, values, and visions of their employers to succeed. Leaders in Enterprise Security Risk Management must get out of the comfort zone and embrace change. It is our place to help our employers make risk-informed decisions and we too must take calculated risks and forge ahead into the future. We may face obstacles as does any business leader. This book will provide guidance on how to move forward to a brighter and better tomorrow.

Security professionals play an important role. As a business leader who manages the security program, understand life safety, asset protection, and have a passion for this career, you have arrived. Now its time to elevate the profession and the positive impact we have for our employers. Be proud of being security professionals. This book will provide insight into how we can accomplish this together.

Understanding how we will work 10, 15, and 20 years from today and; how to adapt to and implement these cutting-edge strategies and technologies is laid out through these chapters. Enterprise Security Risk Management, Artificial Intelligence, and modern leadership are discussed here. Security leaders are professionals in the traditional sense of the word. They are more educated, credentialed, and integrated into the organization than in previous generations. This new hyper-connected and well-prepared group of leaders will advance exponentially in the next few short years. Tomorrow is here, the time to review the topics discussed in this book, explore each topic in greater detail with your peers, and continuously strive to perform as forward-thinking business leaders are now.

I hope you enjoy your road to discovery.

Mike Allen

Corporate security today

1

Defining corporate security

Corporate security can be described as the corporate function responsible for the strategy, direction, and execution of an enterprise assets protection program.

This book examines the dichotomy of security departments, programs, and their leaders as they are structured and function today. It also explores where the profession is heading. There are large highly skilled security teams working for critical infrastructures, such as utilities, financial institutions, chemical producers, communications, and healthcare to name a few. Many large corporations employ security at both the premise level and corporate level, we will explore how the roles and responsibilities differ and yet complement one another. Security departments in the classical sense such as guards, gates, and cameras will be discussed. The key theme will be the departments most often employed at and/or under the head office leadership, responsible for enterprise security risk management (ERSM). This department may be called many things security and investigations, enterprise physical security, protection services, protection programs, and most commonly corporate security. Their leader, the chief security officer (CSO), is often the most senior official responsible and accountable for the department.

This department is less hands-on or operational and tactical in its execution of its responsibilities than the colleagues who secure the premises, vessels, and operations. Corporate security is a strategic function closely aligned with the core mandate of the enterprise it supports. For years, the mission of corporate security may have been driven by the needs of the enterprise, the interest of leadership and the direction set by the CSO. As companies have become more global, threats are more plentiful and the cost of reputational and litigation losses more damaging, corporate security is no longer a luxury but rather a necessity.

Many security professionals responsible for the corporate security function struggle with trying to get the recognition, funding, attention, and resources for their department. Corporate security is a sum of its parts. The performance of the people, the capability and capacity of the chief, the output of the department in its ability to produce large volumes of high quality results quickly are the keys to success. By focusing on enhancing its value to the enterprise, revaluating itself on a regular basis, never losing sight of the mandate, being resilient and always willing to adapt to change the department will continue to move in the right direction.

The Chief Security Officer's Handbook. https://doi.org/10.1016/B978-0-12-818384-7.00001-X

What defines a chief security officer?

This is a question that many ask, few know, and that most of us want to define. The most senior and accomplished security leaders I have had the pleasure of meeting and collaborating with, like their C-Suite counterparts, spend little time thinking about this and instead use that time and energy in doing the great things that make them CSOs. If better defining helps to enhance the future of this role and the next generation of security leaders then I provide you with some considerations here.

Security management directly at or in large buildings, malls, venues, hotels, casinos, amusement parks, cruise ships, and manufacturing facilities, for example, are referred to here as the tactical and operational aspect of security. This is the foundation of a good program. These are often first responders, their experience in dealing with people, emergencies, and often with less equipment and authority than their public sector counterparts could fill volumes with their expert knowledge of detection, deterrence, and response.

Security managers may be in-house directly employed by the corporation or contracted where the security manager works for a third-party guard service provider. These managers may provide security for any one of the few examples listed above.

Security management exists on many levels, as a function of the corporate office for a security service (guard personnel) provider or in the form of people directly employed by a corporation who may report to and work at the corporate office.

These leaders may directly supervise the work of security professionals carrying out and executing the work such as regional and premise management, guarding, loss prevention, etc. This book focuses on in-house the CSO working for large corporations. Earlier publications suggested that the future role of the CSO would be to manage both the physical and information security programs. We now see clearly defined CSO and chief information security officer (CISO) specializations. This book examines the various CSO roles in corporate security, embraces the concept of convergence discussed later and a few different job titles for CSOs. Example department structures, across a range of industries are provided. The book will illustrate the head of security's functions and scope further.

Updated resources are available, such as the *Standard (CSO): Chief Security Officer—An Organizational Model (2013). ASIS Commission on Standards and Guidelines. ASIS International.*

One may ask, what makes one a security director or CSO. Who should be called director security? Is it the person who manages 10 personnel in a major bank including global security specialists, managers, and senior managers all with significant credentials? This director security often reports up to two or three more senior layers of leadership within corporate security. Their team offer a wide scope of services and are often global in their work. Is the leader in a high-end hotel/condo complex with 25 security personnel responsible for security, health, and fire life safety what we define as a director security? Perhaps the level of responsibility is in fact the same, the level of qualifications and compensation does often vary and a global bank's core earnings are significantly greater than that of a single hotel. The mandate and workplace are often the differentiators. In most cases, a corporate security director is responsible for less detail in a premise security program but has responsibility for many locations and are compensated considerably more than a security director in most single premises.

What makes a CSO? Do you have to lead corporate security in a fortune 100 company with cybersecurity, physical security, and investigations under your purview? What about the leader in a large insurance company that owns and leases tens of millions of square feet in office property and manages several areas of asset protection globally? The CSO Center for Leadership and Development of ASIS International outlines some basic parameters to qualify as a member, which is a reasonable example of how to define a CSO. Often the CSO is identified as the senior most security leader in an organization globally. Some CSOs are recognized as directors, managing director's, vice presidents, and senior vice presidents. No different than corporate accountants and lawyers there is no one size fits all, nor is there a need to be.

There are security directors responsible for the physical security for multinational conglomerates with several direct reports. There are CSOs leading security for the worlds largest cruise ships, focused on physical security and emergency response. There are CSOs who are responsible for mid-sized organizations and those with a single landmark premise. Some of the latter, however, are responsible for physical security, investigations, parking, information security, emergency response, business continuity, crisis response, disaster recovery, health, and fire life safety. To date staffing, responsibilities, scope, and title vary considerably and that is no different than many other professional roles across many industries and geography.

As we progress through the foundations and future of these departments, roles and programs the reader will see a trend emerge where the CISO's role will be discussed and then merged with the CSO's role of today, giving rise the CSO of tomorrow.

Corporate security department structures

Provided here are a few structural examples of corporate security departments. Additionally, some larger, very specialized departments at single locations and vessels are included too. The skills found at a medium-sized urban condominium building compared to that of a large hotel and casino complex or large cruise ship are often different. A higher set of skills, compensation, and responsibilities are more often found in the latter.

To simplify the following illustrations and figures, corporate security departments will be broken into two groups. Group A and Group B in no order. In Group A we have banking, financial services, insurance, investment, information technology (hardware, software, social media, and internet service providers), telecommunications and broadcasting. In Group B we have security services, education, manufacturing, health care, pharmaceutical, oil, gas and chemical, commercial real estate, utilities (e.g., power producers, nuclear, hydroelectric, coal, etc.), tourism, amusement (theme) parks, cruise lines, recreation, large urban retail (malls), consumer goods, and retail conglomerates to name a few.

The products, services, and operations may vary between the two groups listed above. The corporate security function will usually remain the same. Corporate security departments are generally concerned with the protection of people, premises, and assets against terrorism, cyberattack, travel safety risks, emergency, and crisis response which are only a few examples. Group A may have three locations in a single country where there have never been any significant earthquakes; this country may be subject to occasional acts of terrorism, mass shootings, and kidnappings. Group B may have operations of different types in more than thirty countries. The company may have faced numerous earthquakes, typhoons, and ice storms. At many of their locations gun violence is almost nonexistent and there are almost no corporate travelers. These companies, their corporate security departments and CSO's understand all the same principles of business and security, although their needs and focus will vary.

In Group A, there may be upward of a couple of hundred corporate security professionals (security experts, investigators, business continuity professionals, and support specialists) in one location, often this is at corporate headquarters reporting to the CSO. Regionally this team may have security leaders who represent entire countries or continents that report to a local business leader and are dotted line reports of the CSO or small teams in these regions of security/investigators who report directly to a mid-level leader in corporate security. Fig. 1.1 provides a simplified organizational chart for the corporate security department under the CSO in the decade from the years 2010 to 2020. I recognize that some large Fortune 100 companies may already have structures and responsibilities ahead of their peers, the figures in this book starting with Fig. 1.1 are used to illustrate where the industry is on average today and within the decade suggested. In Fig. 1.1 you will notice that there is no mention of technology or information security. Very few companies have combined these departments today. Security managers and specialists are a larger portion of the staffing compliment than the support personnel. This means that through most of this decade it has not been uncommon to see a department with more security managers than analysts and support personnel. Similarly, the number of investigators is larger than the body of analysts. The use of metrics and data in this decade has become commonplace in corporate security. It is only recently that the automation of those metrics and reports using special software, databases, and the idea of machine learning discussed in greater detail later has become part of the CSOs strategy. Currently, a single administrator, coordinator, or analyst may be required to gather all the raw data from the security managers and investigators and crunch this data on spreadsheets to create the CSOs dashboard. As data become more abundant, completely digital, and the business model of the industries in Group A change, having a large complement of middle management, manual process driven, tactical, and operational personnel in corporate security is becoming impractical from a fiscal and output perspective.

In Group B a common structure today is to have a CSO at corporate headquarters who may have a team of 2–10 personnel. This group will be strategic in nature creating policies, contracts, and budgets for example. The organizations and industries

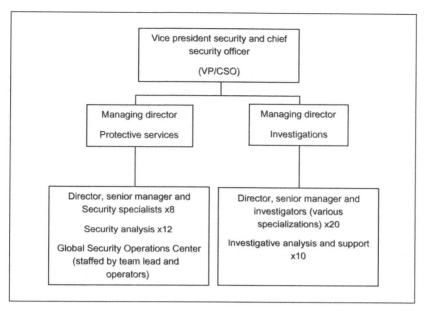

The numbers here represent full time employees (FTE).

FIG. 1.1

Example Group A: Organizational chart (2010–20).

in this group will likely have large security teams in the regions, at the premises or on the vessels. In some cases, such as cruise ships and nuclear power stations there is a CSO on-site or onboard. They will provide leadership to a team of practitioners starting at the guard level, with less focus on corporate security. In most cases, the field security leaders do not report to corporate security or the CSO located at head office. In Fig. 1.2, the corporate security department often has a small number of full-time employees (FTE), who have a large global mandate. There are a few additional specialists which may or may not be found in the departments in these industries. For example, health and safety are shown in Fig. 1.2, which may be a director reporting to the CSO could in some cases be a function reporting to facilities. Instead, there may be a director of crisis in that organization. Few of these programs will have full-scale executive protection, travel risk management, and similar programs. The focus will be heavily on the setting of standards and assessing the risk to the premises and assets. Only the most forward thinking today as seen in some of the largest commercial real estate firms will the CSO have responsibility for both physical and information security. In Fig. 1.2, we see a simplified example of a corporate security organizational chart from the years 2010 to 2020 for Group B.

I take the opportunity here to discuss some specifics of various corporate security departments as they are structured today in more detail.

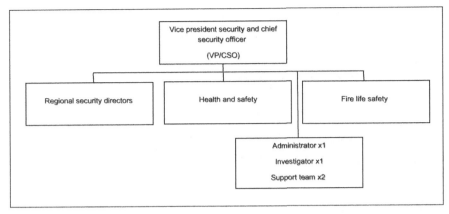

The numbers here represent full time employees (FTE).

FIG. 1.2

Example Group B: Organizational chart (2010–20).

Banking

A common structure for a CSO and corporate security department in a major bank or financial institution is to have a vice president and chief security officer (VP/CSO) or senior vice president and chief security officer (SVP/CSO) leading the department. There may be several assistant vice presidents or managing directors or senior directors. These are often the same level of the role; however, titles may vary from company to company. A leader of corporate security in financial services will often have a more senior title than that of their counterparts say in real estate or manufacturing. Both may very well lead global teams through complex issues. There is not always a clear reason for this. Sometimes how business leaders and human resource professionals view and value these roles from one industry to the next can be a factor. How we as security professional place ourselves, communicate, work, and operate may be a factor. Additionally, title creep has also plagued some industries, which may be a bubble that will burst in the future, this is beginning to occur today where some organizations are eliminating assistant vice president roles where they are individual contributors or only manage one department or function. In bank corporate security today the mid-level leaders responsible for security, operations, and/or investigations may supervise a handful of directors each who can be separated by geographic locations, although have the same duties or they may be in the same office and be responsible for different specializations (financial crimes, financial intelligence, physical security, preemployment screening, security operations center, protective services, and crisis and analysis) to name only a few.

The protective services (common security function) unit may deal with matters such as employee and executive protection, travel risk management (duty of care), workplace violence investigation and prevention, bank robbery prevention and response, physical security policy and standards, event security planning and coordination, security operations centers, and design.

The head office may be home to a couple of hundred corporate security personnel, while there may be regional teams of two to three parties; sometimes a security specialist and a couple of investigators. The head of physical security is often a director or managing director of security reporting up through the chain to the SVP and CSO. Few financial institutions have placed both information security and physical security and investigations under the same department. Fewer yet have placed investigations, information security, physical security, fraud, antimoney laundering, and antiterrorist financing under the same leadership. Where this has been done by a professional with an accounting, law or information technology background may lead the department. This will be explored later.

As seen in Fig. 1.1, security and investigations can be found under the corporate security umbrella. In the corporate security departments of some mid-sized banks, physical security and security operations have been merged the investigations and fraud program teams, under a CSO. Historically this CSO may report to legal, administration, audit and/or human resources. For this example, a mid-sized bank operates in several countries with retail banking in at least one country nationally.

The numbers of FTE used in the example organizational charts are for context. Staffing numbers will vary significantly from a national bank with 53,000 employees to a large international bank with 275,000 employees.

For years, security experts have tried to develop a formula to determine how many FTE they need. Is it based on regions, a ratio of security staff to every 10,000 employees their company has, how many locations, square feet, etc.? A professional will staff appropriately for the volumes and scope of work. CSOs tend to acquire more responsibility, enhance the depth at which their programs go to mitigate risks and have a role to play in the unpredictable nature of the crisis. For these reasons, they will always find plenty of work for their current staffing complement.

Insurance

A general department structure for corporate security in insurance companies today is to have a vice president corporate security who is responsible for both security and investigations as the CSO. Several large life insurance companies own a significant real estate footprint, commonly office towers. Real estate may be owned for corporate use, owned although leased to third-party tenants (sometimes the insurance company may be a small tenant leasing in one of its own buildings), a combination of both and or completely leased from another landlord for corporate use. In some cases, there is a vice president (VP) physical security and vice president investigations. A couple of the most mature programs operating today have a senior vice president of security that only consists of the physical security specialties. These large insurers may have two to three investigation departments operating separately from one another with different focus areas.

Technology service firms

Large tech firms, social media giants, and online shopping conglomerates have medium sized highly skilled corporate security departments. These departments are often headed by an SVP/CSO and commonly have one leader for investigations, people, and asset protection. The information and cybersecurity umbrella are sometimes lead by another group of experts. These departments work closely together and occasionally have some level of convergence. These corporate security departments and their CSOs are often better integrated into the core mandate of the enterprise than their peers. They embrace the platforms, products, and services their own organizations provide, and the department continues to align itself with all other key business units and the corporate strategy. This is where all CSOs need to move forward.

Heads of security in large telephone and internet providers spend less time than their peers sourcing staff who can manage and lead security systems projects (installing access control and cameras in the premises). They do not rely as heavily if at all on integrators. They have access to teams of networking and systems experts and can accomplish a lot of this in-house on existing applications, servers, and networks.

A CSO in a social media conglomerate or software company does not have to venture too far to find an application that will collect, sort, and provide threat intelligence, organize report data, and develop state- of-the-art dashboards. CSOs must learn to borrow these opportunities from one another. Leveraging existing recourses and consolidation will be explored further on.

Commercial real estate

Commercial real estate firms may own tens of millions of square feet in mixed-asset (office towers, shopping centers, residential, industrial, and commercial) premises, which they lease to third-party tenants. These companies may employ in-house or contract security managers at the premise. At corporate headquarters a team consisting of anywhere from 2 to 15 personnel forms a corporate security unit with national or global responsibilities. The team may be lead by a vice president security/chief security officer (VP/CSO). The premise security managers may report to the property director or the regional security director and or have a dotted line relationship to one and a direct reporting line to the other. The flattening of the organizational structure from a classic pyramid design has become a common theme. In this case, dotted line reporting begins to look like a matrix. This improves the flow of communication and breaks down the chain of command. Some security managers may find having more than one leader a challenge when the goals and objectives of the people they report to are not completely aligned.

Like other industries, it is often hard to manage teams effectively from a distance. Compounding this challenge for CSOs and/or their direct reports is when the local security manager/director receives conflicting objectives from location management (e.g., the building general manager or property director). When the budgets for the local security program are owned and managed by the local general manager, this can also cause friction if the CSO is directing the local security manager on how to spend those funds.

These are only a few of the factors as to why we see so many reporting models, titles, budgetary responsibility, and standards of practice today. Later we will explore where this will and needs to go to be successful. If you think of commercial real estate as you examine Fig. 1.2 you will see the simplicity of the department. As we go forward, we will see the general scope, size, and ownership of the departments grow, as well as its complexity which also follows the trend of hiring more experienced, better educated, and more technically inclined leaders. There are tasks performed by a few roles today that will merge into a single position in the near future making some aspect of the department structure easier to follow. We will discuss this evolution in later chapters.

Hospitality

The corporate security function at a hotel chain may be lead by a vice president and global head of security. There will be a couple of regional security directors who perform advisory services to the hotel general managers and security directors, conduct investigations, and threat risk assessments. These departments will set security standards, policies, and provide expert advice on the crisis. The local hotel security director often reports to the general manager of the hotel. The head of security for casinos is usually based at the casino. This role may lead to a large security force, surveillance, investigations, security and surveillance systems experts, and administration. You may also find many large casinos with hotels. On a cruise ship that has a hotel and casino, the CSO is often focused on the overall ship security first followed by the hotel and then casino. Where the casino and hotel exist together, the casino often gets the primary attention as they are "alive" oftentimes more than the hotel where people sleep, the gaming industry is highly regulated, and large sums of cash are in play.

Consumer goods

The enterprises that produce cereals, appliances, cleaning chemicals and nearly every other product in a household, often employ teams ranging from three to seven corporate security personnel. These parties are focused on assets, people, supply chain, and similar areas of protection. The factories, production, and warehousing are often serviced by local proprietary or contract security managers, and their guard force that are most often provided by a contract security firm. Corporate security will design and implement best practices for resiliency at the operations level. This may include emergency preparedness, crisis management, business continuity, and disaster recovery. Business continuity may have a much more information technology-based demand for those organizations listed in Group A and therefore it is often a function of reporting to the CISO or head of information technology in those enterprises. In Group B the business continuity planning function may be focused more on plant and production operations. In some cases, the function reports to corporate security and in turn the CSO.

Retail

The most senior leaders in today's largest retail loss prevention departments are usually global SVPs. Their information security counterparts are often the same SVPs as well. The SVP and CSOs lead multiservice corporate security functions responsible for common areas of corporate security to one side and store level loss prevention programs on the other. Loss prevention management usually working at the regional and store level focus on theft prevention and other key duties related to the direct prevention, detection, and recovery of fraud and product losses also referred to as shrinkage.

These corporate security departments like many others have a few experts leading different practice areas. It will be common to find an executive protection specialist on staff who may manage security personnel, events planning, security drivers, and assess office and residential security for the C-Suite. Travel security and event risk management, threat risk assessment, and other key functions may be led by mid-level managers and or specialists. These leaders have combinations of small FTE or contract to global security risk consultancies that provide experts on assignment.

Nuclear power and chemical producers

CSOs working for these industries are most often employed at the plant level. You may find armed, unarmed, and strategic security all directly supporting operations. The threat assessment, protection services, and security operations teams may vary by title but often provide strategic planning, security systems selection, integration, standards development, and risk assessments. Security and emergency services provide hands-on access control, patrol, and (threat and emergency) response services by uniformed highly trained personnel. The head of the security operations or strategic function is not often the CSO; this is more likely to be the head of the larger tactical side of the department. These CSOs are usually former senior military or law enforcement leaders.

Mining and utilities (power distribution)

These industries may have both site level and corporate level security. The VP and CSO are often leading the strategic direction of all security functions from the corporate head office. At head office, corporate security may be lead by a team of managers or directors. Their specialty areas may be divided as follows:

- threat risk and vulnerability assessments
- head office, protection, and travel and event security
- investigations
- risk and strategy (policies, standards, guidelines, procedures, metrics, etc.)

On-site at the plants you will often find a director of security operations overseeing the various plant and operations protection personnel. There may also be an emergency response team reporting to operations and or director security.

Petroleum (oil)

Some of the most advanced, well-structured health, safety, and security programs exist in the petroleum industry, from oil fields to offshore operations deep in the seabed, to oil rigs/platforms to refineries. With supply chains that span the globe by ship, rail, and transport, this industry invests heavily on the security of its people and product. The work itself is hazardous, the locations and transportation routes are often even more dangerous. Threats to pipelines and constant protests make it target a rich environment. Some of the policies and standards are the most stringent found in operational and corporate security. These departments are multitiered with experts at all levels in geographies spanning the globe. The CSO's often have extensive public and private sector experience, undergraduate to graduate level education and previous international experience. Understanding geopolitics, security, and environmental risk have been ingrained in the entire business, strategy, and operations for decades. Tools used to locate assets, satellites, GPS, and mapping used for drilling and offshore operations have been available to security long before most other industries. This compliments corporate security's alignment with the enterprise strategy and method of operations. The use of global consultancies and private intelligence firms is nothing new to this industry that maximizes these relationships. Like any industry where the corporate security group is chosen from a high caliber of candidates who are already exposed to cutting edge technology. An opportunity exists to enhance the security of field operations with tomorrow's technology and automation as these groups have a very hands-on role to play in securing heavily industrialized work locations.

Airlines

Airlines have operated with corporate security departments for decades. These departments have good relationships with law enforcement, intelligence, airport security and operations; and their counterparts. These departments may work on passenger and crew safety programs, response programs, investigations, and asset protection. Ensuring not only are their crew and planes safe and secure where they travel to and stay but also assessing the risk at airports where they depend on other service providers and hanger operations is critical to their mission. Their operations centers are state-of-the-art. The CSO is often a director or vice president. The CSO of an airline must have up to the minute situational awareness of world security, political, and environmental events. Airlines may be owned by the state, private, and or a combination of the two. This is a highly regulated business, where reputation, quality of service, and a competitive market impact the strategy of the enterprise. Airline CSOs must be sensitive to the pendulum-like opportunities and challenges that move very quickly in this industry. In one minute the executive attention and funding needed to drive security projects and expand often light resources are available and the next the purse strings are tightened and it's all hands-on-deck; a classic more with less situation. This is just another example of an industry where the CSO should be included in key business decisions; and where the CSO must focus on developing their business acumen as importantly as their security expertise.

Cruise ships

I decided to end the discussion of specific departments here with cruise lines and cruise ships. Large, multifunction corporate security departments at head office for cruise lines are rare. On the other hand, a team of security professionals led by a CSO onboard large cruise ships are quite normal. These vessels may weigh over 150,000 tons, can cost more than $500,000 million to build, have 7 to 18 stories on top and carry thousands of staff and passengers. These behemoths set out into the sea crossing vast oceans where the closest land and assistance will often be too far to help in a time of immediate crisis. The high caliber of these CSOs is crucial for a good life safety and security program. The security departments are often broken into groups who control access, entry screening, patrol, response, and management. Knowledge of medical and emergency response, nautical craft, security, law, and ship protocol are important for all levels of security personnel. In time corporate security departments with strong leaders of ship security operations will be employed at the head office will become the norm for all major cruise lines. The design of consistent prevention and response strategies will prove to be quite valuable. Information security already is and will become more important in the future as ships of all kinds including freight and shipping vessels become more and more automated and soon they will become nearly crewless and will eventually be driven completely by autopilots. Autonomous vessels of any kind will need high security onboard to reduce the impacts of piracy and significant cybersecurity investment.

In Fig. 1.3 you will notice less emphasis is placed on the number of investigators and security managers. We see a trend which follows today's federal law enforcement

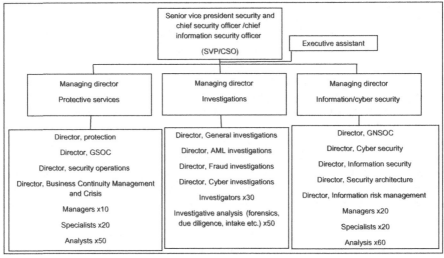

The numbers here represent full time employees (FTE).

FIG. 1.3

Example Group A: Organizational chart (2020–30).

and intelligence models with an increased body of analysts. The generalist role is beginning to shrink at the operations level and the hiring of more specialists is trending today. The span of control changes and fewer layers will comprise the department. Today one may find layers as follows:

- SVP/CSO
- VP
- AVP
- Directors
- Senior managers and managers
- Team leads
- Coordinators/security specialists
- Analysts/administrators

In the future, the layers of management will continue to reduce. Leaders with two programs and two direct reports will now have upward of seven direct reports. Their scope will increase from being responsible for two to three programs to possibly six to eight.

There are several factors from funding to department/agency maturity to training and prerequisite credentials that separate the efficiency and output from corporate security to law enforcement departments and intelligence agencies. A law enforcement organization such as some large urban police force (service) is often better funded than a small security department or a large corporate security department. The requirements to become a security guard in most locations are easier than the vetting and testing to become a police officer. The training at the academy and ongoing training for the police officers are often greater in length, detail, and ingrained in tradition than a security guard licensing course. Some intelligence agencies have a third of the personnel than the largest North American police services. They are however funded with budgets that are at least half or even more than those police departments.

If CSOs could look at this example for a moment, and if you could consider the security team at a premise and or vessel like the local police service, these two groups carry out the tactical and operational work of securing assets or cities in a very general sense. In that example, you may be able to compare the corporate security department to the Federal Bureau of Investigation or in some cases other key US federal agencies or intelligence services that provide subject matter expertise's (SME). CSOs do not need to be great at everything. Do few things and do them well. If you accept that the corporate security department can provide strategy and intelligence, then you may be able to take the first step in building a successful program, by having a starting point to grow from. Intelligence services have an even greater vetting process than your average police services and often hire recruits who must be university educated, have professional experience, may be multi-lingual and have a diverse background in many sense which are all just some of the factors to their success. The use of statistics, analysts, analytics, and threat assessment has long been used by these agencies. Where corporate security has been following a few years behind. Later we will discuss how to catch up and why this is necessary.

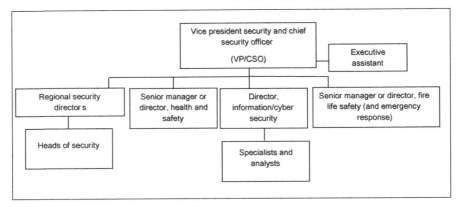

The numbers here represent full time employees (FTE).

FIG. 1.4

Example Group B: Organizational chart (2020–30).

Analysts and analytics will help to change the landscape. Later we will explore how security education will help mold the future CSOs and what this says for the progression of careers within corporate security. This will have a positive impact on the vetting, recruiting, and appointment of future CSOs.

Another scenario seen today is where a CISO leads the overall converged department and the vice president and CSO of corporate security reports into this role. This book examines the benefits, opportunities, challenges, and next evolution of this trend.

Some of the FTE shown in diagrams 1.3 and 1.4 may be replaced by contract employees, giving rise to a staffing model that uses in-house staff and long-term embedded consultants on the same teams performing the same roles. In Chapter 6 we will revisit these organizational charts as we look beyond the next decade (Fig. 1.4).

The responsive strategy

I have provided you so far with a basic overview of corporate security, different CSO roles, department structures, and duties across several industries.

A few authors have written about the intersection of security and law enforcement. Law enforcement is often focused on a response while security is focused on prevention. Security programs have also become very good at response. Response to frauds, premise emergencies, and geopolitical events may impact the safety of personnel and operations. There is a level of predictive thinking built into today's programs. We know there are people who will steal from retail stores, people who will rob banks and that people need support in the event of an emergency. Knowing these factors, we deploy personnel, training, hardware, signage (warnings, rules, regulations, etc.) and a few other controls to help prevent these predictable threats and perils. We also know that the likelihood and probability of some risks are low and therefore the deployment of security personnel to every place, all the time is not cost effective or commensurate to the threat. There are some industries with higher risk operations, locations, and premises which require constant restricted access, entry screening of the highest kind and hardened perimeters. Of course, if commercial office towers, malls, and community centers had to operate in this state on a regular basis the environment would be less enjoyable, accessible, and appetizing the clients, tenants, and customers. If enterprises and their corporate security departments operate completely responsive, we will fail. The risk of terrorism, kidnapping, ransom, extortion, and cybercrime appear to be evolving and growing. These will lead to significant losses of life, assets, regulatory discipline, litigation, and reputational loss. A truly holistic review of all risks to the enterprise, what is directly relatable to the corporate security programs' mandate; and methods of predicting these events using early warning tools is where the industry is headed.

Any CSO who finds themselves constantly gathering their teams to deal with problems, "putting out fires" and searching for answers are setting themselves and their teams up for burn out. This is not sustainable. No CSO should be so far down in the weeds by choice, their working style or the circumstance their employer has placed them in that they cannot provide quick, rationale and expert advice to predict, avoid, and/or quickly mitigate threats and seize opportunities.

Information not intelligence

Having the right information to create a good intelligence product and in turn a strategy is key to any good operation. If the information does not flow through the department in a logical order, in all directions then gaps may occur, opportunities will be lost, and the program may lack actionable intelligence. Basing the staffing structure, number of FTE, resources and methods on a cookie cutter or one size fits all approach may prove inefficient at best, perhaps even disastrous.

The term intelligence is often used by corporate security departments in many contexts. All too often what they have is information, not intelligence. Information is fact or raw data, credible or not. Intelligence is the product garnered from analyzing data and facts, validating that information, determining its useful, actionable meaning and using it to plan accordingly. For example, to say "there is an activist group organized in the city" is information. By observing, collecting information, reviewing history, analyzing multiple sources of data only then may we be able to provide a conclusion which may be considered quality intelligence.

An example of information is as follows. A mining company is informed of the following:

- Activist Group A plans to march in the city this weekend
- They march every year for this cause
- In the past two years, they broke windows during each march

For the mining company's CSO to base mitigation strategies on this information may be inefficient. The vague details would require the placement of extra security personnel at several locations. The personnel could be unprepared and ill-equipped.

By taking that information, reaching out to contacts and sources, searching for more credible facts, and history online and performing a threat assessment; you can develop a plan that more appropriately allocates resources. The intelligence product may look like this:

- Activist Group A plans to march in city X this coming Saturday from 1:00 pm to 3:00 pm.
- The group plans on traveling down the main street from the monument, to a final stop at the bell tower.
- A known group of extremists who oppose the mining project on the moon, known as the TR-Red 481 has a history of destroying public property.
- TR-Red 481, have indicated their intention of participating in online chat rooms and social media groups for the event.
- The route takes the group passed the mining company's headquarters.

Based on the information above the owner of the premise, the mining company and local police can make a better-informed decision than if they had acted solely on the information originally provided.

This intelligence will allow security to better predict what may occur and if not completely prevent it, mitigate its impact and apprehend the parties as it occurs. Activism is a healthy part of democracy. These groups do not need constant supervision. Threat actors can be a party to any company, group, organization, etc. Spending unreasonable resources monitoring all parties by intrusive means may garner little to no credible intelligence. Technology, social media, and good relationships with the leaders of these groups will yield much better actual intelligence about credible threats to help build our predictive capabilities.

In the example above, I used activists and activism to illustrate a point. Many people who march or gather for a cause are exercising their free and democratic right to express themselves, to be heard and make positive change. I myself at one time thought the word activist was a negative term, that all people who protested were young angry people yelling about things that could not be changed. I tell you this not as a political statement, but in an effort for security professionals to move well beyond the days of "strike breakers and security forces" and toward becoming peaceful communicators. In fact, some of the best open intelligence is directly from organizers and leaders of these groups. I have found that they (people leading others to effect positive change) do not associate themselves with those who join causes to spread hate and destroy property.

These leaders are occasionally artists and academics who have something compelling to say. They deserve the same rights, freedoms, and protection as does anyone. They will often cooperate with you to sort out the small percentage of trouble makers if you simply talk to them.

This goes with much intelligence. By connecting with people, seeing what the party of interest is sharing openly and listening you may avoid a lot of unnecessary effort and get timely, accurate, and quality results.

There are many types and sources of intelligence. I do not intend to explore these in detail here. There is plenty of up to date expert literature on these topics. A few simplified examples which corporate security may use and protect against are:

- HUMINT (Human Intelligence) is the gathering of information directly from people
- OSINT (Open Source) which is most commonly gathered on the internet
- SIGNIT (Signals Intelligence) is communications and electronic information interception

As we move through the evolution of corporate security departments and the role of CSO, I will provide a suggested approach on how gathering, organizing, analyzing and dissemination efforts will evolve in the future for corporate security.

Fig. 1.5 is a simple example of the intelligence cycle to help you visualize the process. I will provide a connection to these structures, trends and topics as we proceed. The CSO needs an arsenal of tools to tackle tomorrow's complex challenges. I hope to provide some solutions to the opportunities discussed in this chapter.

As shown in Fig. 1.5 information gathering and the process or cycle to develop intelligence takes time. A CSO who can reduce that time, improve the quality of the results, and limit the investment or resources used to produce this product will be worth their weight in platinum. We have moved away from the time when this was a

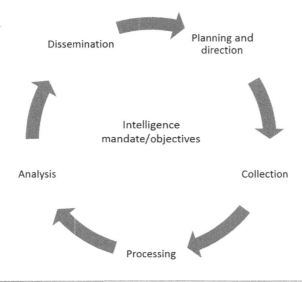

FIG. 1.5

The intelligence cycle.

big mystery when we had to hire the best mathematicians, code breakers, and secret agents to produce a single report. Processes, analysts, and more readily available information have become significantly more efficient. Soon machine learning, software robotics, process automation, and fusion centers will become some of the greatest force multipliers in a decade; revolutionizing intelligence for corporate security departments and the enterprises that employ them.

For many years the public sector has contracted some of this work out to private intelligence firms. They have acquired these services for the collection, analysis, and to simply provide an explanation of how the information is relevant to them. The most forward-thinking CSOs have already started using these same service providers to offer intelligence on a few matters important to the company. This allows them to focus on asset protection, keep their teams lean and agile. These departments will benefit from a pool of other clients all looking to hire top talent who offer a critical view of the world for a much lower investment than a proprietary intelligence team. Many corporate security departments employ a director of intelligence who manages the program.

Now it is time to discuss the next couple of decades for corporate security and how the CSO will move their programs forward step by step. The advancements we have observed in the previous 30 years will now occur in 5-year increments. The global marketplace will become more regulated and competitive than ever. Experts in risk, compliance, and security will be paramount to survival.

Enterprise security risk management

Defining enterprise security risk management (ESRM)

Enterprise security risk management (ESRM) is a strategic practice used by security executives to assess, measure, and proactively mitigate risks to the enterprise. ESRM is an ongoing process which measures governance, controls, and systems that protect the organization where security is integrated with the business. This should include both logical and physical security. It should not be mistaken with convergence. Convergence examines the partial or complete integration of the physical and information security programs. ESRM takes a holistic all hazards approach to identify threats and assign tasks to mitigate them ongoing. ESRM allows leaders to develop preventative controls, make quick assessments on the health of the program, and provide solutions and improvements to better predict and prevent, rather than to react.

A security manager in a hospital or loss prevention manager of a large store can put together the greatest looking dashboard by covering every aspect of their day-to-day operations. You can find artistic ways to graph building patrols. You can create pie charts on how many baggage inspections were conducted in a week. To senior leadership those plain numbers on their own may have little meaning. Even with the most compelling case this may be too rudimentary to share with leaders pressed at keeping the entire business afloat. You may also miss many opportunities for security to ingrain with the C-suite.

The ERSM model

ESRM is not a new name for corporate security (CS) or single functions carried out by CS such as the risk assessment program. It is a distinct and separate but complimentary practice to enterprise risk management (ERM). ESRM is not simply a series of dashboards based on metrics such as budgets, projects, key risk indicators (KRIs), or key performance indicators (KPIs). ESRM is not intended to do the work of compliance, human resources, internal audit, insurance, legal, privacy, or risk. ESRM may be applied the same in principle to each organization however what is a regulation or risk to one enterprise may not be the same to another.

The Chief Security Officer's Handbook. https://doi.org/10.1016/B978-0-12-818384-7.00002-1

Assessing the state of security comes in many forms and is only one part of the ESRM lifecycle. A few examples of what these assessments are provided here:

- Threat, risk, and vulnerability assessments (TRVA)—A quantitative and qualitative process of evaluating security risks, their likelihood, and impact and providing a strategy to address them.
- Security reviews—A subject matter expert review (sometimes more qualitative and subjective) of a security programs' controls and practices, and they are less detailed than a TRVA.
- Gap analysis—A security gap analysis compares actual performance with potential or desired performance.
- Security audit—A security audit may entail a deep dive into the books, reports, and records of a security program. Trust but verify and fact finding are good ways to think of an audit.

To demonstrate ESRM in action we will simplify the security program in the following pages. Few CS departments have physical security, fraud, investigations, business continuity, and occasionally antimoney laundering (AML) under one leader. For this purpose, we will discuss a department where the enterprise physical security domain and the information security domain are either converged or work side by side as partners, in fusion centers and as a center of excellence reporting their KPIs and KRIs in one dashboard together.

Understanding ERM

ERM is an enterprise wide practice of examining all risks to operations and the business. This may include transactional business such as how the company makes money and establishing what ventures are within the risk tolerance. It is an entire discipline with many layers of assessment and metrics. Chief security officers (CSOs) working for financial institutions may be familiar with large robust risk departments who lead the ERM practice. Both ERM and ESRM are task based rather than role based. Just because a company does not have a chief risk officer (CRO) or CSO does not mean that these areas are not being considered and practiced within that enterprise. Where some organizations have a chief risk, officer tasked with leading ERM, the risk department may simply work with leaders and subject matter experts (SMEs) across several departments to set the risk thresholds, tolerance, and track the operational work of these partner departments to practice ERM. If compliance and CS may be referred to as the company police, then enterprise risk and audit can provide oversight, otherwise we will be faced with the age-old dilemma "Who is watching the watchers"? What if this is a privately owned, mid-sized company with one office, one factory and a few stores? The use of a management council, third-party auditors, and program reviews will supplement where an internal body to ensure transparency and optimal results of the ESRM program is not available. The risk department may be split into multiple units, for example operational risk often deals with tracking and reporting the KRIs and KPIs of departments such as CS, information security, investigations, business continuity, insurance, human resources, and legal. Other units within risk may look at due diligence risk and credit risk.

Often ERM is not an operational department executing risk identification and mitigation strategies. ERM provides the executives, board, and even regulators with a report card or snap shot of the current risk posture. Enterprise risk is a key program that facilitates the sharing of information, that helps to set thresholds such as the company's risk appetite and risk tolerance. This cycle of risk assessments, measuring and reporting contributes to the strategy of the business. ERM does not have to be a large department in a corporation. This can be a process and series of tasks assigned to the head of operations, legal, or other professional managers in a completely different line of business. All business comes with risk, this is a fact of life, literally. Will it rain today? Might I get wet? Do I need an umbrella? Small business owners, sole proprietors assess risk regularly, they may simply not over think it, or put a label on it. Why does a shop keeper place their cash in a safe, a hiding spot or the bank? Why does the newspaper delivery person look both ways before crossing the road?

So, what is the difference between ERM and ESRM? ERM programs and departments vary from industry to industry and company to company. A mid-sized commercial goods producer may have different needs from a multinational insurance company. That is not to say that the protection against our food supply chain from tampering is not paramount, it is just one example of two industries that may be bound by different regulators, internal governance, and controls which in part dictate the level of ERM and ESRM programs that they follow. ESRM may be practiced today by a few CSOs without labeling it as or even realizing they are practicing ESRM. ERM looks at all risks to all parts of the business. ESRM is sometimes confused as a replacement practice. ESRM is a practice where CSOs and CISOs may identify their role in ERM, and to provide monitoring and solutions for those risks. ESRM is a not a replacement for ERM where an enterprise does not have a formal ERM department or function. Security professionals do not need to do the work of audit, compliance, insurance, legal, privacy, or risk.

In ERM the CRO may list all the risk assessment, audit checklists, and preventative practices of all departments. Here we will look at a subset of the larger risk picture. The operational risk leader may list all the key operations to the enterprise who deal with assessing and mitigating identified risks. In some organizations information security, physical security, business continuity, investigations, and even AML may fall under the CSO. Few companies divide these up among various leaders. The CSO may simply have all CS and premise protection programs while those listed above are led by internal counterparts.

ERM may start with a list of all the departments such as CS, information security, investigations, business continuity, insurance, human resources, and legal for example. Individually each department tracks their own key metrics. CS may implement the ESRM model to track many KRIs and KPIs. The enterprise risk department may select a subset of these metrics that they believe should be provided in a summary of all risks to the executive committee, the board of directors, and regulators.

Applying ESRM

I am going to provide the details of a fictional company. We are going to take this brand-new company, it's brand-new CSO, CISO, and respective security departments and develop an ERSM program from day 1. The company ILL is a pharmaceutical producer. They are the creators of the "Cure Everything Pill" (remember this book is about the future). They are headquartered in New York, New York, USA, and have operations in Toronto, Ontario, Canada, Tel Aviv, and Jerusalem, Israel. The company employ approximately 1200 full-time employees (FTE) and another 200 contract and contingent workers. In Israel there is an office with a research and development (R&D) team, marketing, production, and distribution center. The corporate headquarters is in NY, along with a distribution center. In Canada there is a production center. The company's key markets are North America, Asia Pacific, and the Netherlands.

The company has hired a large business consultancy and global law firm to set up and commence operations. A large list of business requirements which may include registering and incorporating the business in the jurisdictions it operates will be compiled and provided to the executive leadership team. Another list of rules, regulations, and legislation will be compiled that outline the requirements of pharmaceutical production and sales in all places they will produce, ship, and sell the medication. If the company is public or private and listed on the stock market will possibly add another layer of governance which must be complied with.

Now that all the registrations are complete, the licenses acquired, the insurance in place, and mass production is set to begin. The ongoing regulatory requirements must be identified and assigned in whole or in part to business leaders (who may execute these themselves, via their teams or through third-party service providers) and entered into a process which ensures compliance. The entire list of steps and considerations discussed earlier, along with the business strategy and ongoing practices may fall under the practice of ERM. Some of the benefits of ESRM are to elevate the professionalism of the security departments, align them more with corporate strategy, and reduce gaps in risk initiatives. ESRM is exactly what it says "security," it is not a catch all. The CISO and CSO should not spend too much time worrying about the entire list of rules and the company must follow as laid out by the NY, Security Exchange Commission (SEC) or if we have enough insurance coverage.

ESRM made simple

I am going to break the setting up of the ILL Inc., ESRM program into manageable parts. Let's divide it into two buckets, compliance and assessment. Compliance (or governance) will cover all the internal and external regulations, rules, and polices of the company and security's role in relation to each. Assessment will cover all the protection systems and controls summed up in a document or two and entered as part of the threat, risk, and vulnerability assessment methodology.

We will refer to the formalized working group of the CISO, CSO heads of legal, compliance, risk, privacy, HR, and like departments as the Security Committee (SC). The SC may compile a few lists. List 1 is a combination of a few items found on a possible ERM and ESRM process document which cover the requirements, polices, and regulation that the company must adhere. I have provided some regulations, laws, and regulators in list 1. List 2 provides the potential owners of the policy, program provided in list 1. Some of these guidelines, polices, procedures, and processes are owned and managed by the security departments. List 3 provides the tasks to be completed to maintain compliance. List 4 or column may provide a prescribed interval or frequency of how often this task must be completed. List 5 may provide the task owner(s); and finally list 6 may provide the detailed action. There are many ways to organize and present this document. This is a day 1 exercise. A brain storm between departments. This will help the security leaders integrate with the business, provide immediate value, ask for appropriate resources, and establish a seat at the table. The use of a RACI matrix may be helpful during this process. RACI stands for responsible, accountable, consulted, and informed. It is a chart of all the activities or decision-making authorities undertaken in an organization that lines up the departments and their roles in a given topic, project, etc.

List 1: Regulations and regulators (rule, policy, etc.)

- US Prescription Drug Marketing Act (PDMA) of 1987
- US Food and Drug Administration (FDA or USFDA)
- Sarbanes-Oxley Act of 2002
- New York Securities Exchange Commission
- Company general liability insurance carrier
- Workplace Violence Prevention Policy
- Code of Business Conduct
- Fire, Building Codes, and Ordinances
- Radio Communications Licensing Requirements
- Local Health and Safety Legislation and Guidelines
- Canadian Criminal Code
- NY State Penal Law
- Privacy Legislation
- ISO 27001, 27002
- Global Physical Security Policy
- Global Information Protection and Security Policy
- Travel Security Policy
- Premise Access Control Standard
- Guard Post Orders
- Logical Access Control Policy
- Clean Desk Guidelines
- Security Guard and Private Investigator Licensing
- Established laboratory operating guidelines

- Labeling standards for bar codes
- Drug Master Files (DMFs)
- Contract Manufacturing Arrangements for Drugs: Quality Agreements Guidance for Industry

List 2: Owners

- Information security
- Compliance
- Audit
- CS
- Risk
- Legal
- Human resources
- Investigations
- Business continuity

List 3: Tasks

- Assess general liability insurance coverage
- Assess specialty insurance coverage (kidnap, ransom and extortion, cyber, earthquake, etc.)
- Review insurance limits for contracts (vendor requirements)
- Clean desk sweeps
- Business impact analysis
- Tax assessments
- Training employees on AML and antiterrorist financing (ATF)

List 4: Frequency

- Annually at year end
- Within 4 days of quarter end to provide in quarterly reports
- Weekly
- Every second Tuesday

List 5: Task owner

Note the task or responsibility may be owned by a committee, leader, or department. The department head may be accountable. The actual task may be carried out by others as assigned. For example, you own a building. The general manager you have hired is accountable for a clean and secure premise by leading. The director security is responsible for security and the head of housekeeping for the cleaning by managing. The guards and cleaners execute on the tasks.

- CSO
- chief information security officer
- global head of AML
- CS
- head of facilities

During the review the committee may find that information security is excellent at protecting the confidentiality, integrity, and availability of data stored on the network. Physical security is great at premises access control. Facilities coordinate the installation of safes, lockers, filing cabinets, and door hardware. But who ensures that the business units protect the boxes of files piled by the door waiting to be sent to storage? Who checks that the portable electronics and physical information are locked away? Who makes sure that shredding practices are being adhered to and whiteboards are being erased. Who ensures laptops are secured at end of day, people are locking their screens when away from their desks, and not leaving passwords written down, etc.?

The actions may become part of procedure and standing order documents. An example of prescriptive actions may look as follows:

List 6: Action(s)

- Department heads will spot check that information is locked away and hidden in their office space and portable electronics locked up and out of sight.
- Security guards will patrol the floors removing unsecured laptops, noting those locked up by cable but left on desks overnight and document open drawers, found passwords, information left on desks, meeting rooms, and whiteboards. Items will be confiscated and logged, or the floor secured, and the findings reported.

An example is provided here at how the result of a couple policies and regulations may look altogether:

Rule
- Clean desk policy

Owner
- Information security

Task
- Clean desk sweeps and audits

Frequency
- Clean desk sweeps—quarterly
- Spot checks—randomly
- Audits—annually

Task owner
- Clean desk sweeps—performed by department security officers— department heads
- Spot checks—performed by security guards on patrol—CSO

Action
- Each quarter department security officers will physically inspect their floors, document finding's, report to management, and help in the training of staff where improvements are required.
- At random, while on patrol security personnel will secure unsecured portable electronics, log security/privacy risks, and report findings.
- A randomly selected group of work areas will be audited thoroughly by CS and or during a scheduled audit annually.

Now that you have listed all the rules and regulations, continue by listing what the CSO owns completely, facilitates, owns a task in, and simply supports. No security program can operate by adhering to compliance obligations alone. Laws often move slowly, and the world of business, technology, and security are advancing too quickly to wait.

Threat, risk, and vulnerability assessments (TRVA)

My goal here is not to provide you with the entire building blocks for a TRVA program. There is plenty of literature, courses, and expert consultants out there to help you with that. In the previous exercise we started with a building block to developing the ESRM program. Compliance alone does not identify all the risks to the enterprise or the opportunities for CS to support the business. Identifying all threats, hazards, and perils will help to close a part of the gap. We will go back to opportunities and adding value later.

When starting a threat assessment program, it is always a good idea to engage internal audit or third-party auditors. They will keep you honest. They are experts in beginning to end, that is, cradle to the grave processes. There are many ways to go about this and like many examples I provide, these have been simplified for a larger audience, many industries and people at all career levels in security. Create a list of every department, function, critical asset, and product in your enterprise. Think about its criticality to the company. List all the ways that department needs protection. Does that service or product need protection from the research and development stage to the time it gets into the customers hands? Does that asset, product, or service bring risk to the enterprise? Is your corporate head office the landmark of the city? Are you developing weapons technology? Do you drill for oil? Making plush children's toys and the previous two products and services bring very different attention to your organization, and therefore may require different levels of protection.

After you have listed all your key premises, networks, and the level of criticality for each, you will assign a value to them and determine the frequency in which you will perform physical and logical TRVAs. TRVAs will be conducted and out of those will likely come a series of recommendations which will need to be assigned to the responsible parties to address. Preferably the recommendations will be realistic. Asking for 400 security personnel to protect a two-story premise which houses a very low risk product is impractical. You may force executive to continuously accept the risk or look for alternate means. It would be practical to suggest the right solution the first time. A summary of all the reports may be provided to leadership. The sum of all recommendations for the physical and logical TRVAs may be provided to the CSO and CISO. These should be clearly documented, actioned, and addressed until they are closed.

By now, you should have a RACI matrix listing all the governance matters for the organization driven by compliance. You should also have a list of consolidated recommendations from the TRVAs which have been conducted. Some of these will translate into capital projects, some will be low hanging fruit. This means they should be remedied immediately. For example, "All visitors will be signed in" as stated in the standing orders. The auditor may find a gap in this process. The root cause may be as simple as the paper visitor logs were full, the visitor management system was down, and or new personnel were not aware. These are all easy to remedy immediately. The last number of items may be ongoing, for example, annual tasks for the CSO or new daily procedures for the security personnel, etc.

Something that all CSOs must keep in mind. Not all matters of compliance should rest on the shoulders of the CSO to tackle from an operational and tactical perspective. Not all risk findings are meant to bear down on CS alone. Sharing the responsibilities between departments and department heads is a better way to close the gaps. Two other examples of where this often goes wrong. CS shows up to the premise. Walks around with a 200-point checklist (most of which does not apply to all premises). They make everyone feel like they are being audited, not partners being supported. They pass judgment after only having spent minutes with each department. They conduct the most impressive, all inclusive TRVA ever seen. The report is a literary masterpiece. They issue the report to the property director a month later and are on their way to the next project. CS has another check in the box and the CSO is on their way to another bonus. They may forget that half of those recommendations should fall back to CS for action. All of them will be the responsibility of CS to advise on, track, and report until closed. The property director has a day job of their own. Managing the guard force and systems is only one small but important piece of this. They may become overwhelmed and even feel resentful. When CS come back a month later with a grand idea, or project expecting a cheerful partner to jump in with both feet, do all the work and pay for it, they may not get the warm welcome they were expecting. Another scenario is where security, business continuity, risk, compliance, and privacy permanently or as a secondment assign staff to a business unit. This takes a lot of investment. However, company ILL may do this to drive better results during the critical startup period. After a while the SMEs may go back to their home departments. They are then assigned to support that department going forward. Later this group of departments who we may call the resiliency team, require each business unit or large department to assign liaisons. Like the floor wardens, health, and safety committee volunteers, the often-voluntold parties are now the department privacy officers or department security officers, for example. In time this evolves further. The reasons for doing this may be twofold. One is to teach the departments some independence and secondly to reduce the number of SMEs doing operational work for those business partners. This saves FTE in some cases for those resiliency teams. There needs to be a middle ground, a balance and this is very hard to achieve for many organizations. The CSO needs to know when to completely own something, when to share something, and when completely passing it off brings risk to the organization where less qualified people in areas of risk mitigation are saddled with that responsibility. By making the business more self-reliant you may create a situation where CS brings less value to their partners.

ESRM reporting

In Chapter 3, I will discuss metrics in greater detail. An ERSM program or practicing ERSM is not complete without a way of measuring its progress, success, and opportunities. The CS department and CSO need oversight and guidance. A positive outcome for any CSO who welcomes this is the benefit of executive understanding, additional resources, and support for the goals and objectives of CS.

The CSO will have many dashboards. Later we will examine what metrics and how they are presented can provide a snap shot on the health of the program. Here I wish to stress the importance of putting all this information together. When the CSO starts their day, they may open their incident reporting software, case management system, occurrence report database, or the name most commonly used by their organization. This is the system in place where all security guards write their incident reports. This is the system of record for all the investigators to log their investigation materials and final reports. This is where business continuity professionals and information security analysts can log events and the details of the occurrences. We will examine this under case management in Chapter 5. The CSOs landing page should be quite simple. An easy to navigate page with the CSOs profile, a bar of the newest incidents and an option for the dashboard may be one way of displaying the highlights. In the "Case management" section, we will discuss the importance of what the newest incidents tab will be for the head of plant operations or premise security director and what it will mean for the CSO. On the CSOs dashboard we may see a simple pie chart or bar graph showing physical security incidents, cybersecurity incidents, business continuity events, and investigations as percentages of the total each category shares. A graph may show each by the numbers for each quarter. Another icon or graph may represent those that have exceeded previously established risk thresholds by dollar value, time loss, regulatory risk, or reputational impact (media reported incident with clear impacts to executive engagement of shareholders and stock decline). The CSO can then drill down to the actual incident and move through each layer which may include the summary, report, status, root cause, remedies, losses, and link analysis charts.

For this example, I will speak in terms of how this more often occurs in the decade from 2010 to 2020. The CSO can take the dashboard from the case management system and place this into a PowerPoint slide, which will help to form a quarterly slide deck (deck). This deck starts with a cover page followed by a narrative which introduces the program. I will stop here for a moment and ask the reader to do themselves a favor. Very few of the professionals reading this today majored in English Literature, myself included. Take a minute, go online, and look up the differences of some key terms before you write a deck to your executives. I will not provide you with the answers but rather the exercise.

Using your favorite search engine try some of these and review the most popular results and images in detail when writing your next report or deck. We will use commonly interchanged terms I see used by security professionals. We will use versus (vs) to separate their use and meaning.

- Information vs intelligence
- Policy vs procedure vs guidelines
- Incident vs occurrence
- Threat vs risk vs vulnerability
- Executive summary vs introduction
- Thesis vs hypothesis
- Summary vs paraphrase
- Abstract vs introduction
- Summary vs foreword vs preface
- Overview vs introduction

You now have a cover page, an overview of sorts, and a lay up to your incident dashboard. But that is only a part of the metrics you have available. You should also have a report card on the status of your role in compliance matters and finally a third set of key performance and risk indicators found in your ongoing risk assessments. Later I will discuss the level of appropriateness in reporting to different levels of management and when to report which metrics. These three sets of metrics can be condensed to the most critical items to the enterprise and summarized in a self-explanatory display to convey the most important data to the most senior audience.

This ongoing process will ensure that security is making a valuable contribution to core business objectives. It will help leaders understand the importance of including security at the table. By speaking dollars and cents, risk at an enterprise level and demonstrating your ability to align with the C-Suite; will go much further then short bursts of heroics or reminding them how much the program costs with little to show for it.

Corporate security strategy

Every so often a long-time practice is given a new name. In rare cases this is when something has been studied, standardized, and made its way across an industry. Often it is simply marketing. In those cases, it often falls into two buckets: to gain more attention and sell or to avoid a bad reputation or negative stigma. CS itself is often a subject up for discussion. Many professionals have been trying to find a replacement for the word security. Travel risk management has now been called duty of care. Some who sell services will inform CSOs about laws they must abide by while using a new marketing term. In fact, it often ends up being a local code or ordinance in a couple of states in one country and a province or town in another. Sometimes the law simply ends up being a best practice or suggestion. Other examples may be the cloud, justice studies, and cybersecurity. Cybersecurity has become a separate branch (about 20 years after it starting to be used) from information security or subset. If you read some early articles on people joining the ESRM movement, and knew none the wiser, you may have been led to believe that it was what many established CS departments know as their TRVA program and methodology. Most building security assessments do not remind the security manager to ensure their radios are licensed, their guards are licensed, the guard morale scores high, access breaches tracked, scored, examined, etc.

You have this incredible dashboard once you complete the ERSM process. You have engaged all divisions, departments, lines of business, and leaders at all levels. What are your key pillars? What is your mission and mandate? Is it that of the enterprise? What are your building blocks?

Were you $100k over budget? There is your strategy. Did you suffer a loss causing significant business disruption? That is your strategy. Were you constantly running under pressure by using information to react to crisis and world events; instead of using intelligence to proactively mitigate the risks? That is your strategy. What is the data telling you, what kind of support has it garnered you? Think strategically, act tactically.

I will repeat key themes throughout the next few chapters. When a new and better tool, procedure, application, or methodology arrive to market and are used in security; it is often by those leading the way. ESRM is no different. As I suggest what the CSOs world will look like in 10 and 20 years from now I will explain something about our history. For example, when someone provides us with a new form video media such as the VHS tape, then the CD, then DVD; or when we move through different methods of video compression a few things occur. Some products may not be the best to come to market, however they may have been funded, marketed, distributed, and launched with a vision. I would like to think that security professionals scrutinize things so much that we eventually move forward with the best that has come to market. It then takes that new "thing" to make its way around those industries most in need, for a military application to migrate down to law enforcement and later to security. It needs to make it's way down from the fortune 100s to the masses. To be written about, to be updated, to have its day at a conference. Without a substantial investor, if it does not get a push from the majority it may never fly. Once it stands the test of time, makes its way around the globe and back again then it may become a part of our everyday lives. Thanks to the most advanced generation of security experts, globalization, and the digital revolution that connects all of us in seconds; ESRM will find its permanent home faster in the global marketplace then most any other practice to date.

Strategy management system

In the past decade security executives have come from or sought to understand and acquire top business credentials than the generations before them. The Federal Bureau of Investigation (FBI) engaged top business consultants, academics, and the use of systems to move their corporate leadership into the modern era. One system was the strategy management system (SMS). Published in detail by experts from prestigious institutions such as Harvard, the SMS, strategy map, strategic shifts, and balanced scorecard provided a roadmap and illustration of what the strategy would look like. A few other agencies, Canadian police services and CS programs adopted this as well. It is often hard to know where to start. Adopting a model used by others with like objectives allows you to lay the foundation for a strategy that you can present to leadership. When both the CSO and CS approach this with open mind, great things can be accomplished.

ESRM 2010–20

As this decade ends we look back and see that ESRM may have been practiced by few of the most foreword thinking leaders without having realized or called it ESRM. We can thank some of the pioneers who have authored important text on this subject and paved the way into the future. This decade will end with ESRM as one of the pillars to the future of CS programs. Every professional will be chasing to catch up and perfect their program, as we will strive to understand the world better, explore new force multipliers such as artificial intelligence (AI), grasp the next advancements in cybersecurity, and make sense of a fast paced highly educated generation following us.

ESRM is just beginning to be adopted by large organizations as a case study, standards development, and newly defined process. Courses in the field of security management are now starting to approach the topic. Those bold experts who are driving it to the next level are now evolving their observations to accept new perspectives between ESRM and ERM. We see the difference between ESRM and convergence explained and a roadmap to align both being laid out before us.

ESRM 2020–30

In the next decade ESRM will be a clearly defined series of works and standards. It will become a requirement in a few companies and used industry wide. The term will work its way into job descriptions, full courses in higher education institutions at the graduate level and will become a part of professional security certifications. ESRM will be offered by service providers on many levels such as software applications, consulting, and auditing. Just as we will see formal, professional security departments of one name or another and CSOs in more organizations, they will all practice ESRM.

ESRM 2030–40

By the time we reach this decade ESRM will no longer be something we need to highlight or even see as special. It will be the way we operate. CSOs of one title or another will know no other way of working and reporting. Fortune 500 companies will all have a CSO. Those CSOs will have a seat in the C-Suite. ESRM will just be another core program, an exam one must cram for before graduation. The days of seeing the newest text books being devoted to the topic will be in the past, by then it will be common to see third editions. It will simply be the way we work. There will be plenty of old dissertations and thesis on the subject.

The days of inviting security to the table will be a thing of the past. Security will own a seat at the table. No process or decision will be made without ESRM being baked in, in one format or another. Just as yesterday's information risk management was something you considered, it is now becoming something that is engineered right into the way we do business, design processes, and applications. ESRM will be invisible, just a series of things we do as an enterprise. A requirement, unspoken, unlabeled like the door on a building or wheels on a car, second nature.

All the manual processes we see today which may include pulling data from four sources, compiling it in basic operating system applications and waiting to present it as if it were new news or special will be completely a thing of the past. CSOs will be able to pull down a dashboard in one place at anytime, anywhere in two clicks from a device we have not yet seen and state the health of the organization as it pertains to security risk.

Security consultants will view organizations with the perspective that all risks must be considered to all parts of the operation. Their understanding of how to calculate risk, apply ESRM, and convey that to your executive audience will be beyond compare to the consultants of today. One consultant will speak confidently about your compliance needs, physical, and cyber risks.

Security service (guard, systems, software) providers will understand this process as well as the leading experts do today. No longer will a camera be sold for the sake of selling a camera. The qualifications of someone selling these goods and services will be greatly more advanced than today. They will provide solutions that your organization needs by looking at the big picture just as that of CSO today would.

No longer will the leading experts of today be the only ones who completely understand and in turn apply ESRM to their enterprise. This practice will have evolved and be a task that organizations without CS can assign to the compliance, audit, or risk officer to carry out and; the building blocks and tools will be a quick search away.

ESRM conclusion

Many companies still do not have CS departments or CSOs. If ERSM was a role-based function, then these organizations would not be able to achieve a quality program using the all hazards approach. Today's leading experts have referred to ESRM as a task-based function. It will take todays' forerunners to help further develop and encourage others to help evolve this science. It will penetrate different industries and gain the inertia it needs. Among security professionals it is becoming a term used in marketing, conferences, and the upper circles frequently. Ask another department head what ESRM is and you may find that most of them are not familiar with it and may not be able to define it. ERM however has had a decade to make its way into many industries and into the routine of cross-functional departments. ESRM has come along at the perfect time. When it can be sewn into our processes, applications, or SaaS (software as a service) it joins the digital revolution that will exponentially advance more in the next 5 years than it has in the past 20. I cannot stress the importance for this generation of security professionals to embrace ESRM as one of the key pillars of our success tomorrow.

Artificial intelligence (AI)

3

Introduction

As security professionals, we can look at the future of innovation and technology through few lenses and ask ourselves where this is all headed. How will this help my company and how can I support that? What are the risks of this innovation to my company, its assets, and my program? How can I use, embrace, and deploy it to enhance security? More entertaining examples would be. I have deployed robots to conduct patrols. What if the robots turn evil? Our new artificial intelligence (AI) is identifying, mitigating, and now preventing all frauds by itself. Organized crime group A has better AI than ours and has stolen or secret recipe. All humor aside, AI will provide some of the most important breakthroughs of the century. AI also has the potential to become the greatest threat to a generation.

Often, we are afraid of what we don't understand. For decades, the working population has grown concerned about machines taking our jobs. You must keep in mind that we are also concerned that another person will take our jobs. For every machine, we have built to assist us to assemble cars, wash our clothes, and print newspapers there has often been a higher paying and more skilled job to come with it. Who repairs and maintains the machine? Who engineers the machines? Who does the programming? For as long as there are people, we will need people. It is our great creativity that will always allow us to invent new things to sell, to make life better, and fulfill our basic tenet to evolve.

I have never been intimidated by computers. That is because when I was first introduced to a black and white game stored on a cassette tape, played on a device called a data recorder all I had to do was press the keyboard arrows to slide my spaceship back and forth and press the space bar to shoot the asteroids and invaders. I once cared about the results on the screen, not how it works. That is probably the same for most people using phones today. You can talk, take video, play games, and do so much more. But not many are really concerned or aware of the engineering, scientific, mathematical marvel they hold in their hand and how it works. For some, its seems too daunting and for others its almost magic. The first time I stood in front of a fire panel fixed with nearly 50 toggle switches and nearly twice as many tiny colored light bulbs I thought I had been dropped into a nuclear submarine. I was both astonished and intimidated. When I experienced the first alarm, it was my role to make building-wide announcements on the enunciator. My colleague who was more than twice my age, who I would learn later could not use a computer, came in

The Chief Security Officer's Handbook. https://doi.org/10.1016/B978-0-12-818384-7.00003-3

during the alarm, cool, calm, and collected. He looked like one of the great pianists from history maneuvering his way between toggles, lights, and small displays. As I made the first announcements triggered by him, the fire department walked in. He took charge by explaining to them what device caused the alarm, where and that he has no other alarms activated. All I observed was a lot of beeping, buzzing, and whirring. I felt quite stressed when I was told that I too had to master this mechanical monster. Later when I was retrieving video evidence on our new closed-circuit video system (CCTV), which was no longer using a time lapse video cassette recorder (VCR) and television (TV) but rather a computer; that same colleague looked at this contraption as if I were from the future. In time toggles were upgraded to large plastic buttons on that fire panel and later to a soft, flat panel of 20–30 buttons. The indicators had gone from little light bulbs to light-emitting diodes (LEDs) and then to information mapped out in detail on monitors. The smoke detector sending a signal and the panel controlling the event performed the same function. It had simply gone from something more manual to something we referred to as computerized. When I was at the ASIS International Seminar and Exhibits in 2014, the event was hosted in concert with and under the same roof as my ISC^2, Certified Information Systems Security Professional (CISSP) colleagues. I was expecting that a bunch of retired police personnel, physical security experts and doctorate level, information systems, cryptography geniuses from a three-letter agency would be lined up together for the keynote speaker. Somehow a little bit of knowledge about information systems and information security and I was intimidated by computers for the first time. No one wants to admit that they are completely lost in the conversation. I thought I was at risk of becoming a dinosaur before my career had even began. Was I out of a job if I was not an elite hacker by night?

I was first put at ease when my friend a respectable information technology professional turned crime fighting CISSP, told me that he had started working at a young age in a salt mine in Poland and was no PhD, nor did he ever imagine that he would have ended up being considered an expert in information security in his wildest dreams. Later some recent graduates of the CISSP program confided that they struggled with the physical security sections of the materials to become certified. Astonished I asked why. For lack of experience, interest, and the ability to confidently conceptualize the physical mechanics involved in the process, they could not make the connection of how it all worked. When they explained to me how logical access control worked in it simplest form I realized two things. Understanding the principles of information systems was helpful in pursuing a career in information security at that point in time and; would be a necessity for any career in security soon. I had also realized they worked very similar. One opened files on a screen the other released an electromagnetic lock. Everything in between was nearly the same.

Why don't we make information technology and cybersecurity a tad less intimidating for us? For those of us who do not live in the world of information systems or wage wars in the cyber-battleground, I will try to provide some context. What if we look at the history of vinyl records as an example. I encourage you to go online and watch a short video or two on that very topic. The visual and auditory story may help to trigger the part of your brain that allows you to grasp the simple operations of mechanics, which some of us tend to overcomplicate. In the earliest days of the record, sound vibrations were captured through a cone and membrane like the eardrum and caused a needle to etch the sound waves onto a medium. One of the earliest inventors to work on these marvels was Thomas Edison and his team. What if we slid or spun the record back along the needle or stylus? The grooves would reproduce the same sound that has helped to create them. In time, the materials used, the math involved, and craftsmanship were perfected over generations. Over the next 50 years, we had become good at taking images recorded on film and displaying them in your home on a black and white TV. Recording songs on magnetic tapes became something for the masses. It was not to long until someone put data on those tapes and connected it to a monitor. As this evolved, we learned that we could store this data on better materials. Materials that could store more data, that would last longer, store it in layers and work at greater speeds.

When the first machines were invented to perform calculations, transmit data or crack codes they were very mechanical. Pulleys, levers, gears, valves, etc. Small electrical miracles were invented called micro transistors. The early versions were not much more complicated than a light bulb or LED. We now had a way to store small amounts of data, one such way was magnetic materials. We had a small micro transistor connected to a basic circuit board connected to electricity on one end, a button in the middle, and a screen on the other end. Push a button, connect the circuit, and the effect could be seen on the monitor. Using an old system of counting called binary which is a simple form of mathematics, we could use 1s and 0s to create an endless combination of results. A 1 is a bit and 8 bits is a byte. The organ is a large musical instrument, when different keys and pedals are used together it produces different sounds. The first counting machines were quite mechanical. Let's build our own machine that can stamp numbers. We could use a series of interconnected presses, levers, and pulleys. By pulling lever 1 we may stamp a 1 on a page. By pulling level 2 we may stamp a simple 2 on a page. What if the operators pulled 1 and 2 together? We could create a series of tubes and valves or brackets and arms to trigger the number 3 to stamp the page. By mechanically engineering this machine in a manner that allows combinations of levers to create different arms on a machine to move; and by using binary as the logical sequence of events; we could make those levers attach a handle on a car door rolling by on a conveyer belt in a factory or to squeeze blue and red paint together into a bucket. This is no different than an early calculator. Press a large button. A small electric signal on the circuit board produces a number to appear on a screen. Press a function button which then triggers a simple math equation using binary grids and micro transistors. By entering another number and pressing the equals sign, the electric signals connect on different transistors to create a number like the levers on the press. These are very simplified examples to help remove some of the mystery of what is happening with all this clicking of the keyboard. We have come a long way from the introduction of the compact disc (CD).

Eventually, languages were written using binary. Massive rows of 1s and 0s written by coders in various formats that formed the most common computing languages today. A few very long rows of these numbers could simply represent the letter A. Several rows could represent the actions of the space bar.

So how do these people we hear about do all this complicated hacking? They must be computer wizards? Some and some not. There are many things one can do to change the way a computer or website behaves. Some things referred to by the layperson as hacking is not necessarily hacking.

What if I had some books on the coding languages. What if I clicked on every website I could find. In two clicks, you can view the HTML source code (I implore you never to do this, unless you are a Certified Ethical Hacker who has been hired to do this by the website owner). What if I found a website that someone had forgotten to lock the code? Using the book, I could easily decipher the digits in the code that represent the background color. In many cases, you may see this literally. What if instead of the word blue or code for blue I changed it to orange. This could be embarrassing for the webmaster. What if I read, toyed, and tinkered enough that I changed the little button that allows you to link to the more secure portal for online credit card transactions? How would this online business who conducts 90% of their online sales transactions via credit card do if the link to use credit cards option was down for several hours? In Chapter 5, we will discuss information and cybersecurity and provide some assurance about how we can protect ourselves.

Data analytics and big data

For generations the leading minds from many fields of academia including but not limited to mathematics, economics, geography, and political science have helped to pour over large sums of data to provide intelligence, patterns, and trends. This refined data would help to form strategies that would win wars, put us on the moon, and create entire intelligence services.

Like the gun that became the great equalizer for the physically weaker opponent. That is until we made more guns, better guns, and readily available to the masses. The scientific calculator in the hands of the average person helped them to quickly solve equations previously only managed by mathematicians. The internet leveled the playing field for intelligent youth who lacked the same educational resources as their peers in the well-developed countries. These devices and many more in the hands of great minds can be force multipliers. It then became a race of who could build the better rotor machine, the better bomber, and overall better technology.

Data analytics is a discipline which helps us to process sets of data sources and specific information. A chief security officer (CSO) no longer needs to find a subject matter expert in data analysis to organize and translate large sums of data. A security analyst using spreadsheets, software applications with sophisticated algorithms that are designed to provide trends, patterns, and metrics for immediate use have become day-to-day functions in corporate and information security departments. These massive raw datasets can be crunched, reworked, and layered with other refined sets of data to provide almost endless combinations of possible outcomes. We can model red force and blue force scenarios. We can search for more sophisticated frauds, codes, hidden money, and uncover opportunities. The final intelligence product is used by the CSO to enhance and optimize the corporate security mission. A data driven, intelligence led business unit.

Corporate security provides many services to the enterprise. Each unit must use every advantage to stay ahead of business world changes, criminal enterprise, climate change, and evolving workforce dynamics. How can we do things more efficiently? How can we add layers of protection? How can we uncover misconduct? Manual data analysis has been a a fundamental method of getting these results, until now. Automated, digital, computerized data analytics has been a must have capability for CSOs in the last decade. Data analytics on its own today is becoming obsolete.

A CSO will use descriptive analytics to tell a story. Aging fire equipment, may have led to numerous false alarms. This has led to call center, production floor, or trading floor down time. This equates to lost revenue. Investing on the equipment upgrade is an immediate return on investment (ROI). Multiple elevators entrapments can lead to law suits. Baggage inspections, may have led to the prevention of successful thefts. In retail, this can be important. In diamond mining, this could be critical.

When there is a fraud, the investigators are triggered into action by the reporting of the loss, an anomaly noticed by the client, a hotline tip, and many more starting points. Once they have responded, investigated, and concluded, the root cause will need to be determined. Is the loss still occurring? What caused or allowed the fraud to occur? Was there a control in place? Was it not followed? Were controls lacking? Is this a new scheme? How many have gone unnoticed? One tool used by the Fraud Risk Management team to help answer these and many more questions is diagnostic analytics. Why and how did this occur?

A CSO needs to be able to assess what threats are on the horizon. If the long-time, beloved leader of a dictatorship society passes away while the CEO is in town, what may occur? If the dike breaks during the hurricane, what will be the immediate impacts and long-term fallout? If an employee becomes the subject of a misconduct review and patterns or red flag behaviors are discovered, escalating in severity and frequency synonymous with violence, what level of immediate intervention is appropriate? Predictive analytics helps us to see what may occur based on history, previously seen outcomes, successes, and failures. What is the likelihood and impact?

There are highly sophisticated enterprise case management systems. These supercomputing, data-mining systems offer many services in one platform. These may include threat modeling, threat analysis, link analysis, and collaboration. Conduct hundreds of threat, risks and vulnerability assessments, and enter the findings. Enter the most optimal solutions to the recommendations. What if we enter all the possible threat model scenarios? What if we enter the best mitigation strategies? What if we do this for fraud, anti-money laundering, and cyber-threats? We now have computers that can take symptoms and provide extremely accurate diagnosis and suggested treatment in the medical field. CSOs can build a powerful mechanism comprised of human experts and data analytics to offer prescriptive analytics. Prescriptive analytics can help train newer or more junior members of the department as they will receive the most optimal recommendations to solve investigations, assess threats, and mitigate losses.

The leading security teams have used these forms of analytics over the past decade. Many CSOs will tell you that you need to "feed the beast" with plenty of good information. You will need an army of analysts to do the work where the process starts before the digital automation takes over and where it ends to wrap it all up. By using good metrics, you can be certain to optimize your program.

Who uses data analytics in security today? Banks apply good data to analyze bank robberies. CISOs use large volumes of data to detect network threats rapidly, determine which are low, medium, or high, and deploy defensive actions. Retail loss prevention use data to reveal patterns and trends to find internal loss, identify various frauds, and narrow down suspects.

At the beginning of this decade, the phrase big data was used often. It seems redundant now. Ten years ago, a terabyte (TB) portable hard drive was a few hundred dollars and the size of a tablet. It seemed a technological marvel. Who could possibly have so much data? By the time you read this book, I challenge you to go online and see the cost, size, and availability of a 1 TB drive. Then, I welcome you to go to your department shared drive or SharePoint site for the team and see how much data you are using. What are we doing with all this data? Security professionals hoard knowledge and data. We save every piece of intelligence we can get our hands on like squirrels. Storing big data without purpose, simply sitting dormant in a forgotten virtual machine (VM) is as useful as keeping piles of corporate money in noninterest-bearing accounts. Essentially this brings little to no value.

Data sets (big data) were a reference to high volumes of information too complex for early data-processing applications. When you have a lot of cases (rows), you can create a statistical powerhouse. There were several challenges when this was first introduced to the consumer and corporate market. How could we effectively increase the speed at which we could process big data. The ability to pull anything useful out of it. Understanding the importance of making the right investment to protect it. Not implementing measures to protect it that rendered its value useless. Occasionally, we received a result that may have been referred to as false discovery rates, I will clearly state that some of it was garbage. Security professionals cannot do these things alone. You will need to bring the great minds in your organization or a professional service provider to aide you in these projects. Information experts who specialize in virtual networks, engineering, security, and data scientists need to become a daily part of your strategic regiment. The CISOs, coders, and engineers of tomorrow will be sought after like yesterday's doctors, lawyers, and accountants.

As we have moved away from the term big data, we now refer to predictive and behavioral analytics. We think less about size and more about results. As a CSO, we were not in the least concerned about this at the beginning of this decade. Today, we would be crippled without it. Corporate security departments did not have to run out and buy massive server farms and string together now outdated hardware and software to produce early results. The constant evolution of Excel for example became a go-to for many security managers. Large corporations began to make investments into systems and data processing software that eventually trickled down to corporate security. To this day, the CSO has those people on each team within the department who get it. Those who are technically savvy enough to manage the database use the software and walk the talk. Tomorrow that will be the entire department. There are case management and threat detection and analysis software service providers out there who can offer CSOs services superior to anything that can be developed in house (by most firms). They offer this as software as a service (SaaS), where you can log on from a virtual private network (VPN), straight through a mobile application and even from a browser. They host all this data, in a secure environment on the cloud. They continually update the storage, security, and analytical capabilities as part of the service agreement. I can assure you that they are probably securing and backing up your data better than you have been historically. In 2002, my entire security program was on an unencrypted laptop. It was secured by a Windows password. I thought this was much better than the piles of bankers' boxes or printed procedures I had been using earlier when the file drawer was too full. This was the same computer the entire security team used to check personal free email services. We probably clicked on everything that popped up on our screen and thought it was great or annoying. Many CSOs still struggle with the confidentiality, integrity, and availability (CIA triad) of their data trusted offsite in someone else's hands. Now, many CSOs have experienced or known someone who have lost the entire access control database for a building or company; or the totality of the incident report database in the late 1990s or early 2000s. These were backed up nowhere. A RAID 5 (redundant array of independent disks) configuration was not something that most physical security CSOs had heard of much less deployed. Today, the vendor risk assessment process is one way to ensure this is done to acceptable levels. A paragraph in the master services agreement and occasional data dump will alleviate your fears about getting your data no matter what. What a CSO can find and accomplish today using a mobile phone and a couple of these applications during their morning coffee; is more than the entire department could do at their desks in a day 20 years ago. Pull down a dashboard on the status of TRVAs for the year? Review all the occurrences for properties around the globe in order of severity for the past 24 h? Review the status of countries political, environmental, and security stability? Track every corporate traveler and locate lost corporate phones? Thanks to the basic foundations laid above in the past decade this is all possible.

Machine learning

"Machine Learning (ML) is one process by which a computer can learn its trade. ML is about providing AI with lots of data. It refers to a wide variety of algorithms and methodologies that enable software to improve its performance over time as it obtains more data."

(Hyacinth, 2017)

When you enter a query into a search engine, several results are provided. When you use some free email services, search repeatedly for similar topics and engage in one behavior of discussion on social media forums you may find related advertising, media, and services appearing based on a collection and analysis of data, targeted to your needs.

When working with specific software and popular operating systems, they begin to offer settings most optimal to your task, recall which of two or three screens you prefer to open your email onto, correct your spelling, grammar, and recall where you most often save certain types of files.

Today, a specialist in a Security Operations Center (SOC) can start the night shift. Each day between 23:00 and 23:30 h they drag camera number 43 to monitor 1 and select full screen. They then proceed to drag a grid across a box in a hallway and geofence it. If the scene around the box changes or the box itself is moved, an alarm will sound, the camera will be duplicated on monitor number 2, will rewind 10 s and will automatically replay the event.

What if the operator performs this 4 days in a row. What if a new operator takes the console on the fifth day. By setting a schedule, what if the system offers these settings by popping up an on-display prompt? What if when an event occurs the system automatically follows the moved object and subject by activating an alarm and creating a primary event with each sequential camera they pass allowing for total continuity, rapid detection, and dispatching of the response force? All by machine learning (ML).

Financial institutions use software to process day-to-day banking transactions. Over the past decade, fraud analysts have used fraud detection software to analyze data which had been extrapolated manually to another system for further review. In time, a level of integration was introduced by layering the fraud analytics over the transaction data. Some automation was offered in the early stages to identify patterns and possible red flags. These still needed to be verified by human specialists. The stakes are getting higher. Losses of client money and data may impact shareholder confidence. These losses or breaches will bring empires under scrutiny and create uncertainty in the systems we rely so heavily upon. We are already using ML to identify threats and to fight fraud. In the future, we will expect that the predictive and preventative analytics are built right into the actual financial applications themselves, and not be something to be integrated later. Using ML, we can automate several safeguards too numerous and large for humans alone to efficiently manage. We are now seeing features built into operating systems to protect the network from cyberattacks. These are becoming a necessity and not a luxury.

ML uses supervised learning, unsupervised learning, and reinforcement learning. Let's go back to an earlier example. In all, 1 or 1000 of our wonderful coder friends and their allies who make the world better, write a series of codes that allow us to drag tabs or screens of emails, websites, and file folders across the two to three screens we stare at each day. What if someone wrote an algorithm [a process or set of rules to be followed in calculations or other problem-solving operations, especially by a computer (online dictionary)], that said for every 10 times I drag my email from my laptop screen to the monitor positioned to my top left when I set up each morning, to open my email on that screen on the 11th time for me? This could be a very basic step in ML.

What if we connected all the physical security systems in a building. We then placed them on a network and synced them together. We instruct the machine to duplicate the actions of SOC officers after 20 occurrences. The doors have contact alarms, can sense door held open and forced open actions. The cameras can detect changes in motion, direction, and lighting. The motion sensors, glass break sensors, fire systems, and safe alarms can create an alert if triggered in at the control display. An adversary breaks into the building from an exterior door by force. The thief passes by two cameras and turns left. The adversary makes their way to a critical asset located in a secure room. Meanwhile back in the operations center. The officer hears a tone indicating a door forced open alarm in sector 1. The officer looks at the camera but sees nothing but a swinging door. The officer plays back the last 30s of video and observes the break-in. They use the radio to call all response force units to move toward sector 1 and to be on the lookout. The operator enlarges the next camera, rewinds it 2 min and looks to see if the intruder turned left or right into sector 2 or 3. Just having completed a perimeter patrol our response force has now entered through the broken door and are in sector 1. Our intruder is in sector 4, seconds from breaking through the door. This is our server farm and he is armed with two giant magnets and a large toy water gun. The officer now sees that the intruder turned right down the hall to sector 3 and dispatches the team to this area. The officer enlarges the next camera, checks a motion alarm in a hallway near the restricted area which alarms after hours and rewinds that camera. By now I can assure you the servers are gone, fried, and dead.

What if we wrote a program that synchronized the alarms and cameras. What are those cameras enlarged on a second screen and rewound 30s by themselves and automatically replayed? The response force during the next 19 break-ins and enter incidents may only be 10s behind the intruder instead of 20. Many of you have been in a building with automated fire alarm announcements. A smoke detector is activated on the 10th floor. The fire panel receives the notification and plays prerecorded messages to all occupants, followed by another specifically identifying the 10th floor, smoke detector and instructs people there to evacuate. What if our security system could send a phone call, SMS text, email, and radio alert to all response force personnel? What if these messages were triggered when any device is activated after hours in the restricted areas without being shunted by the patrol officers access card and biometric authorization. What if our system could learn from our communications by natural language processing? What if the security system was programmed with enough algorithms and we applied the previously mentioned ML principles? By occurrence number 21, the system would have immediately and automatically copied all the actions of the officer in millisecond. The system would even generate the calls to the response force with up to the second information. The response force would arrive 10s before the intruder made it to sector 3. The intruder would be neutralized, and the servers saved. What if we used blue tooth technologies on the patrol officer's phones to capture paths of movement? What if we captured access card data, alarm activation data, occupancy sensor, and lighting sensor data? What if all these systems were tied in together in one smart building? Can you imagine if we recorded 2500 scenarios like this at this premise? We applied the best of response procedures, the most optimal physical protection system principles and had the system learn the most efficient ways to respond to all scenarios and to dispatch those results for future events in the most optimal way to catch intruders. We could apply this thinking to fraud, money laundering, and cyberattacks. What if half of the response force were actual robots, connected to that system and covered in 1000 state of the art sensors? What if active barriers were a part of the buildings defense system? All automated and constantly learning to optimize. You might be thinking this is all make believe? This sounds expensive. Why would I develop myself out of a career?

When one CSO invests in a brand-new technology, they may end up paying high prices for the development of a product that only delivers a tenth of what they developers hope it will one day achieve. What if the designers of those technologies took us along in small steps? What if we all worked together to elevate the industry, practices, and technology? What if in 20 years from now this set up was common for all premises? Could the technology and services be provided at a much more reasonable cost? What if I could reduce the size of the human response force?

This is not make believe. This is happening slowly today. This is working and/or being tested in the most highly secure or forward-thinking premises. This will be available to the masses in the next decade.

What if the CSO of tomorrow is significantly more technologically inclined and has a broad but much higher average level of education? What if they are treated more professionally and are in higher demand? What if they spend more time advising on these scenarios to continuously perfect these responses and technologies? What if guards no longer are assigned other, non-security-related duties to justify their cost? What if the premise invests in less guards, however, those response force personnel are much better equipped, protected, informed, trained, and respected?

Can criminals use ML against us? Can they use it to support their criminal endeavors? The answers are yes, of course and they are. Therefore, we need to work together, with other subject matter experts and CSOs. Therefore, developments for the good need to be funded better than criminal enterprise. What can I do about it? I suggest we do not get into a deep technical debate where the CSOs of corporate security of today are limited. Instead you must recognize that there is someone out there running scenarios with this technology on how to defeat your systems, your processes, and team. By getting past your fears and discomfort, by supporting the movement to develop and embrace these technologies for better defensives is doing your part. Educate yourself and look to others where you do not specialize. The next time you find yourself sitting in a room where the phrases blockchain, cryptocurrency ML to combat fraud or ML for information security are uttered. Do not glaze over and wait to hear something familiar. Speak up and ask questions. Use an online search engine and enter those phrases. Read a couple of news articles, watch a couple simple explanatory videos. Ask those departments or service providers to keep you in the loop on how those can create vulnerabilities to your organization. What you can do to reduce those risks. How you can use them to secure your information, advance your program, systems, and what others in your field are doing with them already. Let's get ahead of the threat actors as early as possible together.

For many of you aspiring and new CSOs, the era of ML is the perfect place to cut your teeth. There are many online introductory videos and courses. I recommend you get lost in them for a while. Brain storm with your peers. Are you the head of security for an office tower in New York? Find your peers, connect with them. Do you lead fraud investigations at a bank in Toronto? Find your peers, connect with them. Are you a brand new CSO for a fortune 100 and perhaps new to the private sector? Find your peers and connect with them. If you're in oil, Tokyo, manufacturing or London it does not matter. Get connected, talk about how one another are using ML. Reducing loss should not be a competition. If every CSO today, could take one process and automate it via a ML process, create a standard out of it, and share that knowledge we could completely change how that task or process is done. We could create a sharp trajectory of how that will now evolve here forward. What if that was a better way to predict workplace violence or enhance access controls?

ML will improve the lives of the corporate security personnel, enhance morale, and extend careers.

Artificial intelligence

There are many very similar descriptions for AI being used today. AI is a branch of science which aims to create machines that can think and act like humans. The most successful area of professional study to get us there is computer science. For some time now, the acronym AI has been overused as a marketing term or one that is misunderstood. Now leading experts have divided this narrative. This helps to make the science more consumable and to have realistic expectations and applications in corporate security today.

Here are some explanations in the form of easy to relate to examples:

Artificial narrow intelligence (ANI) or AI weak is found in our everyday lives. Do you have a portable device or product in your home who you can be voice activated, that you can ask for today's weather or when your favorite team plays next and they will tell you as though you were speaking to a human?

Artificial general Intelligence (AGI) or strong AI is observed when thousands of nurses can rely on a supercomputer to diagnose and recommend care or medications with remarkable accuracy.

Artificial superhuman intelligence (ASI) is what we have been reading about and admiring in movies for years. This is a conscious entity that can think cognitively, make its own decisions, create new choices, and merge the best of human and computerized thinking.

What if the world's largest developers of computer technologies fed all the fraud investigators, anti-money laundering professionals, cybersecurity, and threat risk and vulnerability data from threats to mitigation strategies into one supercomputer. What if every CSO volunteered on committees to help list every possible attack, criminal, and loss scenario they could possibly think of. Every emergency response plan, business continuity plan, crisis management plan, disaster recovery plan, all the scenarios, and all the many solutions they could think of. Now imagine placing well-rounded operators in a room, with access to this computer. Imagine that this fusion center was equipped to conference in the department heads leading the specialties above or the senior executive vice president of security who leads all of this. The SOC and the supercomputer poised to tackle any event, any query for the CSO who is up in the command center with the senior leadership team who are all hands-on deck to tackle the next crisis. What if we were maximizing all the technologies discussed so far in this book. The rate at which we could solve problems and provide the most optimal strategy to address them would be the greatest force multiplier to date.

So how can today's CSO implement these technologies? Where do I start? Why don't you conduct this exercise with your team and colleagues who will most likely help you, partner with you, and benefit from these developments as well?

1. Create an information package (as you may be turning the pages of this very book, I will suggest you make this package paperless where possible). In this information package with a few articles on what AI is, how it is being applied to your area (physical security, crime analysis, cybersecurity, etc.).
2. Form a committee, the corporate security AI working group.
3. Host a kickoff meeting, talk about your homework and about how each person uses technology in their lives daily. Get a consensus on what they think of the existing technologies and the wonders of tomorrow's technology.
4. Set up a meeting schedule (perhaps a half hour meeting, once a month), take minutes, draft agendas and distribute.
5. Include something interesting each meeting, a short video, a guest speaker (this can all be done virtually), and a live demo.
6. Use the audio feature on your phone to look things up online, encourage your team to do the same.
7. See if your company has approved the use of a virtual assistant or smart speaker to use in the office, don't be afraid of technology.
8. Install near field/bluetooth enabled readers on the corporate security office door. Have more than one door? Install a door which requires a card and biometric to access the office, embrace technology.
9. Buy a department drone, play with it, study it, and talk about it.
10. Does your company have a virtual phone? Start using it off the desktop, have Skype? Using it to its full extent? Why not?
11. List all the ways your company is seeking to use AI.
12. List all the ways corporate security may use AI.
13. List all the ways AI may be used against you.
14. List all the ways AI could turn against you.
15. List all the ways you could defend against those scenarios, what impact will that have to the work and processes it is doing for you? (I have built the most

efficient computer to run the bank. It was corrupted and now it is doing bad things. Can I just shut it down? Will that cease all transactions?).

Before the end of this chapter, I will provide you with some more suggestions on where to begin. For some of you who are well ahead in this journey (if we view this one as a race we may miss a big opportunity for the next generation), I will aim to suggest some things you have not tried just yet. If you want to see what great minds have to say, I suggest you go to the "Future of Life Institute" website at https://future-oflife.org/ and hear what they have to say.

In the time I have spent researching this topic I have seen those aiming to profit off AI, those aiming to better the world, those completely opposed to it, and those who have accepted that someone will create it but want to be sure it is done right. If we think about all of the work, resources and investment being placed into AI today and the near future; we need to ask ourselves what will it do when it wakes up, thinks, has self-awareness, consciousness, and cognitive thought? As a security professional, I wonder if we will even know when this happens. The entity may be running, thinking, and working on its own agenda long before we realize it. If it is as smart as we believe it will be; I am not sure it will bother with or take interest in us, much more than we interact with ants.

With all these computers being used to beat humans at board games and the other computers running war game scenarios; I must think if someone has already written a plan to respond if AI gets to the nuclear codes and starts to play a game.

There have been a few suggestions for the Laws of AI. The world's largest search engine has just produced a list of seven guidelines. It would be perhaps in the best interest of everyone if a global standard could be agreed upon and followed. This may be an optimistic statement. As security professionals we are constantly looking at history, trends, and trying to determine the likelihood and probability of risk. Based on our history of trial and error, weaponizing technology and "putting guns in the hands of babes" (this refers to many inventions made available to almost everyone which should have possibly been better controlled).

I could not image any of the world's largest companies having become as profitable as they are today without computers and the internet. I can now say with all certainty that if you're not working on AI-based applications today and working to use advanced AI in the future, you may find yourselves out of business. I highly recommend that the security industry, courses, leaders, and academics completely embrace it, study it, and integrate this at all angles.

If it does turn against us, I hope we can still flood all the servers and become farmers.

Drones

In the past decade, the use of drones in day-to-day commercial applications has become quite normal to see. They are used to survey land, inspecting hard to reach places, in video and film production and now security to name only a few.

If you were not aware, here are some of the interesting drones and drone-related technologies commercially available today:

- Fixed wing drones (airplane-like models) that can fly much further and faster than their rotary operated cousins.
- Indoor drones which are surrounded by a soft, stretchy soccer ball sized skeleton.
- Drones that can fly over 10,000 ft (there are many regions with altitude restrictions in the 300–500 ft range).
- Drones that can take out other drones.
- Systems that will take over hostile drones and land them on a predetermined pad.
- Automated drones with complete patrol routes, times, and that can be activated by an alert system.
- Drones with facial recognition that can follow the synchronized mobile phone of the operator.
- Drones that can carry packages pick things up and put them down.
- Drones fixed with military-grade surveillance cameras, including infrared and heat detection technologies that can take clear video at 20 mph.
- Drones with eight arms/rotors (Octocopters) that can mount larger batteries and carry heavier payloads.
- Lower noise producing drones.

By investing in drone technology or by engaging the services of a reputable drone provider, a lot of residual benefits can be gained and some ROI may be observed for the entire company. I recommend brainstorming with others to compile an arsenal of ideas. Some are provided here:

- Does the maintenance department need a rapid visual of the rooftop? (damage, snow accumulation, sun damage, a missing worker)?
- Would events and marketing like to get some live ariel shots of the company picnic, a commercial that ends in a beautiful pan out of head office?
- Are two climbers stuck on a glacier and need reassurance, water, or supplies?
- Do you need to lift a cable across a ravine?
- Do you need to scan a building for broken windows?
- Can surveying drones also be used for security patrols?
- Search and rescue? Imagine a missing child at a theme park. Imagine using the facial, behavioral, and profile recognition systems, the images of the child entering at the front gate and every camera on premise and a fleet of drones to scour the area.

Some of the interesting, new, future, and typical uses outside of government and military I found were:

- Advertising
- Animal herding

- Coffee delivery
- Utility tower inspections
- Delivering tools to people working in high places
- Deicing
- As an elevated light and speaker at events (tethered)
- For wedding videos
- To battle other drones
- Disaster relief and recovery
- Oil pipeline inspections
- Studying animals

Take a survey, ask all the departments what they may use a drone for. Ask your counterparts about the applications they have seen, heard of or use today. This may spark future conversations when each party learn more. This will like many topics open an ongoing dialogue between like-minded professionals with similar goals.

Drones have been used to drop items over the fences of prisons and to conduct hostile surveillance. They have interfered with aircraft and wildfire fighting operations. In some places, shooting down drones and/or confiscating drones is unlawful. In some of these places, a drone could conduct flybys of your corporate office windows. Local law enforcement may not yet be equipped with grounds, laws, or the technology to assist you. However, taking a positive action against the drone by security may be unlawful. In Chapter 5, we will discuss the need for laws protecting us (the private citizens and corporations alike) in the virtual world which needs to catch up to the rate at which technology advances and can become a threat. We need to address the threat of technically savvy adversaries and what seems like our limited ability to deal with them head on. We need to spend some time and resources on addressing the need to allow security to take countermeasures.

Have your security committees and associations speak to local law makers and law enforcement to ask:

- What happens when a security officer uses another drone to take out an unknown drone that is a perceived threat?
- What happens when a drone intentionally strikes a pedestrian, a vehicle, or aircraft?
- What happens when that very same drone acted on its own volition?
- Are we waiting for these things to occur to then react?
- If corporate security has the technology and knowledge to act and prevent or at least stop a crime in progress will they be authorized to act by their less technologically capable partners in these matters?

Security is about preventative measures. We should not sit idly by waiting for others to act or make the rules. The CSOs of the global fortune 500 companies work for employers with greater numbers of workers and gross profits than some countries have in gross domestic product (GDP) and nearly as many people. We should offer to help our partners in laying the foundations to deal with these matters now, before it is too late. The netguns, anti-drone operation technologies, and drone signal jammers should have a defined use case. Does your company have a policy on the use of drones? Do you have a stance that has been communicated with leadership on what action to take with hostile drones? Is this yet a line item on your budget? Do you have a contract and due diligence template ready to go when you want to engage providers? Have you sat down and seriously looked at drone detection and early warning systems?

Today's drones can sense and avoid obstacles. They are fitted with global positioning system (GPS) can sense their docking station, the controller and retrace and map their original flight path without human intervention. We have computers that can beat any human at chess, the game of Go and complex videogames. These computers are self-taught. What if a military drone is programed to neutralize any being not wearing a beacon. What if an area is geofenced to control the parameters of the mission. Now what if someone uses ML and AI with two simple objectives. First is to crack the security of the drone operations controls and second is to target any beings with the beacon? What if you deploy a drone for patrols? What if that drone is commandeered by an adversary and simply crashed into a populated street or traffic?

I have conducted threat, risk, and vulnerability assessments around the globe. The laws on recording video, recording video on the exterior, retaining that video, and having video at all varies. What type of data can the drone collect? Do you have and apply corporate compliance requirements to those records as any other computer? Canadian and European privacy laws are very complex.

Just as you would ensure that your security officers are trained and licensed, you should understand the basic requirements for your drone service providers and verify that they are compliant.

In 2017, drones were deployed for the Boston Marathon. These drones were tethered to cables providing signals and power and could hover continuously providing the bird's eye view. This is only the beginning. Some cites have taken a stance not to have police patrol copters. What about drones? For those of you who investigate bank robberies, I ask how often are banks robbed on days where it is warm and sunny versus those that are in a state of complete torrential downpour? I will lean more to the sunny side rather than when its pouring based on some experience investigating robberies. When you see a movie where the suspect is running away through the rain or a river, the search dogs lose the scent. Cameras images are not quite the same on the exterior during storms. What if immediately following a bank robbery one of several long range, surveillance drones, which are centrally located between clusters of banks owned by either corporate security or law enforcement was deployed? What might the chances of apprehension and recovery be? Not so serious when banks have other detection measures are self-insured and the losses are low. What about when the suspect discharges a weapon? What about when the decision makers who decide against such ideas are in that bank or their loved ones? Could this concept be used during active shooter events at campuses and other large open areas where many visitors gather at once (theme parks)?

I suggest you educate yourselves on the current state of laws being put in force by various civil aviation authorities, the evolving state of licensing and operations.

Drones are not the same as a remote-control car or truck. Responsible training, licensing, and registration seem to be some of the more reasonable motions discussed today.

Robots and robotics

Robotics is the use of robots (yes, those robots) to automate simple and repetitive tasks. You walk up to a door, the sensor sends a signal, and the door operator opens the door for you. A car chassis rolls down the production line and simple robots weld parts onto it.

Today's inventors have either a very tough audience or a road paved with adoring fans. For nearly as long as there have been TVs we have been watching sci-fi movies costarred by pretend robots. Sophisticated humanoids that we have adored or feared. Robots are not supposed to be hostile. Industrial accidents are just that, accidents. When we equip them with weapons and televise them destroying each other in student competitions. When we militarize them. I am not sure what the logical outcome will be when the first superhuman-intelligent robot watches this show with its' human companion.

Not many people have heard of the "Three Laws of Robotics." They were from the fictional work of Isaac Asimov. We later could see a couple of more laws added to these in fiction. For fans of robot themed movies, you will have heard them but until now not paid any real attention. They are:

1. A robot may not injure a human being or, through inaction, allow a human being to come to harm.
2. A robot must obey orders given it by human beings except where such orders would conflict with the First Law.
3. A robot must protect its own existence as long as such protection does not conflict with the First or Second Law.

Ask your household virtual assistant what the three laws of robotics are. They will recite them. If we had stayed true to these principles, our worst fears about robots and AI may never be realized. This, however, is not in our nature. Robots do not break these rules. People who design and control them do. If people can weaponize a family sedan, I ask you to think critically and take responsible steps as a future CSO to question what they may do with the robots of tomorrow?

Since we have been watching highly advanced robots from the imaginations of writers come to life on the big screen for decades, robots or androids dreamt up 50 years ago that are still more sophisticated than anything we see today; it will be hard for anyone to impress us. Our expectations are too great. On the other hand, the application of the computer sciences in the very near future will advance robotics in astonishing ways. Much of this book was written just feet from the docking station of a household robotic vacuum. That simple little cleaning marvel has more computer technology than the first rocket. Thanks to those very same movies that have created a sense of lackluster in us about robots they have also desensitized and conditioned us to not only accept but also expect them. There will always be those of us who have a healthy sense of skepticism right down the spectrum to those who remain off the grid and unplugged.

There are currently industrial sized, commercially used floor scrubbers, lawn mowers, and soon snow blowers all autonomous. What risks come with all this great technology? What about the unconscious or sleeping person in its path? What about the bored grad student who thinks the hacking of a service bot to be hilarious? Does your security department have a plan written for dealing with accidents where a robot was at the root of it all? What about adversarial bots? Do you have policies for workers and students on how to and not to interact and interfere with them? As a parent have you spoken to your children about autonomous lawn mowers?

This book asks a lot of questions. The answers need to come from all of us. We need to ask the questions and answer them together for a better tomorrow. Some of these may not apply to you and many will vary for different industries. I can assure you that our slow crawl to having physical safety and security concerns about AI and robots are soon over. I encourage you to embrace them and to reap all the benefits. Plan for the worst and hope for the best.

Imagine what you could do, gain, and learn from sticking a security camera on these autonomous workers? What could you gather from the sensor data? Can we add sensors that tell us if a human is in the area? Can we check on workers, working late, and alone to enhance their safety?

Currently, I can run away from an evil floor scrubber. What happens when we equip it to use door operators and/or upgrade its' technology to open access-controlled doors and drive up ramps? Please now go back and list every piece of equipment, machinery or electrified tool that was the cause of an industrial accident, fluke accident, or residually caused destruction while it exploded in a fire or fell into water and ask yourself how ludicrous that question is. Have you ever heard someone say, "we never saw that coming," "not in my wildest dreams," "who could have though that would have ever happened"?

When you start down this road make sure that the information security and engineering team are with you assessing the risk and suggesting controls and failsafe's the entire journey. You may have come up with some questions about the technologies and recommendations so far. These may include:

- What if the virtual assistant or the robot security officer is hacked?
- Who can hear and see our critical information?

Some counter questions may be:

- Do you have security guards standing in your most private executive strategy meetings?
- Don't you clean off white boards at day end?
- Do you realize that many cameras and intercoms at duress and parking stations, elevator emergency intercoms already can be used to dial in to speak to you and hear you while streaming live video? Now think back to every elevator ride you have taken, the conversations you have had, the adjusting of the belt.
- Do you have to have it placed in or patrol the most restricted places?

- Can a security guard patrol the washroom? Yes, you can stop recording in private areas.
- Should you be saying some of those things at work at all, talking about those secrets outside of the meeting room in the first place?
- Does it provide a false sense of security? I think for the human operator watching several screens of cameras can become monotonous, but watching it through the eyes of a couple robot coworkers could be interesting.
- The robot will never take a bribe, be too afraid, take sides, lose their cool, or be blackmailed (well not for the next 20 years).

Robots in security 2010–20

We always expect there is some space station, university, military base, or government lab where the technology of tomorrow is being hidden away, until it has been replaced and upgraded several times and then the first generation is sold to every business and household for less exciting applications. As I look across the countertop at the lineup of small appliances in my kitchen, nothing analog about them. Black, stainless steel all fitted with little LCD screens. I can only image what they are saying to one another. "So where are you from"? "I was checking pressure valves for leaks at NASA last week, now I am here making cappuccinos on command."

In the early part of this decade, we did not see much in the way of security robot applications in the main stream business world. In the last half, we have seen a gradual shift in this area. We are not talking about the autonomous vehicles driving around the campuses of technology conglomerates. We are referring to the innovators who took the mall patrol guard off there motorized two-wheeler and stuck a robot on top. The malls and buildings from the United States, the United Kingdom, and the Netherlands who have introduced two generations already in robot security guards. They can recognize your face, scan your employee access card, identify hazards, report missing items, transmit your commands, and identify humans. They can patrol for hours and be equipped with other safety sensors.

They received little attention beyond their initial marketing and PR efforts, that is, until social media blew up in 2017 when one fell into a water fountain. The online jokes ramped up to calling it robot suicide. This was some pretty good press.

The intelligence that can be gathered from these robot's sensors and patrols will prove to be very valuable in the future. This data will aide in further development of these robots, and the understanding of your indoor and outdoor environment as never thought of before. The ability to detect threats using already available sensing technology for items such as explosives is available today. For those familiar with bomb threat response protocol, we know to turn off all transmitting devices. Police remote control robots do not approach the scene until all people have been cleared. Transmitting devices such as radios and cell phones could be a possible trigger to detonate the explosive. What happens when an autonomous robot on patrol, passes by people, while transmitting and receiving and comes into proximity of an abandoned explosive? What about when they intentionally approach one or a suspicious package thought to be lost and found or rubbish? Will security now have access to and control a robot traditionally used by public law enforcement? Are you as a future CSO prepared to address these issues?

Robots in security 2020–30

Like many technological assets such as cars, drones, robots, and portable computer and communications devices there is one major factor in their limitations, power. The research and investment currently going into making highly efficient, low consumption devices or light weight, extended life batteries, or rapid charging contactless batteries has become a major branch of study and industry of its own.

Around 2013, a rush of concept videos exploded online. These showed prototype robots of all sorts of designs connected to power, attempting all kinds of physical feats. Articles were few and the technology seemed some years way. The applications appeared limited and power was clearly a major factor. For those robots that had some more athleticism, they seemed to lack the computing power compared to their large bulky cousins. If you have not watched any of the dystopian movies or shows on any of the very popular streaming services, I suggest you do. What was astonishing were the following developments. These robots unplugged, received some battery upgrades, lighter and stronger materials and learned how to crawl, walk, run, and jump.

One of the leading US-based service providers of patrol robots operating in 2018 found a way around the computing power. Put an onboard computer inside capable of handling the heavy lifting and then connect cellular, satellite, and other transmission and receiving capabilities to continuously stay connected, update information such as GPS and diagnostics. These forward-thinking innovators have started security robots on a path to do great things including 1 day saving lives. One of these robots can be subscribed to for 24/7 support for the same as it would cost to have just one security officer annually. An officer who only works one shift.

By 2020, we already start with robots that can already run more than 20 mph. Robots that can jump a 3 ft vertical. Robots that can patrol a mall autonomously. What about a robot with a defibrillator? Robots with tasers? In the first half of this decade, we will see robots with utilitarian upgrades. Better all terrain capabilities, longer battery life and faster charging. Weather resistant, more durable, lighter, and faster. In the latter half of the decade, we will see partners outside of security and robotics become involved on a mass scale. Aesthetics looks and design will go through many enhancements. The application of ML for problem solving, the cross technological sharing from systems designed for autopilot, self-driving cars and self-learning will allow the robots to use existing technologies and apply them to more complex tasks. The first automatous robot will have followed a suspect, extinguished a fire, and been accepted as part of the team. These robots will talk to the smart buildings they patrol in. By the end of this decade, we will have implemented our first laws solely around these devices. We will have seen our first criminal court case and destruction of property law suit involving these robots (where the robot is the victim or did not look where it was going). There will be groups calling for their destruction and those discussing their rights.

CSOs will already have onsite team members tasked with working with the robot. Procedures and standing orders will include the robot. They will have renewed their old service agreements and requested additional robots. We will have personally named them. Sound far off. In 1975 we named rocks, in the 1980s we named quilted dolls and stuffed puppies, those that all sold out and were all the rage. If in 2018 the toy robot in my home can be synced with a cell phone, avoid staircases, recognizes faces, and says your name, the security Robot of 2029 will be running facial recognition of every most wanted list while patrolling past hundreds if not thousands of people in every mall, train station, airport, and office tower. These security bots will be able to activate fire alarms, vacuum hazards, and wipe spills. The will be able to conduct license plate recognition searches and record incident reports for their human partners. They will have collected court evidence and been requested to court for examination.

Robots in security 2030–40

By 2030, some of the topics discussed here which includes data analytics, big data, and ML will be obsolete. We will be entering the second generation of AI. Computers are wonderful at taking a single task and learning to do that single, simple task more efficiently. Once game theory, a decade of historical robot data and our imaginations are poured into multiple streams of quantum computing with a goal of teaching the robot to improve itself the results will surpass what a human programmer can do. These robots will be using sophisticated internal processors and a link to the cloud where a portion of the computing power of one of tomorrow's supercomputers will provide continuous situational awareness and updates. Meanwhile those separate tasks and streams of data that are being compared to the design, processing, and performance of tasks of those robots will be merged into one analysis. By the end of this decade, the enhancements the system will recommend on its own will grow in rapid, large exponents. The computer will be telling you how to upgrade its own robot body better than you can ever have imagined designing it. It will have printed its own replacement part on a three-dimensional (3D) printer while on patrol. It will walk for hours and charge in seconds. It will have its first law enforcement counterparts. It will be able to chase and detain people.

This super robot will also have been hacked. It will have harmed its first human (without intention). It will complete at least 60% of its routine tasks more efficiently than its human counterpart. It will, however, lack TLC, empathy, and civility. Although it may not lose its temper, it will also not sincerely care. It's logical, unemotional decisions will be its strength and weakness. Some of these will look very human, sound very human, and be treated like one of the team. Armed with nonlethal weapons and defenses they will have saved their first human partner, quelled rioting crowds, and stopped a rabid animal. They will have earned respect of many and faced extreme prejudice of others. They will have become a major factor in the first human guard force reduction as we end 2039.

How can I be so confident? I am not. However, when I first mentioned seeing a video online nearly 8 years ago some of my colleagues scoffed and reminded me these were just concepts, far from deployment. A few years ago, I watched one patrolling around our conference. The next year they were in a handful of commercial premises being supplied by three different providers. A couple years ago a peer asked me with all sincerity how much they cost, with a deliberate intent to know and not just curiosity. Today, I can find white papers, more than 30 videos online, multiple service providers, enhancements already made in the past 6 years since the first generation. They are here to stay and only improving. I have already apologized to my robot vacuum for getting in the way twice and felt slightly guilty for old faithful collecting dust in the corner at least once.

Robotic process automation

Robot process automation (RPA) is a software form of task-specific ML. It can take the most mundane, routine tasks that have many steps and great volumes of work and automate nearly the entire process. I am going to take you through the foundations of several interconnected technologies, explain how they work and how to apply them. Then, I will tell you not to use most of them. If you have not used any of these so far, three things may be happening. First, you may be using them already and do not even know it. You have either purchased a case management, security audit report writing, or global threat awareness tool that is automating several functions for you. Second, you may be using a database or receiving useful data from another department who applied technologies such as RPA years ago. Finally, in our third bucket are there very small group of you who may not need it for your current security program, but may one day for the one you are going to build.

So how does it work? Not in terms of coding, but how do I use this software, what will it do for me? Before I get to that, I will give you another option. Now that I have covered step one to understanding coding and binary earlier in the book, here is an option. You can study the coding languages, buy the software and write thousands of lines of code to make one action (clicking the red box on your screen), and produce one simple result (and the screen border turns blue). Alternatively, you can be thankful for the programmers and coders and buy one of the top five RPA software applications in the market today. When I say today, I literally mean today. If you are not applying RPA by 2020, you may as well move onto an application that handles all your tasks from beginning to end.

The employee opens the RPA software. They have a simple graphical user interface (GUI). Some features allow you to hit record and then go about doing the steps to a daily task from beginning to end. Then press the record button to stop again. You can select options for the GUI to recognize when you click on the keyboard or mouse and much more. Let's use a few simple examples. Assuming the employee is using the GUI to record their steps and is toggling between very simple to use and follow features they may do the following.

Everyday employee A compiles a list of online threat intelligence directed at the company and show how it is trending. They open an Excel spreadsheet. They open Facebook and search for every mention of the CEO. They repeat this for the name of the company, company address, and senior leadership. They repeat all of this again on Twitter, LinkedIn, Snap Chat, Instagram, etc. They perform online searches using Google and review the top results (this is an example, many CSOs have departments with much deeper search capabilities, automated systems, and service providers doing this). On the website, they can use one of a few options and filters. One of these is referred to a data scraping. This can retrieve specific data on each webpage. You can then populate a spreadsheet with all of this data. You can then graph the data you have chosen to populate. Finally, you can set up and automated email to send each day once complete to a distribution list or safe on a deck for the quarterly report. Once this is complete, it can be tested for quality control and there after all these steps will be handled automatically by the system. This entire task has been automated in less than 20 min.

What if you created an online world map in Excel? You applied conditional formatting. When the risk increases, the country is red. When it is low, it is green and there is an entire spectrum and legend to support the risk rankings you find in the online in the threat trending. Again, there are many sources of data. If we use Twitter for example and look online for clusters, continuous mentions of key terms (terrorism, bombing, vehicle attack, murder, strike, etc.) and organize these we can get an idea of what the security situation may be. (This has been simplified.) By applying the RPA software to your analyst's daily steps, you can nearly automate the entire process and have the map change colors in real time, all by itself while you monitor it. Please note this is to help you understand it and start to apply RPA to many opportunities. There are, however, service providers using Twitter, for example, to produce some remarkable, real-time threat intelligence. In all, 500 mass shooter-related tweets in one small area, in a short time can be a very helpful early alert system. These providers have nearly perfected a valuable service and provide these at reasonable costs. Facebook has access to a significant amount of data. Although no one wants social media to become big brother, the data can provide trends, capture red flags, and identify escalations in behavior that could possibly prevent human-initiated catastrophes by giving us early warnings to act on and intervene. Intervention does not have to be minority report. It can be offering health and wellness to those who indicate an intent to harm. The signs are not always there, but when the red flags go up and begin to escalate in severity and frequency, help can be offered.

Are you the security manager, director, or CSO responsible for the department budget? Reporting and tracking of spend? Do you have a sheet that calculates ROI? If your company has invested in accounting software that can provide all of this, then I suggest you learn it and maximize its potential for you. However, the ability to pull information from many spread sheets, chart and graph it and place into your deck can be automated. Can you imagine investing some money and a little time to reduce hours if not days from your work year?

What about a corporate investigator trying to search and sort threat or fraud information from an email. Then populating all of this onto a spread sheet or report. Instead of 3 workdays you could automate this in less than half an hour. What if you have a spread sheet already made from previous files complete with tabs, pie charts, and all? You could automate the populating of the email data to the sheet in 15 min. You need to get out of your comfort zone and embrace these remarkable force multipliers.

Credit card fraud detection uses this technology to automate the process that identifies anomalies, cross references it, and acts against possible frauds by suspending the card until the account holder is notified. Years ago, this took teams of human analysts.

Consider the following. Your company already has RPA software and experienced users, you can leverage this and get one of your people a software license. Have it installed on their profile and get them training. Choose one small, monotonous task and have them automate it. Imagine that they could do this for five tasks in corporate security. What if those tasks previously took an average of 10 min each day for those two staff? What if we multiply those five tasks by 10 min? If you already have the software, your team performs many repetitive tasks, are using disparate databases, then this is a great option. A second option of many is to connect semiautomated applications using the network and may possibly require some customization such as writing scripts and code. You may get the same results; however, you often spend more money and lose some of the out of the box functionality. If you upgrade one system, the others may have to follow. You will need to be mindful of how the various server upgrades and patches impact this chain linked creation.

My suggestion is that you go to the case management section in Chapter 4 and consider skipping all of this as a future CSO.

Applying metrics to the security function

Data, data, data I cannot stress this enough. Good actionable intelligence. Security departments of any size, scale, industry, or specialization have access to great amounts of information. If you are an aspiring security manager or security director and have never reported any metrics or are not sure what to do with them, then I hope I can impress upon you, the importance of this part of your security program.

We will start with a building security department. Create an Excel spread sheet for the month. Make it a 31 days month. Leave a space for the title "Security Incident Reports" in the top left. Under this leave column A, blank and from left to right enter numbers. In column A, I want you to write the words incident type. Under this all the way down the page, I want you to write the 10 most common types of occurrence.

Fire alarm, flood, power failure, medical, trespass, crime, bomb threat, property damage, natural disaster, etc. There are many books, lists online and later we will discuss software that can provide you with many more good examples. Under each main heading, list subheadings. False fire alarm, arson, fire, etc. Throughout the month, each time you or your team complete an incident report place a number under the day of the month. It may start to look something like this:

January					
	1	2	3	4	5
Incident types	Monday	Tuesday	Wednesday	Thursday	Friday
Fire alarm					
Arson	0	1	2	0	0

Make sure to copy this tab for each month of the year and the first tab can be a total summary of the year. Have the end of the rows total and all incidents total (use the math functions built into the sheet) at the bottom.

If you're not certain get an Excel guru or someone in your office who works with Excel to teach you. There are also many great online tutorials.

Armed with this year's worth of security incidents, you can now try graphing the data in different ways. Ask yourself are there any patterns? Maybe loitering outside drops in the winter, however, trespassing in the colder weather increases. What do all the maintenance deficiencies tell management? If you have "calls for service" increasing by 10% a year, this may help the business case to add a split shift officer somewhere.

The security manager notices a spike in overnight thefts for 2 weeks. A closer look reveals they are all from the same office floor. Take a closer look at the access control, visitor logs, contractor logs, work orders, and cameras. This may reveal an overnight project by unsupervised contractors.

Another example could be as follows. Food goes missing for 2 weeks in the staff canteen at a factory. The incidents all seem to occur in the middle of the night. By all indications there is no one coming in or out. A search by a team at 2:00 am revels an employee living in a mechanical room.

By charting out employee schedules, work assignments, door lock interrogations, and missing fridge items, a hotel security director can narrow down internal thefts of minibar items.

A building has a high security perimeter, turnstiles and guards posted at every entrance. Despite these barriers and controls, there still are several cases a month of unauthorized persons found inside the barrier. Good data may be able to help you see that the guard walks away from their post for hours, unattended. The turnstiles need photoelectric sensors and alarms. The staff are swiping in friends or holding doors open or people are tailgating. Someone has found and is using an unauthorized card. Doors are being propped open and alarms ignored. There are so many more examples. These access breaches can lead to workplace violence and lost data.

What about business and compliance metrics? You can use a couple of key factors to calculate the risk for a premise. You can set risk thresholds and document how often you perform a security audit on a scale of low to high risk for those premises. You score the measure of the security at a premise against the threats, risk, and measures to prevent those. You can track how many security assessments you completed in a year. How much it cost to use consultants versus in-house FTE. If you need resources and funding, you should be armed with good relevant data.

There are service providers who offer training and software to assess the propensity for violence and/or help you to identify pre-incident indicators and more. The Center for Aggression Management who offer the critical aggression prevention system (CAPS) or Gavin De Becker and Associates, who offer the MOSAIC threat management system are two key examples. Data are not just numbers. All the metadata, keywords, and cell phone numbers are an analysts treasure trove. You can look for obvious red flags before many acts of violence and sometimes even suicide. Preincident indicators can be used in a chart, counted and scored. If you determine that the red flags are the midpoint, then an expert can look at the person's life in totality (relationships, stability, history, criminality, social media, web searches, possible triggers, etc.) and see a pattern that may lead any normal human being to that midpoint. After one red flag and a few more triggers, you may have another red flag. This could be the point where the person in duress sits and contemplates claiming their own life or their perceived antagonist. Something in their makeup, psyche, or a final trigger could push them to act in one of the two of the previously mentioned ways. You can quantity those triggers, stabilizers, red flags, and pre-incident indicators. At what point is social intervention needed to get this person well, help or other care? Leading experts, using the incident data from thousands of cases, criminal and psychological assessments of these situations have quantified these probabilities into scoring systems.

By already having the data in the risk assessments, incident reports, investigation reports, and other records you can offer a way to better predict and prevent several perils to your organization. Start by collecting the data now. I am often asked about what metrics a security a manger should be collecting and reporting. In financial services as an example, your regulators will require certain information. You may have an internal audit and risk department who report metrics on a regular basis. These are highly skilled professionals which include accountants and actuaries, people you can leverage, for their expertise. Specific security metrics can be hard when you need a starting point. With good data you can chart it out and tell a story that compels your audience to see a measurable set of facts. Then, you may soundboard off other leaders to be certain they are relevant to the audience. Do not get hung up on pretty graphs and charts if it is not the right data. Knowing every single incident at your premises in the form of a small chart can help the CSO determine how to allocate resources. No different then the crime analysts' report to the chief of police. The crime analyst may compile the entire city's crime data, organize it, and learn that there is little to no crime in precinct 1. This may indicate to the chief that in this area they can deploy less patrol officers. The statistics may demonstrate a high crime rate in precinct 8. This may inform the chief to deploy more patrol officers to this sector. I know some of you will be chomping at the bit to remind me that the absence of crime does not mean there isn't any, this is just an example. This just as easily be applied to a mall or building where thefts are occurring. If the same wall is spray painted every night between 2:00 am and 5:00 am, then it may be wise to post someone there or train a camera in this place to help deter or identify and then stop the aspiring artist. Police and security budgets are only so big and resources only so many. What sounds good in crime theory is not always what the chief has to work with. Going to the executive leadership team of a fortune 100 company and talking about the number of slip and falls, elevator entrapments, or trespassers is a sure way to find yourself unemployed. The slip and fall that cost millions, that you have now implemented a prevention strategy is noteworthy. The entrapment of a person with medical fragility, that lasted 10 h or was instead 30 entrapments in one premise that went unreported, un-escalated, and resulted in a law suit or death; after analysis you have now come up with a series of preventative and or response strategies, that is data worthy of your executive report. Breaches to data from stolen laptops, stolen files, system breaches, on premise homicides, emergencies that cause significant business disruption. That is what the CEO, board, and regulators may need to learn about.

Book author, George Campbell and the Security Executive Council (SEC) have published online resources that not only provided me with some of the best metrics to use, but also helped others to start thinking about security data in a whole new way. If your company has data scientists, get to know them. Take your data, from systems, reports, threat assessments, incidents reports, and loss reports. Have them crunch the data separately, together, in layers. Have them help you develop a way of looking at it and reporting it. Take your engineers, your RPA and now automate that incredible dashboard.

There are providers who offer both services and software for case management. There are providers of global threat data collection and analysis applications to monitor world events, travellers, and crime. There are applications to write and report threat assessments. These are canned, well-developed versions of the resources listed above. What if you could use the RSA Archer Platform or the Palantir Technologies suite of services to capture, sort, and provide a dashboard on all of this. Companies like TrakTik and resolver are now offering customized ERSM platforms very much tailored to corporate security departments. The research, whitepapers, and security community involvement that some of these companies have been doing is cutting edge. They are trying to lead us into the future and embark on things that have not been done before. Their founders are heavily involved with industry peers. Not just as clients and providers but at the table as partners, trying to create and continuously improve the way we do things. Big data, information, intelligence is all a part of good security metrics. You can get tired of hearing the terms community policing and crime analysis; however, it has revolutionized the way police have evolved from reactive responders to data driven-crime prevention and investigation experts.

Robert Hasting, a Canadian security executive, early adopter and advocate of security metrics and ESRM. Robert has written and contributed to the use of metrics in security. In April 2016, he authored a LinkedIn article titled "The Value of Security Metrics and Why You Should Care," Hastings lists some considerations and steps in the importance of collecting data and creating metrics. One key thing that stands out is his statement "Don't be afraid of numbers" the author goes on to say… "math and statistics is scary to a lot of people. It doesn't need to be. Many commercially available programs will perform the bulk of the work for you"… From this, you can see that you don't have to face it alone. There are many professionals using metrics and software that can aide you in the quest to become an intelligence lead professional.

The benefits and risks of AI

Now, we can circle back to the topic of AI with better understanding. You may have heard the expression, "don't put all your eggs in one basket." A lot of the small steps we are taking to get to real useful AI are telling us to do just this. Big data, ML, blockchain, and robotic process automation all require us to compile or link massive quantities of our most precious, quality data into one machine. You may very well need a supercomputer protecting the supercomputer who is providing you with this great automated processing power.

At a high level the CSO of tomorrow, hopes to have a system that will process all the department collected data and turn out a finished work product with less resources and of better quality then today.

We aim to understand the risks of AI, and hope that when we achieve true superhuman intelligence that we can coexists, let alone work with or pretend to control it.

As a CSO you have that sixth sense. That well-tuned, risk adverse super ability to detect when something isn't just quite right. Be bold and brave and help drive change but trust your gut instincts and know when to pull the plug on something, literally.

Now speaking to the very large audience who are tasked with not only protecting enterprise, but those in national security, intelligence, and defense. We all have an idea, training, playbook, and failsafe for as many scenarios as we can imagine. For decades, few firefighter's response plans or manuals included a response procedure for responding to downed or observed unidentified flying objects (UFOs). Why shouldn't we have a state of readiness in place when someone tries to take the second generation of AI technology and use it to attack our systems and infrastructure?

When the power grid, airplanes or medical implants are under attack by corrupted advanced AI what will be your defensive and offensive strategy? Will we have to think of system continuity and recovery while we neutralize the invasive threat? I do not foresee antivirus software stopping an entity smarter than we are driven to shutdown pacemakers. What if the AI we send after it decides it likes the other team better?

Possible ways of slowing down or stopping this threat:

- Attack the power source
- With simple, multiple sources of brute force attack requests, essentially a denial of service attack (DDoS) by simple AI systems

- Can we place logic bombs in its way without impacting the system we are protecting?
- Inject an infinite loop equation

There are many articles online today asking these questions, some with a hint of sarcasm while others on the verge of nervous curiosity. We need security professionals coming into the fold today who are up to the challenge. It is in fact a very serious question. For every enterprise and nation state investing so heavily to be the first to win this race, a level of caution and a backup plan should be demanded of them. I recall back in the 1980s few of us believed that way ahead in 2020 we would have cured cancer and landed on Mars. In fact, we have only taken a few steps forward. I predict AI will be the first major accomplishment that occurs suddenly and without warning well ahead of when we are anticipating. I hope it is a pleasant surprise. We will, however, do it almost by accident. Like penicillin or the microwave that were pleasant accidents to develop one thing we may discover another. As the entrepreneur rockets toward the moon the chief risk officer steers the rudder to avoid asteroids and the CSO shines the light and hits the alarms, but the rocket forges ahead swaying from side to side in a forward motion. We are not here to stop progress, just to make sure we get there alive.

Let's look back at what we do with great discoveries:

- We split the atom and then made a bomb.
- We discovered nuclear energy, weaponized it, and tested it on our own plantet and in our oceans.

Nothing to see here. At this rate, humanity will ensure that the role of the CSO will be here forever. Tongue and cheek aside I tried to think of as many scenarios as possible. AI as a threat, what are all the things that could go wrong and how could I stop them. The list on the left was much longer. That was not a good thing. I don't know if placing, unplug the computer on the right will work once its in our critical systems and spread across the net. If we all just took our hands off the keyboard and left on the power what would happen? Perhaps, it is already connected and alive.

On the lighter side of the cons list were issues already addressed which include the employment that may be eliminated by this automation. We forget that we have a choice to make sure the next generation have new careers to grow into. Where a job in a call center may close a career in digital technologies will open.

But what is the purpose of all of this? Sure, it is making some things cool and convenient. But if all else fails, I can stick my head out the door to check the weather. We certainly use technology for social media, to drive consumerism and develop more technology. What about that essentials of life? What about food and shelter? How does this relate to security?

It relates in two ways. Some of the experts working on these technologies will use it to solve the global food crisis, to increase the fresh water supply and build better, abundant, cost effective homes. When our essentials are being provided by this great apparatus, we should look back at the original point. Don't put all your eggs in one basket. If for whatever reason it all goes wrong, it may be like a pilot having to check 60 controls as a plane is descending when the autopilot goes AWOL. Society is civilized until we a natural disaster strikes, and we are rioting in and demonstrating our worst while using a stadium like a shelter. If this machine is providing our basics of life, and according to Maslow, safety or security of the person is one of those foundations, what does that mean? Do we lose our security? Does it turn against us? Lock us up for our own good?

I am a big supporter of technological advancement. I am not one to stand in front of a title wave, but rather try to surf it. In the many interesting concerns, I found the one that stood out to me as todays greatest concern is social manipulation. This is the sort of thing that can topple governments and cause us to question democracy.

Now let's shift to the positives. As the biomedical engineers help to take us into the next decade, advancements in AI may mean a level of human and medical machine integration that the system may one day be able to monitor, assess, diagnose, treat and cure the patient its connected to. It may very well be able to fight or at least give us leaps ahead in the battle against cancer and heart disease. If today's CISO and CSO believe that protecting a banking system is critical, wait until a billion people are being monitored by devices that read their vitals, are connected to life support, have medical devices installed and are being cured by these technologies. Security engineering will have to be a part of how everything is designed, developed, built, and deployed.

Can you imagine that over the next decade machines will depend on our input and cognitive thought, while we enjoy an improvement in the quality of our lives? Perhaps, you can set up your computer to run a few tasks for the evening to get through year end while you make a dance recital for a change. The computer won't get sick, tired, or make mistakes. What if we had roadways like those seen in the movie Minority Report? A separate place for bikes and pedestrians. No more distracted driving, speeding, or variation in driving skills. No more driving under the influence, no more vehicle borne attacks, completely autonomous.

The future role of AI in CS

As corporate security moves through the next two decades, it will evolve and expand into a department likely to encompass all related departments. In Chapter 5, we will explore some things to come. Here, I will provide my vision of what it will look like in action as a seamless transition of interconnected integrations connecting the virtual and physical space. I believe we will continue to try to find ways to increase our privacy laws, secure vital systems holding our records and accounts and dread hacks, breaches, and data loss like no generation before. I also believe that same generation over the next 20 years will unwittingly share more of their lives to the interconnected world both online and through lifestyle devices. Your phone and vehicle will talk to one another, to your home, office, and other traffic. As a CSO you already know this scenario. In room 1 an employee sits and explains to your that they do not want your big brother like systems knowing where they go or seeing when they leave. In room 2, the same employee tells you they are being cyber-stalked somehow, as you see they have placed their every step, meals, plans, vacation, likes, and dislikes online. Do not watch me, but let me tell you what I am doing, thinking, and feeling 24/7. Don't you dare lose my data, but I will enter it everywhere online and email it to myself at home. This will be an ever increasingly complicated paradox for the CSO.

The security systems will talk to the building, the vehicles entering, the phones scanning, and the hundreds of external cloud servers speaking to it. Imagine that creating an access card is just two clicks. Imagine the camera can follow everyone, everywhere without human interaction. That a fire alarm activation will provide the security manager with the building occupancy on their mobile phone with 90% accuracy. Imagine conducting a threat assessment on a tablet by checking 50 boxes and receiving a completed report with the best recommendations possible a minute after the last entry is made. Imagine incident reports are corrected, automatically sent to the CSO and all the correct parties for that report (insurance, legal, C-suite, compliance, etc.), where all receipts, read receipts, acknowledgements are automated.

Computers like the Sierra or ATS-2 supercomputer protect nuclear arsenals today. Tomorrow this computing power will secure our corporate networks and optimize life safety. This will require acceptance from the security industry. It will take our understanding today. We cannot expect professionals, who have grown up with these concepts, were schooled in them and know nothing but an interconnected world to just suddenly secure it all, use it to secure us all and create an AI security supported program. We are the generation who need to lay that foundation. We need to not tolerate it but accept it and even embrace it. Why is it we go to work and someone asks the seasoned corporate security team members to use a new software application, update their hardware and deploy new methods and they grumble. Those same people go home and throw out the VCR and get a DVD player. They discard the DVD for the blu ray and then toss the blu ray for streaming on the TV? You might think with the adversity to change observed in the office, they go home to a candle lit house and a wood stove.

If you are operating your security program in a vacuum. If you are fine just the way you are. If you see your peers as competition, ESRM, technology, and modern era management as fads or soon to fade trends then you are in a race by yourself. If you are not running to get on this train, then your peers will without a doubt will shift into hyperdrive while you continue to stack your boxes of paper. You may as well show up to a drag race with a bicycle. I can assure you, you're not hiding it. Those who are at the table know very well who isn't. It will take an industry wide, unified effort to make this change over the next 20 years.

AI in corporate security will soon be a menu of exciting pathways to explore. The next generation will be able to accomplish workloads, behavioral analysis, and financial crime detection in a tenth the time and with much better results than we see today. I know that many of the CSOs already doing these things today are willing to collaborate and help get us there. You are reading my commitment.

The chief security officer

4

I anticipate that you are reading this because you are a security professional, an aspiring chief security officer (CSO), or a CSO looking to improve in areas you may not have considered or to gauge where you may be in the development of your program. For those of you who are none of these things but are here on this journey with us, we are happy to have you as a partner and hope that you may consider joining us.

Throughout this section I will refer to security officers, security guards, and professionals of similar roles and titles as professional protection officers (PPOs). I will try to avoid referring to PPOs as entry level, or security managers as mid-level and CSOs as senior. I will discuss the evolution of each role as a career professional. What I mean by this is to view those who will enter and remain a PPO for their entire career as a *professional or career* protection officer. There are many people who enter as a security guard and remain a security guard and that is fine. You are the first and last people I see each day. You keep me safe and give me the heads up on what is happening and where the action is. There is a difference in someone who works today as a security guard and sees it just as a job, something to pay the bills or get them through school until they reach their calling or find something better. There are those who believe they are stuck there, had to start or fall there. Those who want to climb the security ladder. I have had officers tell me that they want to do more, in the sense of taking on a role with some variety such as moving up to supervision. I have spoken to officers who wish to continue being an officer but to rotate positions. I have had officers who want to remain exactly in their roles. I have had those who want to move up in the sense of being the best of the best as one put it, however remaining an officer. Let's discuss some of these.

I will pause. Some of you are asking yourself "I am a CSO and was never an officer" or "I am a security manager and did my time." The both of you may be wondering why we are discussing officers? Well many will rise through the ranks today and more so in the future. To be a good leader and manager of a security program, understanding the industry at all levels and your people better will help. Let's break down a few of these examples. If you have not talked to your officers about how they are doing, what their aspirations are and explained to them the great big security world out there, you can start today. This applies to people at all stages and levels in information security, business continuity, risk, cybersecurity, financial crimes, general investigations, and all similar branches.

As the CSO you should encourage the managers you lead and you yourself to get in touch, write it down and see what you can learn from this. Be open to criticism,

The Chief Security Officer's Handbook. https://doi.org/10.1016/B978-0-12-818384-7.00004-5
© 2019 Elsevier Inc. All rights reserved.

67

listen, don't argue. While explaining their hopes, dreams, and aspirations you may learn their interests and motivators. They may also share what they see as their own personal obstacles. Some of those will be workplace related, some maybe you and sometimes they are correct to some degree. This is a moment when the both of you really speak, reflect, and grow. Many of us want to be Atticus Finch, here is your chance to listen, don't judge, and lead.

1. I am just working as a security guard as a job, just to pay the bills or to get me through school.
   - Make sure that this person is aware that there are many different specializations in security, an entire career can be made in this profession.
   - Treat this officer like all others, I have worked with many who went on to manage other departments, work their way up to becoming the general manager of the building or a community policing partner.
   - Tell them they are always welcome to come back, to stay on a while and perhaps bring some different perspective to the team.
2. There are those who believe they are stuck there, had no choice but to start or fall there
   - *I was a police officer back home, I moved here for a better life, for love etc., and I am not a citizen, am learning the language and I feel stuck as a guard*
   - *I retired from law enforcement, made a mistake because like you I am human, I am deaf in one ear, going blind, and have a bad stomach the army don't need me anymore...*
   - *I come from humble beginnings, never went to school and had to get a job*
   - *I was laid off from (insert any major employer here) and this is what I could get*
   - Does this person have a development plan?
   - Now that they are here are they trying to leave, or have they accepted it and may be ready to hear how actually awesome it is?
   - They do realize that their public-sector counterparts do not typically conduct terrorism related threat assessments, fly with executives to foreign destinations or master a control room of sophisticated technology?
3. Those who want to climb the security ladder, stay the same or move around
   - *I want to be promoted (and move up the ranks)*
   - *I want to rotate positions (I do not want a promotion, just to move around the department [in time many of these people do move up])*
   - *I do not want change (I am a single parent, my spouse has a busy career, I love my day shift and feel comfortable with this level of responsibility, this is a second career I am done soon)*
   - *I want to be one of the elite (I am young and do not see so much as a promotion for now but want to go from condominium guard to Nuclear Response Officer or bodyguard to the CEO)*

Here is where you can make every effort to educate your team on this massive industry that employs millions, operates in the billions, and protects much more. I will focus mostly in the physical security space here. Once I began pulling out my boxes of conference materials and reaching out to many colleagues (who I am very thankful to) I realized that an entire book could be written on the following few pages. Throughout every year of my career I was amazed to learn about another industry specific association, club, periodical, magazine, trade show, conference, etc. In some cases, I wished I had known about each one earlier and in other cases was embarrassed I did not already know about them at that stage in my career.

I suggest you start by reading up on the following online, reaching out to peers and leaders to learn more. Join, subscribe, and get involved. Share the news. Discover an association, a security author, a new company or CSO. Follow them and connect with them on every social media platform you can. The lists below are not all inclusive but give you an idea.

Associations

This highlights some of the more general groups and does not include the many specialized groups for banks, financial services, nuclear, critical infrastructure, military, health care, campus, and many more. By searching the words security association and then adding a county or continent to your search you will find a very extensive list of resources.

ASIS International https://www.asisonline.org/

ASIS International CSO Center https://www.asisonline.org/membership/cso-center/

CANASA Canadian Security Association http://www.canasa.org/canasa/EN/

ISMA International Security Management Association https://isma.com/

IPSA International Professional Security Association https://www.ipsa.org.uk/

British Security Industry Association (BSIA) https://www.bsia.co.uk/about-us.aspx

BSA British Security Association http://www.britishsecurityassociation.com/

The Security Institute https://security-institute.org/

International Association for Counterterrorism & Security Professionals https://www.iacsp.com/about.php

Overseas Security Advisory Council (OSAC) https://www.osac.gov/Pages/AboutUs.aspx

European Corporate Security Association https://www.ecsa-eu.org/

Other great resources https://www.securityguard-license.org/articles/security-organizations.html

Magazines (white papers, journals, digital only editions too, etc.)

Security Management https://sm.asisonline.org/

Security Magazine https://www.securitymagazine.com/

Canadian Security Magazine https://www.canadiansecuritymag.com/

SP&T News https://www.sptnews.ca/

Security Director News http://www.bizreport.com/magazines/security_director_news.html

International Association for Counterterrorism & Security Professionals—Counterterrorism Quarterly https://www.iacsp.com/select-pay.php

The Counter Terrorist Magazine http://www.thecounterterroristmag.com/

Security Journal https://www.springer.com/social+sciences/journal/41284

Unmanned Systems http://www.unmannedsystemsmagazine.org/home

Security & Border and CST & CBRNE https://tacticaldefensemedia.com/security-border-cst-cbrne/

Armor & Mobility https://tacticaldefensemedia.com/armor-mobility/

Security Buyer https://www.securitybuyer.com

Campus Security & Life Safety https://www.campuslifesecurity.com

Campus Safety https://www.campussafetymagazine.com/

Locksmith Ledger International https://www.locksmithledger.com

Security Today https://www.securitytoday.com

SDM https://www.sdmmag.com/

Security Technology Executive https://www.securityinfowatch.com/magazine/stec

SD&I https://www.securityinfowatch.com/magazine

LPM Loss Prevention Magazine https://losspreventionmedia.com/magazine/

Fraud Magazine https://www.fraud-magazine.com/fm-home.aspx

CSO https://www.csoonline.com/

Frontline Safety & Security https://security.frontline.online/

See also Security Journals for different industries. A few security companies produce their own papers, newsletters, and journals available to staff and subscribers. Magazines for building managers, real estate owners, and facilities. Magazines printed out of the United States, United Kingdom, and Canada that focus on business, men's lifestyle, tech and special interest magazines also run cyber, spy, and security articles, a quick search of their website will yield some interesting results.

A few associations (e.g., the ASIS CRISP reports), schools, large corporations, government and not-for-profit organizations sponsor ongoing, peer-reviewed white papers. They also produce standards and guidelines on several important topics. The US Department of Justice have published and participated in a few papers with direct relevance to topics crucial to corporate security executives.

I highly recommend writing. Start with book review in a security magazine. Interview a peer about their journey or program and submit it. Write a 12-page field manual in your area of expertise. Join a standards and guidelines committee and actively participate. There are many opportunities to get involved in the community by not only reading but by contributing.

Books

Security books written for education programs (text books), books from the subject matter experts point of view, interest subjects, and hot topics have been available from most major publishers and associations for decades. If you have completed a professional designation or browsed your associations online store you may have found a few. I have included some recommended reading in this book. Some of those texts may lead you down a wonderful path of learning and self-development. They often open the doors for aspiring CSOs. Having read a couple of them multiple times, they bring on different meaning and understanding at different stages of your career. I have been asked about my extensive reading in the field. "What is the point of all that reading if it is not for a course"? or "Why are you doing all this writing, if it is not for a course"? We do not always need recognition for our self-improvement efforts. The reward is simply knowing how to do the job. Several academics and experts have shared their expertise, experiences, and points of view and I suggest you soak it all in. I have connected with many of the authors in security, heard them speak, and follow them online. You may find this is an easy way to keep on top of the latest hot button topics, from reputable sources.

Videos

There are many videos for sale. Videos a security manager or human resources department can use for training. Workplace violence prevention, responding to active shooter events, bank robbery prevention and response, security guard 101, etc. In the past decade online video streaming services have exploded. You can type in nearly any security course, topic, keyword, and find dozens of helpful videos, prerecorded webinars, and even security poking fun at security. Use your judgment to gauge what is of quality and what is not so great. These have provided me with a quick understanding of many topics on the rise, peripheral to my core skills and helped me to hitchhike onto other materials on that topic. Entire information security and security management course materials have been uploaded for your viewing pleasure. I would not recommend trying to earn the "documentary diploma" however use these as one more aide in your learning arsenal, and to keep you up to date when your too busy to commit to another course.

Conferences, exhibits, summits, and trade shows

The largest security associations host annual conference and exhibit gatherings around the world. If you are in corporate security but focus on emergency management, investigations, disaster recovery, etc., they have their conferences too. There is vendor hosted events, shows that are technology focused and member's only summits for CSOs and government personnel. I recommend not only attending, but also actively listening. In time I suggest not only attending all the sessions that are important to your line of work and objectives, but also participating on a panel, speaking, volunteering, and getting involved further. The doors that will open for you, the contacts you will make and the feeling of satisfaction when you give back to the security community, share and mentor others is only understood once your ingrained in the energy.

Education

Like the role of the CSO itself many professionals come into the field from different paths. This goes the same for their education. No different than any other industry, the CSO of today is not always the most educated member of the department. There will always be highly skilled experts including technologist, information technology, or financial focused roles who may require certain education. Career colleges, colleges or city colleges, universities, and some private training corporations offer certificates, diplomas and degrees in security, security management, risk, cybersecurity, organizational resiliency, emergency, and security risk management, and much more.

No different from any other educational program, there are some that are good and some that are great. Do not be tempted to invest in a diploma or degree that is not recognized under the same accrediting bodies as the larger main stream universities if you wish to be competitive in the global job market. Some of these unaccredited degrees or accredited under bodies that are not recognized by other higher education schools or employers could impact your ability to get hired, apply to a master program or in some cases apply to law school or a professional accounting designation, for example. There are online websites that you can check to see if the major accreditation bodies list the school. Do not take the schools' word for it, or the online blog posts of current students or graduates of that school.

2010–20

For as long as the past three decades there have been law and security, criminal justice, and justice studies programs offered by higher learning educational institutions. For years many of these were heavily focused on public law enforcement and taught by current and former law enforcement. These focused-on entry level or young students.

During the end of the last decade and the begging of this one we observed several certificates, diplomas, degrees, and even masters programs at the graduate level in security management. It seemed that only the upper echelons of security were enrolled in and graduating from security management masters programs by the mid-2000s.

It is common today to see many PPOs with 5–7 years of experience entering the job with or completing a diploma in a police or security-related program during that period of tenure on the job. Most security specialists and managers in corporate security departments by the mid-to-late 2000s had a degree from any field of study. By the end of this decade, we will see hundreds of people around the globe who have graduated with a Masters in a security management or closely related area of study, who are in mid-level security management roles, teaching, consulting, and/or leading national and/or global security departments.

A security guard in many places in the 1980s may have watched a video, signed a form, and received a security permit or license. In the 1990s some site orientation and perhaps a first-aid and CPR course would have rounded off their training. By the early 2000s some predeployment training, on the job structured training and a college diploma were much more common. By 2015 several countries required protection officers of all different kinds to obtain a license or permit. The licensing authority required approximately a week-long course, first-aid and CPR, an exam, and passing grade. The officer would be required to adhere to a code of conduct and a few uniform and registration protocol. Almost all these officers have had training at a career college or employer offered orientation in emergency response, customer service, use of force, and more. Licensing and training standards will expand globally and improve where they already exist today by the end of this decade. As people who are often the first responders, make arrests, and provide life safety in both proactive and reactive services, this is one of the best things to happen to those professionals. The level of training for an officer working at a warehouse compared to an armed response officer located in a critical infrastructure facility still varies significantly today. Regulation, justification, and cost are often key factors. This will change. Armed or unarmed, all of these roles will be more educated, better trained and will have a greater level of responsibility soon.

2020–30

If you told a CSO in 1975 that security guards would all be educated above high school, be licensed, have mandatory training, use defibrillators, make lawful arrests, write parking infraction notices, use sophisticated security systems, send photo evidence and messages around the world from a handheld phone in seconds, and use a phone or fingerprint to open a door by the end of their career, they may have sent you for a psychological evaluation.

PPO will be a career that you must want to join, not a job you pick up. The entry level requirements will be significantly more stringent in the next several years. The job market will be filled with a generation who have all graduated from a 2-year college program. Major enterprises will require their contract and contingent workers to go through the same background checks or equivalent as regular full-time employees in almost all operating jurisdictions.

Nearly all building security management will be college educated in a security-related discipline, have several years of progressive experience in the security field, and have completed a designation. Most corporate security managers will have a related degree. The number of CSOs with a master's in security management will have doubled. All CSOs will have a degree and a designation.

You will see convergence in security management programs that will focus in either security management or information security management. Both will offer business, leadership, and information technology courses. They will also cross over into one another's domains to a degree.

2030–40

By this time there will be two decades worth of security management graduate classes at all levels of diploma and degree. Employers will demand a higher education and prefer to hire career security professionals. The roles and education will have merged into programs that leave the graduate capable of advising on top security matters and projects, conducting complex investigations, writing business continuity plans, handling the incident command, speaking cybersecurity, and understanding MBA 101.

The lines between law enforcement and security programs will be completely divided. Criminology departments will no longer own the security and risk arena. This will be a business, law, or technology discipline. CSOs who did not work their way up in the field and did not study security management will have accounting and or legal backgrounds.

Certification

Professional certifications or designations are often earned in security by years of service, sometimes rank, education, and only after studying for and passing an examination. Several of the larger associations listed above offer these designations. There are certifications for general security management, investigations, integrators, fraud specialists, anti-money laundering experts, security consultants, PPOs, business continuity, emergency management, campus, hospital, hotel, banking, information security, and other areas of specialty.

Currently there are thousands certified professionals. It is important to understand the difference between certified and licensed. Currently there are many certified professionals with postsecondary education and those without. There are those with the minimum years of service and supervision and those with much more and higher than required. I highly recommend the following. After completing a degree, earn the highest and most relevant credential relevant to your role and stop there. Many professionals feel the need to earn several to be accepted as an expert. Accountants, lawyers, engineers, and architects for example do not do this. The burden of continuing education when you have several is too great when you have the workload of a CSO.

You may earn one every few years through organizations which include the IFPO or ASIS International. They have programs for each career level or specialty. It does not mean that a 7-year veteran of the certified protection officer (CPO) program who is now a security supervisor or team lead who has just completed their exam and is now Certified in Security Supervision and Management (CSSM) needs to also maintain the currency of their CPO thereafter. You may by choice, but it is unlikely it will be raised in your future job interview for CSO.

You may enter a bank as a corporate security investigator and earn your ASIS International Professional Certified Investigator (PCI) designation. Over time you may work both the fraud and anti-money laundering (AML) desks. In this case it is understandable to earn these designations. Having the alphabet behind your name for ego or for seeking some validation is not necessary. Trust me personally on this.

2010–20

In the fields listed above and related practices there are more than 20 certifications available today. You should ask yourself, do I want to be a career security expert or leader? You can move from expert in an area to leader or you can remain an expert and become thee expert. Certifications are reasonably priced, are acceptable in duration to earn, and show your commitment to the field.

In the beginning of this decade most exams where either proctor based or completed at testing centers. The curriculum was a stack of books and papers. Finding authors and volunteers to move the curriculum and program along was a challenge. Today there are volumes of material available. Testing is at centers and or online. Materials can all be delivered online and in soft copy. Not only have these been a nice to have in employment job descriptions, they are now must haves in some cases. A couple designations in physical security and security management can be found as requirements (must haves) in some locations for critical infrastructure security professionals and site designers in the cannabis industry.

2020–30

By the time we end 2025 at least 5000 more security personnel will be CPOs by the International Foundation for Protection Officers (IFPO). The ASIS International designations will have made their way to tens of thousands of professionals on every continent combined.

Information security will be a part of every designation in one form or another. Corporate security departments will have adopted certifications such as the Physical Security Professional (PSP) and or the Certified Fraud Examiner (CFE) as a baseline requirement (graduating from the academy if you will).

Instead of more associations and certifications penetrating the industry, discussions will start about consolidation.

2030–40

By this era, we will see that these designations are the end goal for most postsecondary programs. It will be hard to find a job without one. They will be significantly harder to obtain and will require more to enter the programs and testing. Some of these will meet or exceed testing for licensed guards and investigators in several regions. Many more career colleges will offer the study programs as a course.

In the future colleges will continue to provide practical education to security professionals and universities will offer more security programs. Designations at the entry and mid-career levels will offer an opportunity to those who postsecondary education is still unobtainable immediately following secondary school. Designations will also highlight those looking to specialize.

Under licensing I will highlight where this will head for CSOs by 2040.

Courses

Courses may be offered to upgrade skills, help introduce people looking to make a career or specialty area shift. Courses are also helpful to earn continuing education points. These are offered by all the parties listed above. If not working toward a diploma, degree or to learn about nonsecurity matters, courses offered by the associations themselves are an excellent way to remain certified and current. Continuing education should be a career long activity.

It can enhance your self-image and have a positive effect on your life. There is no doubt that continuing education benefits employers and employees in many ways. Whether it is to improve proficiency in the workplace, improve employee promotion options, or learning new skills; continuing education has many benefits.

Licensing

Currently licensing or permits are often observed in the ranks of security officers and private investigators. In the future many more countries will have a formal training, testing, and licensing process. Those who currently have one will continue to require higher standards. Several locations today have standards or restrictions on security and investigation professionals. Some were suggested by police personnel. The uniforms, chevrons, ranks, and the name "officer" are not trademarked by the police. In fact, most of this came from long military tradition. It is understood that some security personnel were titled, uniformed, and equipped so that it was hard to distinguish between the two. I am not fond of the word officer being restricted from security. Therefore, I would suggest the multibillion-dollar industry advocate for a more professional, globally recognized name in the years to come. This should then be reflected in the licensing. I will also suggest that security professionals of the future will no longer try to mimic law enforcement. They will be a separate and distinct group of career professionals.

After speaking too many of my colleagues, listening to some great ideas, and coming to my own conclusion or opinion, I recommend the following. In the next 20 years, every CSO have a security management degree. The ASIS International, Certified Protection Professional (CPP) designation course and exam grow into a four-exam process like the fraud examiner or accounting programs. The largest security associations work with ASIS International to provide a standard that consolidates all other top security management certifications as the Certified Professional Accountants did. The CPP then becomes a global standard and professional license, yes, a license no different than medical professionals or architects, for example. Our colleagues who have earned their masters and those who will have their PhD's will be qualified to teach us. As another Canadian security expert said to me that it needs to be tied to life safety to be taken seriously. CSOs are responsible for the strategy and sometimes real-time decisions that directly correlate to life safety. For example, what is our active shooter training strategy? Should we evacuate the entire campus or not? The CPP could be offered to those with fewer years in security, still requiring management experience and a relevant degree will be a must. If you think this will deter many from striving to achieve the CPP, you are mistaken. It will become a requirement. A goal, well worth it for those AAA personalities. It will motivate the universities to support this idea, knowing you must pass their program to apply to be a CPP candidate. I open this discussion up for those with the leading information security designations. Perhaps at that stage they will all be consolidated into one. The public are becoming more aware. Corporations and their leaders are being held more accountable today than they were 30 years ago. When a network breach occurs or a loss of life stemming from violence, companies will need prove they have highly qualified experts in place already. They will need to show what efforts have been, are being and will be made to prevent this again. True career security professionals will be highly in demand to mitigate these matters as best as can be expected.

In conclusion, CSOs and many other security professionals consume a lot of time focused on what courses to take, what is the best degree to have, and which designation to earn next. If you look at classic career professionals such as lawyers, accountants, architects, doctors, and engineers they complete a degree, law school, and their designation and that is it. Most of these professionals rely on trade journals, peer to peer networking, and the required continuing education guidelines to remain current. Like their law enforcement colleague's security professionals often continue to feel the need to be recognized by their peers, employers, and society as experts and professionals. We are experts in areas of life safety, emergency, and crisis response and are responsible for the protection of trillions in assets.

CSOs will all have degrees in the future, a professional designation such as the CPP offered by ASIS International and may have some second language, computer, and business skills. The need for multiple advanced degrees and designations is excessive. As one gets more senior in their role, no different from any other executive the skills of leadership, technological prowess, global awareness, social, and emotional intelligence are far more valuable. You should at this point realize that you are a business professional who leads the security function.

If a CSO moves between industries and a short program or certification is required unique to this field, then a clear need is present. Credentials are helpful, although not a guarantee of success.

More and more security professionals are joining associations such as ASIS International, are getting certified, and taking an active interest in security as a career.

There are many entry level, mid-level, and advanced courses and designations available today. Some of the other professionals mentioned above regulate, mandate, and license their graduates. The industry should make sure that there are reasonably obtainable programs for entry-level professionals while enhancing the requirements, materials, and testing for the most senior professionals. By regulating and enforcing requirements for certifications such as the CPP like what has been done with the Chartered Professional Accountants (CPA) only then will these carry the same weight with employers.

There is no room for insecurity or competitiveness among the ranks. Today's CSOs should be embracing our more technically inclined, ambitious, and connected future successors and mentor them to help build a more professional and recognized career that will be given a seat in the C-Suite.

Convergence

I will try to avoid defining convergence. I am however referring to the partial, gradual, or complete merging of the physical and information security disciplines. No matter how you do the math, the more corporate security tries to be less like a law enforcement function and drives toward innovation the conclusion is inevitable. I understand my peers who do not see it, want to see it, or don't get it. I was on the fence for a long time. But by the time this does occur, I am sure I will be near retirement and who are we to stand in the way of progress? Information security professionals are not taking over. Data centers need physical protection, networks terminate somewhere. These have become the bank vaults of the 22nd century. If there are people in the physical world, physical security expertise will be needed.

Everything the corporate security department does should be planned, documented, analyzed, and stored on a computer. Even the protection of people, the assessment of violence and the response to emergencies will be enhanced by applications, algorithms, and mobile devices. Information security professionals will need to rely on someone who can interview subjects, translate computer crimes into real-world lawful actions, and conduct inspections with a certain bravado.

If CSOs of today help to pour all their knowledge into the supercomputers of tomorrow; and the CISOs help to automate the work, enhance the analysis, and bolster the capabilities of those programs; the combined efforts of public and private sector allies will tilt the scales in favor of the good guys.

By 2030 most of all operational work, notes and protection assignments will be managed on mobile devices. The future of wearables that you see in the movies, from waving a hand across a glass wall to control images, to accessing files in a contact lens. I predict this is 20 years away. What should be 60 years will be significantly accelerated by machine learning. Like the movie Minority Report, life imitates art. The empty upper quarter of your vision span will be put to good use with intelligence information. Augmented reality vision will change the game for protection professionals. Investigators searching for clues, performing digital-forensic inspections, and conducting subject interviews will be given superhuman abilities.

The CSO of the future only know a world where protection professionals have been schooled in cybersecurity. When service providers in the market today can offer threat management and threat monitoring tools that can cover the logical and physical world seamlessly the movement to consolidate systems and operation centers, and analysts will be inevitable. Educational programs are already merging the two disciplines. The more senior the security professional, the easier it is to merge the two roles. Their common languages will be business, leadership, and strategy. The ability of the future information security specialists to access a wealth of real-time information, security applications, and critical corporate data will be put to good use in partnering with their physical focused counterparts. The data that will be accessible to them in seconds and relayed to their teammates who will be working in joint, state-of-the-art fusion centers. All of this will be commonplace in 10 years. Protection professionals of tomorrow will be equipped with networked, advanced technology; this will help to change security forever. Think of what an executive protection (EP) team can do today with a mobile phone. GPS, weather, natural disaster alerts, suspect databases, up to date images and bios of the board of directors, threat warning applications, mass notification systems, building layouts, guest lists, security camera live view, access system alerts and much more at the tip of their fingers, all here today. Imagine trying to explain this to an EP team leader 30 years ago.

In Chapter 5 we will discuss future technologies including completely networked, buildings, vehicles, and security systems. It will take a team effort to protect and operate these. If information security professionals do not consider the threats from the real world, understand how to protect physical systems, and humanize their interactions with employees, they will lose the point of their message. If PSPs do not learn all they can about technology and do not grasp how to protect their systems and data online, the gap will grow into a canyon.

The future converged security programs will close many of these gaps and bring together a truly holistic view of security for the organization. Enterprise security risk management (ERSM) will help to demonstrate the value of this inevitability.

Management

If you do an online query there are many articles explaining the difference between management and leadership, the qualities, practices, and styles. There are specific things different for the role of a security manager compared to managers of a different kind. There are also many areas security managers should be just as skilled as their business educated counterparts. Some people are great managers. The paperwork is perfect, payroll, scheduling, governance all done on time, error free, and with a bow on them. Some people are natural born leaders, a joy to work for. Getting some of these leaders to write that recommendation for you, to make sure they approve your expenses on time or remember you booked vacation may get lost in the motivational speeches. At times you may switch from one extreme to the other through your development to becoming a CSO. You may also manage well for one part of the team but lead better for another. Finding balance is the key. When you have it all figured out, please let me know, I am still trying to tackle that one.

When interviewing security professionals, I have been known to go off script. Security Officers who binge watch mob movies often have a different view than ones who obsess over detective shows. For those who want a career in the field I have asked questions related to policing. Patrol, SWOT, or detective who would you want to be? SWOT or army? Detective or spy? Traffic, patrol or first response? Why?

After working at a site for a while I have asked do you like nights, afternoons, or days? Desk, patrol, gatehouse, or control room? Responding to alarms or monitoring cameras?

Many entering the field have all watched TV and believe they have some semblance of what our public-sector counterparts do but have little idea at all the different aspect of the security world. Understanding career security professionals at all levels will help you both manage and lead them. As a CSO you may lead managers and directors. Knowing that many of today's security managers do not live for the excitement of budgeting you may need to manage that aspect of their development and monitor this part of the practice a little more without micromanaging. It is fine to be friendly but not friends. Knowing when to shift the conversation back to work and to direct to the task at hand is simply being a good manager. Allowing staff to fall behind, get overwhelmed, and lose focus is in part a shortcoming on the management the CSO provides. Do not be afraid to delegate, share the workload, and give assignments. How will they ever become a CSO if they have no exposure.

Education, experience, and exposure are key to development. Do not reward your superstars with more work and scold them for the one thing they forgot, are behind on, or did poorly when they have 10 times the workload. Do not reward laziness and incompetence with a participation badge. These are grown adults. If they need to be politely guided to work harder, work smarter, and or do their share, that is your place to tell them. If they need to be placed on a performance plan, then you have already failed them. This may sound harsh, but if you have spent your time guiding them, coaching them, helping them documenting discussions formerly and they are still not getting there, then I am sure you can confidently tell Human Resources you need to have the chat. Waiting until year end to blind side them with a plan is unproductive. This has its exceptions such as those good workers who have fallen off track due to life matters, etc.

So where will the realm of management sit with the future CSO? Later we will discuss the future of the working day, agile teams, and the impacts of technology in greater detail. As all the systems that provide the CSO with a single view of the organization and the ERSM

Why don't we do a couple of exercises that may help bring some sanity to the daily grind. Time management is often made too complicated. Here are some effective tips I have used in the past decade. I have had the benefit of reporting to some brilliant people, each who were kind enough to bestow some wise advice (most of it eventually sunk in) and who I was able to watch and learn from.

As a CSO or when helping one of your aspiring CSOs they may feel overwhelmed at times. It seems all that technology has brought the office worker of today is more emails, always feeling connected to the workload and an expectation that since you can instantly receive the request that you must instantly answer it. Feeling overwhelmed? Don't know where to begin?

1. Get some perspective and remove yourself from the situation—Step back from the office, step away from the desk, distance yourself from the screen.
2. Get organized—(A) You need to prioritize. Using a whiteboard draws in collaboration, it encourages creativity and allows the world to see how important and busy you are. If you use one, make sure that everything you write is professional, that you transfer it onto a computer or at least take a picture and save it when you're done, and then erase it by day end. I see a lot of security managers with lists. We are task and goal oriented. I see lists on sticky notes, three different notebooks, on the whiteboard, on the computer, in the calendar. Keep these lists and papers in mind, they may already sound familiar. You now have several disparate lists, you continue to carry a bag back and forth to the office each day with a growing pile of notebooks and sheets of loose paper you hope to work on later. Starting tonight you will take a picture of all those notes and lists. You will then shred that paper. Each day or night you will take one or two sheets, lists, etc., and type them up and

email them or add them to one electronic list. Your task list in Outlook may be a good pace or a log on your computer. Not on your desktop, but in a drive or system that is backed up. If you have an app on your phone even better. Use one place to keep this list. No paper. Paper is where some of you may jot it down, but then it must go somewhere that has pop up reminders, security, and is backed up.

(B) What about all that paper and those files? You know that laptop bag full of who knows what? How about that organized chaos on your desk. Say good bye. I will give you two options, the first is to stop what you're doing. Go get a stack of file folders and labels and organize all that paper into something your proud of. Then sort it alphabetically into a secure file cabinet. This includes any scrap paper and notes written on napkins in your bag. If a file goes home, shame on you. But if it does you will only realistically take one from now on and when your done the work, it will be shredded, because all the actual company records will be on the network. By the way, you no longer keep information stored on your desktop or personal drive. Corporate approved, network drives, and secure sharable resources are their new and only home.

3. Your desk should be absolutely clutter free. No more stacks of paper, no more lists. Everything filed, scanned, and sorted. Create email folders, rules, and alerts and use the calendar for everything. If you get a call, an impromptu meeting, request, etc. Make it a calendar entry. Set aside an hour in the morning to do work, have that in your calendar already. Block the time and let people know your busy. Then actually do that admin. Your boss asks to see you in that time? Go back to your desk or use your phone, shift the original work time, and enter that meeting with your boss. Learn to track and review where your time is going. Organize your virtual folders and email every day. No more electronic clutter. Create folders, use SharePoint, OneDrive, etc. Your bag, office (work and home), desk, drawers, nightstand, and even car should be clutter free. Sometimes you look at a pile of notes, all out of order or a desk with stacks of paper on, in and around it and feel so overwhelmed, so unmotivated you don't know where to begin.

4. I want you to go to your phone. See the 40–60 apps. Delete the ones that are nonbusiness that you have not used the longest. Good bye. Embrace minimalism.

5. Do you have five internet tabs open, the company intranet, several folders, Outlook, a dozen emails open, and another Microsoft application open? Have only one to two open max from now on. Completing 5% of a few things a day does not help.

6. Go through the team drive. See all the very old notes, extra materials that are now outdated and found online? Delete nearly everything that is not fresh, a record, or in progress. Simplify the folders. If you are behind in case management and ERSM software, use a spread sheet to track each program. Go no more than three folders deep.

7. Now make a list. Your to do list. Divide this into three parts. Timely, urgent, and routine. Under timely list all the things that need to get done soon and in order of due date. That report to your boss is timely. Those submissions to set up your new employee, timely, the audit report for the regulators, timely. Urgent can be matters that are urgent or not. These requests come from all directions. Some people will reach out for information urgently. As the CSO you will understand what an actual crisis is, what it means to help the boss or colleague before they head into a meeting with up to date information and what it means to please those people who think everything they are doing is urgent. Do not be afraid to speak up. Ask the boss, how urgent it is, when it can wait until and remind them of the other top priorities you are working on for them. Let the requestor know you will get back to them or one of your people will and then give them a day and time. Let them tell you it is much more urgent and why. Last are daily or routine tasks. Place these in your calendar with reminders. Block time for emails and administration. Time to submit, review, and approve expenses. Time to review reports. When someone calls you for your time, let them know to schedule something and that your calendar is up to date. Leave 15 min to a half an hour between meetings. Allow for no more than two important meetings a day. Often, we work on what we like to and not what we need to. We review the ESRM dashboard but avoid expense reports. Get the thing you do not want to deal with out of the way immediately. Do not procrastinate. Just get it done. You will sleep better, and you can stop dodging people in the halls.

8. Go to your to do list. Pick the top item on the timely list. Open that one single email, or that one note or one file folder or one deck. Have nothing else unrelated to this task on your desk, open, etc. Now just complete one task.

9. Here is how your week should look for the next few weeks. You will clear all items in your email inbox. Organize and sort emails, files, and paper each day. Go to your meetings and keep good, organized records. Complete one item on the timely list and one item on the critical list each week. Only one each on top of your day to day. When someone comes to you at year end with 10 urgent matters, assess the following. Is this a time to help and roll up the sleeves, are they completely disorganized, do this to you constantly and must they learn to respect your time? If yes, then in that case you need to say no. Is this something they should carry over to the next fiscal year objectives and add it to performance plans?

10. To recap—Organize, remove all clutter, stay organized, control your time, speak up, and just complete one thing at a time.

There are times when a CSO and their team face crisis, launch a new system or project, and are short staffed. This is when you really will take work home every night, come into the office a few weekends, and pull some consecutive 60-hour weeks. There are weeks of disappointment, weeks you may struggle politically and months that the monotony will drive you mad. Here is a fun exercise I like to do when I see new staff glaze over with the invasion of projects.

- Days in a year 365 minus the following:

Have fun, put a local spin on this.

- Vacation days 20
- Civic and statutory holidays 11
- Personal/sick/other days 2
- Weekend days 52
- Conference attendance 5
- Team building/town hall/development course days 4

    = 271 days in the office on average
    Things to look forward to:

- Training course
- Cool project, investigation, award ceremony, meetings with peers, company pick nick
- Conferences
- Occasions in the office
- Business trip, lunch with peers

You can also make a list like the one above for your personal life. That trip, birthday party, reunion, etc. Small rewards to get you through your days. Don't over commit, volunteering, and attending industry and workplace events, committees, and projects make you feel more involved and makes it all the more enjoyable.

The bad work day:

- Running late, walk in, boss wants to see you, forgot your laptop, colleague annoyed with you, proposal needs work, forgot umbrella, missed little league. The average work day:

- 8:00 am—came in got coffee, got settled, started the computer, got caught up, went for bio break
- 10:00 am—went to a meeting, presentation went awesome, get coffee, caught up with team and boss, bio break, lunch
- 12:45 p.m.—read reports, finish deck, another meeting, get a signature, sign something, respond to a dozen emails, bio break, snack time
- 3:00 p.m.—host a call, go to a meeting, (surf the web, do personal banking, sign your kid up to sport, check the score), send the minutes, write the next agenda, submit expenses, sort more emails, scan some documents, say hi to Bob (or insert other random coworker name here)
- 5:00 p.m.—did that one last urgent thing, edited a report sent it back to team, took edits from boss, fixed deck, clean coffee mug
- 5:30 p.m. (if you made it this long, enjoy your night, if you left early for other commitments, wrap up the emails on the mobile later) I will see you tomorrow!

As you can see there is quite a bit of time away from the office. Several things to look forward to and a day that has some variety. Try to keep this in mind and keep your team aware that everything in life is temporary. When it seems like it won't stop, when you're on the wrong side of the happy boss campaign and when the days are long, it is just temporary. When you're the Rockstar…it is just temporary.

Example 1
- Employee A—Leads all security and investigations for Asia-Pacific
- Employee B—Leads all security and investigations for the Americas

Example 2
- Employee A—Leads all travel security globally but is based in New York, NY, USA
- Employee B—Leads the global security operations center but is based in Singapore

Example 3
There a lead for each area of the department, located in each region, responsible for their region.
- Employee A—Leads travel for China and is based in China
- Employee B—Leads financial crime investigations in Canada and is based in Canada

Having too many generalists is often hard. Assigning your team members specializations can be helpful. You can also divide them up by geographic regions even if they sit feet from one another. If your company and corporate security department are large enough you may need subject matter experts for each region.

Allowing for cross training, encouraging collaboration, and creating a rotation or secondments is a good way to prepare people for promotions, create continuity, enhance knowledge, and break up the monotony for career veterans.

If you are a security expert, who can also lead people then you are two-thirds of the way there. If you need to practice good management or take some business courses to help become a great manager as well, then speak up. Discuss this with your leader, invest some time in this area of your personal development. We all want to be great leaders, but if you cannot manage the department first, you may not have chance to get there.

Leadership

All too often we read up on leaders versus managers and believe these must be cast by two very different people. In some cases, they are. You can work on becoming both. Having the skills, confidence, and self-awareness can go a long way in determining how long it will take you to find some balance. I have seen well run programs lead by the quiet, calm, reassuring, wise leader, and managed by the high energy department cheerleader who corrals the troops. I have also seen the energetic, charming visionary lead the team while the quiet, reserved task-oriented business person drives the paper grind along. You may need to toggle between both functions from time to time yourself.

When your appointing department heads some great soft skills for a CSO are to be a great talent spotter and to know how people will fit with the team, where they will fill gaps, complement each other or even butt heads. Employees often know they need to listen to the manager but want to follow the leader.

You should have your human resources department help you enroll your department heads in some leadership and management development courses. Make sure they have a component that assesses their styles of management, personalities, and offers some interactive material they need to work on with their leader (you). Additionally, you should inform you leader you would like to attend a similar course for executives. Sometimes these workplace personality tests and exercises can tell you a lot about yourself. Look for honest feedback and be willing to accept that you can still improve yourself. Being voluntold, rather volunteering to go to some leadership training can be a hard pill to swallow, but at least they have confidence you have the potential.

Look up some words that describe great leaders. You may find, civility, transparency, integrity, honesty, confident, committed, passionate, inspirational, good presenter, communicator, strong decision maker, visionary, accountable, delegator, empowerment, trust, creative, empathetic, and innovative. Have your people complete a survey and see what they come up with for a manager and leader. Have them tell you what they believe is their strongest quality and where they wish to improve. Makes sure to provide some follow-up and feedback, create an action plan, and commit to it.

As CSOs we often have strong personalities. You will need to adjust this for the corporate environment. Becoming a great leader takes some work. You will be leading your team to accomplish something great. Leading your peers to see your vision and to gain their support. You will lead top executives through crisis and sensitive matters. The CSO of the future will be seasoned, well rounded and for all their technical savviness, they will still need to remain human.

Revitalizing the programs

Throughout this book, I have talked about where we will be in the future. I have had the honor of listening to and speaking with industry leaders in technology and innovation both in business and the security arena. I will try my best to provide prediction based on history, trends, and todays' torch bearers. A few of my colleagues reading this will have had been doing these things and deploying these technologies for a couple of years now already. When a couple of the fortune 100s are doing it, they are pioneers. When 50 of the fortune 500s are doing it, that is a trend or a practice at best. I am referring to the time when these new technologies and methods are as common as security guards and cameras at a building. When I talk about ESRM in 2040, it is when I believe it will just be a baseline for all security. From the condominium to the social media giant.

One of my favorite publications for helping us see the future technological world through visionaries is Wired magazine. They are great at being bold and anticipating what the future will hold and they are the first to admit when they may have gotten it wrong. I hope that when Lawrence (Larry) Fennelly and his army of experts give us a look at the next few years in security that they and all of you prove me wrong. Wrong in the sense that my predictions for 2040 are all long accomplished and even better by 2025. That the class of 2028 will all be graduating together with their master's in security management, organizational resilience, and similar programs. I hope to see leaps and bounds in ESRM applications and a complete market penetration of its deployment. I hope that all security guards are certified protection officers (CPOs) and we refer to them as professional protection officers (protection officers). Please band together, elevate this profession, and prove me wrong.

My home is far from being a complete techno-marvel. I can, however, program my coffee maker, speak to my virtual assistant who can control my thermostat and other things. My wife can use her phone to randomly run the vacuum. Smart homes, TVs, and buildings. It is all happening around us. We all know some people who are averse to getting out of their comfort zones and embracing technology or a new way of doing things. I too have been this person when it suits me. Perhaps, I have watched too many dystopian sci-fi movies. I recall hearing more than once colleagues speaking about their former security chiefs at other corporations and basking in the failure of their attempt at some ridiculous idea. As I now begin to walk in the shoes of my former chief security officer (CSO), I think back to something he had asked us to help accomplish nearly 7 years ago. Ric Handren sat across from us talking about his vision for a case management system and a fusion center. I had some experience in security control rooms and incident databases, so I was very interested. He explained that fusion centers could include all like departments, shared resources and more. Fraud, anti-money laundering (AML), cybersecurity, physical security, business continuity, and all sorts of experts, he added that we should have public and private sector teams working in them together. He went on to tell me that everything needed to go into the case management system. I thought sure incident reports. But no, he meant everything. I thought that he may not have the big picture. It took me nearly 7 years of trial and error to realize; I was wrong, and he was right. He had access to leaders in security and intelligence operating years ahead of us. That is exactly what the leaders in corporate security (CS) and financial crimes software development and the most forward thinking, driven CSOs are doing today. They are building vast intelligence repositories that work smart. If you are reading this and thinking big brother, you have it all wrong. Your mothers' retirement savings, you would expect that her bank is doing all they can to stay ahead of the bad guys. The engineering site your loved one works at. You want to be sure that if a band of rebels or pirates come to storm the grounds that they are met with a formidable force of futuristic systems and personnel that scare the intent right out of them. Sometimes people are ahead of their time. For this reason, we laugh them and their idea out of the room. We look puzzled and confused and say, "I just don't see it." Packaging and delivery can go a long way. You may be able to invent it or dream it up, but you may not be best suited to sell it. As a CSO if you have someone who is simply a better salesman then let them be your ambassador. Think of Kirk and Spock. Kirk was not the smartest, but he was a great leader. Many CEOs can lead, but they have armies of people who are much smarter developing the products and they have many selling them. A CSO can be confident enough to bring out the best in people. To know when they have a genius in the ranks who can provide strategy and when they have someone who can help sell the ideas to the masses. Stick juice in a bowl and freeze it. Now pull it out. "So, what am I going to do with this"? Now your brainy friend takes that idea and pours some into a long plastic sleeve and others into a narrow mold with a wooden stick in it. Then, your chatty pal gives them a cool name, suggests you make different flavors and colors. For decades, we have had a childhood, household summertime staple in the freezer, from just that. Some great ideas never fly because of the way we introduced them, and others get put on the backburner until the rest of us catch up. When the very first portable cell phone, microwave, or home PC were even conceptualized as something everyone would have in their homes one day, they were laughed out of the boardroom. How about the touch screens we use today? At one time, it was thought that would never fly, the screens will get dirty. But here we are. Sometimes people will talk about past prototypes as failures. Many were in fact just pioneers, early additions, or seeds of great things to come. Sometimes you must get it wrong a few times before you can get it very right. I applaud those who have taken their shot. In case management, I will talk about the Federal Bureau of Investigations' (FBI) Sentinel program. Many may think of the Virtual Case File as a series of disasters and failed attempts. Louis J. Freeh in good FBI tradition wanted his agency to be a technological innovator. Challenged with bureaucracy and budget constraints he pushed onward. His successors took those recommendations and forged ahead on a very bumpy road. But their perseverance paid off.

When someone on your leadership team asks if they really must invest in that new way of doing things or that technology, ask if the business itself is modernizing. If they say no, you may need to rethink if your company will be there in the next couple of years. If they say yes, then ask them, "Why should the security programs be treated any different?" For as long as there have been caves and castles, security has been a necessity, a cost of doing business. I am sorry to inform you, but that will be much more clear and apparent in the next decade. The rise of dangers posed by climate change, terrorism, and political shifts will come on much faster than years past. When you draft a proper business plan for the next 5 years that includes a step forward, you may be asked why? Be prepared to answer this and consider all challenges and opportunities. Be reasonable but firm. If that fails let them read this. Is the protection of the company assets, reduction of losses, and preservation of life not worth the investment? Get that in writing. The company wants to do great things and the CSO wants to help them get there. We are business enablers.

In 2015, Dean Mini and I stood in front of a whiteboard mapping out the future. We vowed to stay in touch with the next generation of security and not to become dinosaurs. When we walked in with our colleagues to the ASIS Conference and Expo, at the Kay Bailey Hutchinson Convention Center in 2017 in Dallas, Texas, I had temporarily lost hope. As we entered the exhibit floor an indoor drone flew by, a robot security guard was the talk of the town and what I could only describe as National Security Agency (NSA) looking operations platforms were on display, available to security departments. I myself almost screeched like a Velociraptor in good humor. You really need to attend some conferences, take some courses, and read the security trade periodicals and magazines to stay in touch and up to date. So where is this all headed…?

Access control

It is all just data. If you keep in mind, it is all just strings of 1's and 0's making things happen on a screen, to the door, or in cyberspace, then we will all be on the same page. When we say access control it does not matter if we mean logical or physical, it's just data. When we talk about video imagery, again just data. Start there and work your way out.

2010–20

Coming out of the late 1990s and early millennia, many proprietary systems dominated the commercial market. These were simple, reasonably priced, and had little integration. In time, the market demanded open-architecture systems, so they were not tied to one integrator or software. The synchronization of access control, alarm, and display with closed-circuit television (CCTV) systems to better assess alarm conditions became a minimum standard for most mature security operations. As the options and features became more abundant and, in some cases, complicated, the graphical user interface (GUI) became easier to navigate, available in many languages and compatible with common operating systems.

Most large campuses (any group of buildings, belonging to a school, healthcare provider, corporate head office, etc.) centralized their systems on one platform, one card (facility code) and designated an access control coordinator or security control room to manage the full-time management of the card programming and system.

2020–30

In the earlier part of the next decade, networked access control systems will have been phased in across the board. This will help the developers and providers ability to move us into the next generation. Software based, cloud hosted solutions may be the only service delivery available from the largest integrators. The ability to load the software onto any working and network connected client will change the game for many still using stand-alone systems on outdated servers. There will be the occasional high-security user who decide to create their own closed ecosystem (e.g., nuclear stations), however, they will still network that system and integrate it completely.

Accessing the software from a web portal will also be available from some larger providers. This will limit the work that has to be done by the IT and Information Risk teams and will allow large companies to allow contract security personnel to use the system without onboarding them to the network as full users.

New players will enter this space who will provide an end-to-end solution. These will be able to take over all your disparate existing systems from multiple previous providers and offer one GUI. Others will provide solutions at a fraction of the cost that you can purchase systems for today. The usual questions and rumors will be raised. These questions are healthy but often driven by competition or political agenda. Why is it so cheap, it must be inferior? It has the following limitations (so do all others), or well if it is sold by a state-owned company it must be spying on us and therefore, a security risk.

Preconfiguration of edge devices and panels will reduce set up time. The mapping, architecture, and programming occurs before the physical installation is complete, which means that the configuration steps will be almost eliminated, and the testing and commissioning will occur minutes after the panels and readers go live.

Completely IP-based systems will make the integration with elevators, duress, parking, printing, and other building and company networked devices easier. The age of the Internet of Things (IoT). Machine learning will come into play. Today, there are a couple major players including HID and AlertEnterprise who have helped to revolutionize incoming features such as behavioral analytics into the system. Access control systems that can flag behaviors of credential holders that may identify possible fraud, breaches in the code of conduct, and workplace violence. Today's pioneers are working toward a future of true intelligent access control. I anticipate that in the next 10 years a few accurate, peer reviewed, independent white papers will offer clear direction on where access analytics are headed. By the end of the decade, these features will be built right into your base access software.

Information security or engineering will have taken on the control of these systems in large enterprise where most premises are leased. All fortune 100s will have connected their systems globally and be able to centrally manage credentials from several redundant control centers. Although it is expensive and challenging for CSOs, many major software providers are abandoning the software's ability to work with legacy systems. Old servers and panels will need to be replaced for enhanced security and better performance. This drives everyone to be more innovative, forces companies to migrate obsolete technologies, and ensures that systems security and integrity keeps up with ever advancing threats.

Access control can be used to assist in a few other ways. These may include but are not limited to, understanding who is still inside a premise during an emergency, to count occupancy rates and few other applications for healthcare, schools, and business. By the latter half of this decade, this will be less about big brother and more about data collaboration and life safety.

This will be the decade where the cards go to die. Biometrics, mobile devices, and fobs will take over. User acceptance and the quality of these options will surpass today's best products in the very near future.

2030–40

In the future not too different than today speed, convenience, and competitively priced products will attract the customers, who will be comfortable with reasonable security. We can sell you a very expensive door for your business, its 2 ft thick steel. It costs a small fortune. Alternatively, I can sell you a frosted, tempered glass door, which looks great, is easier to open and costs a tenth the price. Everything will eventually be hacked. How many years did police services deploy new radar detectors and the market came back with a device to detect that and so a game of cat and mouse began. Whoever continues to make a better device will bring on all challengers who want to be the first to break it, crack it, or defeat it. Edge devices and the IoT will play a very large role in physical security systems. We will have overcome many of todays' challenges and technical limitations and have found ways to secure these systems using peer-to-peer edge technology. We will have done this and still created a system more resistant to cyberattack than today. Video data will be accessible thousands of miles away, quick, secure, and without bogging down the network.

By the middle of this decade, wireless security devices will be much more available. Wireless, point-to-point devices may be less secure, however the cost savings may tempt many buyers. We will have perfected rapid, contact only charging devices. Biometrics and mobile devices will start to dominate the market. Cameras and facial recognition technology will replace some card readers. Biometric devices built into a door handle or door will also reduce some of today's card readers. What about hackers? What about security? People will always tailgate. People will always hack. If we continue to deploy convenient doors that are easy to walk through, then criminals and curious people will continue to exploit this vulnerability. Fire codes and accessibility practices will ensure the safety and inclusiveness for all people. The challenges we have today to comply with some fire codes, while trying to secure the space will have been solved. Door design and hardware will meet the needs of the codes and provide optimum security. Access control cards that double as ID cards will be gone. A virtual card can rest on the user's phone, amongst other more modern and secure options. When someone tells us that they can hack the reader or our credential, we will no longer overreact. We will realize that first, you could always just follow me in. It is much easier, but if hacking is your thing great, we will have two reasons to arrest you, for both hacking and then trespassing. Second, hacking, spoofing, bypassing, cracking, and phreaking have always been a thing and always will.

Today, we are already installing virtual lobby attendants. We already have turnstiles that can be fitted with alarms, ground elevators and entrances that can lock you in a glass booth. We are moving to a world where we can achieve a high level of security at entrances and reduce the need for reception and guard posts. Future, professional protection officers will spend their time on much more productive tasks.

Almost every door will have electronic access control, capable of remote operation and enhancing our ability to produce audit records for many more areas of a premise, all in the future of smart buildings. In the future when most areas of a facility are controlled by electronic access control and under view of security cameras, more crimes such as office theft will be reduced, recorded and or thwarted.

Questions

Why is relevant to me?

If you are a CSO or an aspiring CSO, involved in corporate IT or real estate or a business leader, I am sure that doing things better, less expensive, enhancing user experience, and security may interest you.

You will need to think critically about what annoys you about access control systems today, the whole process of getting from the curb to your office and to think like the bad guys. If you can support better, demand better, and develop better than take one small step.

Write it down and share it with those working on these solutions. Share your knowledge. Be bold, try new technologies. Help build a better mouse trap.

Steps

- Gather your team and write a survey for the employees
- Do some research, speak to your integrator, read up, watch a video, hitchhike from this book
- Issue the survey and see the results
- Share your learnings with your technically and mechanically inclined colleagues
- Try to install one of each device at different, low-traffic areas [Near-field Communications (NFC)/Bluetooth, hand geometry, vascular, facial, etc.]
- Try an edge device transfer of data from a laptop to phone using new technology.

Now you can start to develop a strategy for the future of access control for your enterprise. Most CSOs of today have never programmed an access control card. At least we can understand it.

Considerations

Always include partners, INFOSEC, Legal, HR, Privacy, Compliance, Information Risk, Marketing, and Communications, etc. If your going to do it, do it right.

Conclusion

Electronic access control in 2040 will be an information security function. A digital, completely integrated service. Physical security responders will be a force to be reckoned with. As we will see in the cybersecurity section of this chapter physical access control breaches will be treated more seriously and logical hacks will be better understood.

Alarm communications and display

I remember the first time I walked into a security control room. It was what the worse stereotype I can think that a nonsecurity practitioner may expect. The desk, not console, desk was lopsided, full of crumbs and coffee stains. The room was cramped, poorly lit, not ventilated or cooled, and fitted with obsolete equipment. The best part was that it was unstaffed. Just a place to check cameras on a VCR and hand write reports. By the third site I had seen this, I simply just settled in and was happy if the coffee was free.

A few years later I walked into a security operations center (SOC). Before we entered the control room, the boss turned to me and said, "don't act shocked, just go with it." I thought I had just walked into a submarine command area. This was a multi-console, 24/7 operation with two to three operators. It had connections to every duress, elevator, parking, and door intercom in the complex. Multiple radio consoles, access, video, fire, alarm, and more. The operators had three screens each in front of them and another 100-inch monster in front of them. The desk was a real console when sit/stand was unheard of. Still one event and the dozen communications systems and alarms could overload any team of operators. The 100+ cameras were dizzying for anyone 7h into a shift.

Near the end of my term in on-premise security management I had finally toured and found those control rooms that many CSOs have sought to create. One of those that are depicted as the NSA operations center in every movie. I immediately fell in love with it and found several more the following 2 years. I believed this to be the standard. The only standard for any control room.

2010–20

In the first part of this decade, in the post 9/11 era most major companies and premises had some form of control room for security. It was not uncommon to see the card programming module of the access control and alarm system open 24/7.

Card programming and changes seem to be a never-ending task. Rarely do you see the screen with all the devices and alarm points or the alarms logs open as the primary monitor. Most of these rooms boasted some form of big exciting screen or many, rear projection, multiple LCD screens, and cube video walls. Really grand, impressive video walls with all the cameras on display, some on tour, some integrated with alarms and all of them capable of giving operators a bad case of overload.

Today, many of these rooms are well designed, properly lit, appropriately sized, certified, and properly furnished. Most systems are integrated, there are less manual controls and fewer operator panels, premise specifics maps in the form of digital, interactive floor plans on the GUIs make the operation easier for the officers. It is still common to find more than eight screens in the room filled with multiple cameras.

I have asked many operators around the world, at many different types of premises if they feel they have received enough training or if they receive annual refresher or updated training, and the answer is always no. This is common in so many industries. This is often the on-premise emergency dispatch center. We often see a scenario like this. A two-office building complex connected by a small retail atrium, both towers more than 40 stories tall with a daytime occupancy of 7300 people. The dayshift has two guards facing 100 cameras, two alarm panels, two fire panels, and phones ringing off the hook. Then, we have one emergency call, trouble at the dock or a fire alarm and watch all monitoring and alarm scrutinizing go out the window. For those of us who worked our way up each progressive level in the field we understand these pressures, but sometimes forget as CSOs. For those peers who have never worked one of these consoles (which means nothing as we all bring a different perspective and set of skills to the table), it would be good to spend a full-shift working, not observing, but working down there. We tend to get stuck in the 100,000-ft view and enjoy talking about world events while the building we work in, is need of some attention.

2020–30

As this chapter progresses, I will speak more to the future of security control rooms. Setting convergence aside and will focus only on the building's physical security systems as we will look at life in the next decade.

In the next few years, there will be no more than four screens on the main display. These may be the building approach or main lobby security desk. Additionally, the most vulnerable locations which may include vaults or executive office entrances. A quick slide across a touch screen panel will allow the operators to slide across screens, bring up entire sectors, and increase and decrease the number of cameras on display. All other cameras will be connected to all the various door, motion, intrusion, duress, and other alarms and will take over when there is an incident. Rooms will be designed with all the appropriate ergonomics. Operators will be able to sit, stand, and move around. Fatigue matts, wireless headsets, and moveable touch screens will help make sure operators are comfortable but do not drift away. All cameras, alarms, sensors, and doors will be shown on a large GUI. The simple touch of the screen could allow the operator to open a door, lockdown the complex, or view all images in the alarm area.

2030–40

It is hard to give a really great example of today's forerunners without discussing many service providers. Based on what is already being beta tested today and who is currently looking at these technologies, it won't be later than 2035 when we are using Spielbergian technology. The control rooms will have completely interactive technologies. The ability to wave your hand across a screen to slide between applications will be common. The entire room will be activated by voice, gesture, and even eye movement. A nearly touchless operation. There will be almost nothing on display except for what the operator is working on. Only systems related to breaches or alarms will be shown when needed. Interactive glass wall displays will cover the entire room. The room, seating, lighting, and temperature will know the operator's preferences and automatically adjust for them upon entry. These rooms will have twice the capability but use half the power we use today.

The operator's ability to view an intruder in a hallway, lockdown the area and dispatch the response force will almost be completely automated, although when and where a human operator integrates with the room and building it will be with fewer than five motions and a voice command. They will no longer spend hours starring at multiple cameras or programming cards the entire shift. Analytics and machine learning will have advanced these controls and displays to a point where the operator can make a proper assessment of alarms and action them with ease. No more overload, white noise or excessive false positives.

By 2040, the purpose and use of these controls will have completely changed and the monitoring and response of the physical protection systems (PPS) will be done by automation.

Questions

What is the difference between the control room, the individual systems, and the alarm communications and display (AC&D)?

AC&D is about the interface for the operators, the ease of use, and seamless integration of the controls.

There are not many specifics here, where am I supposed to start?

Starting could mean conducting some benchmarking with peers and seeing if there is a need for a SOC in your enterprise or not. Try to understand what you should or should not be monitoring and assessing today you may already be wasting valuable time and resources and there is no point in doing the same thing in a fancier room. Go see what is in the market today, consider the return on investment and see if it's time to upgrade. A good business case in any event is always a good way to convey your thoughts.

Steps

• Engage your operators and discuss the current controls, look at it from all shifts, functions, operators, and during a crisis.
• Do some research on everything from the displays to the furniture.

- Go through all the systems and devices that can produce an alarm, are they all on the same GUI, are they being used to their full potential, been shutdown due to being annoying?
- Analyze the alarms, false alarms, and troubles to see how this can be improved to ensure the operators receive timely, quality easy to identify alarms.
- If there is an alarm, there should almost always be a camera for assessment, or quite close (don't put a camera in an executive office where the duress alarm is but perhaps feet away in reception).
- Engage a consultant with experience specific to this area of security operations.
- Reach out and tour some modern and cutting edge SOCs; your peers, integrators, security providers, and consultants can help you locate these, bring your leader and the parties you would involve if refurbishing one.

Considerations

- Remember that not all premises and operations are the same. Having alarms active in the middle of a mall or even factory by day may not be practical. Alarms in a gold vault or data center that are always armed may be practical. High security premises should have alarms and detection as far to the perimeter as possible.
- Keep the display simple, the alarm tones obvious but not disturbing, unless it is the most critical of alarms are tripped and then you can bring on the creepy alert tones.

Conclusion

- Career SOC experts are a unique breed of super multitaskers. They have incredible concentration skills and are great under pressure. Show them the latest and greatest and allow them to help with the development and upgrade strategies.

Active shooter/active assailant prevention and response

Active shooter situations have been defined many times. I have included active assailants, since there have been some horrific edged weapon (knife, sword, machete, etc.) attacks globally in the past several years. These incidents are too numerous, tragic, and senseless. It is going to take the work of law makers, psychological experts, mental health care, law enforcement, parents, security experts, and many more to reduce these, identify them earlier, mitigate their impacts, and hopefully almost eliminate them. Once the threat actor is in motion these occur swift and have dreadful impacts. I implore everyone reading this to educate themselves to know what to do in such an event, share this with others, and take a step in making this problem a thing of the past.

2010–20

At the beginning of this decade the only significant books, government provided education or direction for the public and analysis of such events were found in the United States. The history of mass shootings, multiple stabbing attacks, and prolific bank robberies turned shoot outs seemed to have peaked to unprecedented levels over the previous 15 years (1995–2010). It would have been unimaginable that global incidents involving students, terrorists, and random strangers would more than double in the next decade (2010–) from the previous. Police in many places changed from standing down to proactively pursing the perpetrators, this is complicated when you must determine if the suspect is on a moving shooting spree and must be stopped immediately or if they have barricaded themselves with hostages. Our police often have split seconds to make tough choices with not only little information but also sometimes incorrect or rapidly changing scenes. A profile of events, the shooters and victims has been established and used by leading experts to study these tragedies. Law enforcement, criminologists, and security experts began to develop response procedures. Table top and live simulation scenarios become routine at previously impacted and/or the most forward thinking, proactive companies. Public and private alliances formed to tackle these issues. By the end of this decade, we will have not eliminate this threat by any means, however, we are learning that preparedness saves lives, mass communications are critical and there are often very subtle red flags that something isn't right. These may be one of the most dangerous and terrifying events for law enforcement to respond to and amongst some of the most emotionally hardest to deal with in the aftermath. We should be thankful for their service everyday. This is one area where CSOs and law enforcement leadership must be on the same page and continue to work fatigueless together.

In the last part of this decade, we have seen more public agencies, police agencies, and cities create public awareness campaigns from Australia, Canada, the United Kingdom, and the United States. Children's schools include lockdown drills. Faculties are trained in what to do during such an event. The number of corporations ensuring their security departments know how to respond and their employees know what to do to enhance their chances of survival, have improved dramatically. But there is still more work to be done.

2020–30

In the next decade, published standards and guidelines for these sorts of events, and those guiding private enterprise on how to develop an active shooter program will be in their second and third generation. CSOs will need to help develop and update these standards. The National Fire Protection Association (NFPA) and the American National Standards Institute (ANSI)/ASIS International Standards on Active Shooter will be amongst some of the premier materials for developing a program. There are currently several leading books today, which will have been updated to reflect the most current event data and response protocols. CSOs have learned by this point in their career when to approach sensitive but important topics with tact. This is one area where a CSOs passion for life preservation may take over and allow them to drive home the importance of duty of care. The right amount of training, communication, and resources must be devoted to allowing for a reasonable program that touches on the entire organization.

Today, gunshot detection technologies (GDT) are considered superfluous or even a luxury. By the end of this decade, these technologies coupled with weapons detection technologies in the workplace will be much more prevalent. Companies like SITUALIS will revolutionize public and private emergency communications combined with (GDT) can reduce notification times and enhance response with better situational awareness. Every workplace will have clearly defined polices, training programs, and routine drills for corporate responders and leaders. Building management, security, human resources, business continuity, corporate communications, risk, legal, and other critical partners will share the responsibility.

2030–40

Imagine a world where advanced detection algorithms that analyze patterns behavior using keyword association and other measures comb social media for preincident indicators. A time when we have the understanding and resources to identify high risk or vulnerable persons and get them the care they need in advance of the execution of an attack. In the future, protection officers will be able to respond to greater threats and will be equipped with better training, protection, and nonlethal weapons. No longer will we soften the message. We will train all citizens on what a preincident indicator to an attack may look like, how to react, and what to do in such an event. We will address the matter head on. Smart buildings will allow operators to potentially lock down zones in a premise and isolate the attacker. Although open concept workspace gives less places for concealment, they will offer little barrier between the assailant and response force. Quick observation of the threat will help to find them and neutralize them faster. Gun control will not mean taking away firearms or citizens' rights. It will mean keeping them out of the hands of the wrong people where it is obvious including children. It will mean deploying already developed biometric technologies. Military service personnel may still be deployed with unrestricted weapons for those who are under fire and injured who need to return fire under any condition. Domestic weapons can be fitted with control systems to only be used by the authorized party. Stockpiling of weapons and the movement of weapons will be better administered.

By 2040, the first robot will have stopped an attacker.

Questions

How do I deploy a training program to reach employees in a global organization?

Steps

- A CSO must work with their key internal partners to effectively deploy any training.
- Draft a plan to roll out training at all levels of the organization.
- Compile the best resources and engage consultants where needed.
- All employees will need to be trained in person or online or by video, in the response protocols to enhance survival. Include all contract and contingent workers.

- The building management and security officers, health and safety committee, fire, and floor wardens are often first responders to notify employees and evacuate them when needed. Determine who needs to be trained on how to make announcements, call the police, lockdown the premise, etc.
- Train the CS, business continuity, crisis management, and the key senior officials on how to manage the situation from an incident command, business continuity, and disaster recovery perspective.
- Engage your security company and crisis counselors to develop these plans.
- Host table top drills at all levels for responders.
- Host live drills for those responders outside of business hours, include local emergency services, have a mock media scrum. Put everyone to the test, repeat this as needed until there is a level of comfort in knowing their roles.

Considerations
- Depending on the size of the enterprise this may be a 4-year plan.

Conclusion
- This matter is a real-world issue. It will require a tactful but firm approach to make sure that you get to buy in from leadership to appropriately prepare staff. Fear mongering is never professional. Be factual and take the process one step at a time.

AML and anti-terrorist financing

In the past decade, this has become a very important topic. Regulators have been working to set higher standards for financial institutions (FIs) to comply with. If you want to hurt crime and terrorism, cut off the flow of money. If you want to get to the source, follow the money. Corruption, the proceeds of crime and the underground economy put a strain on the efforts of billions of good people trying to earn a living, who pay their taxes and play by the rules. No matter how digital, no matter the amount of money somewhere in this web of laundering is violence.

2010–20

At the beginning of this decade, many enterprises were either introduced to AML compliance or were faced with greater regulation. It took several years after 9/11 for law makers to come out with clear guidelines with prescriptive steps for many industries to follow and a few more years to develop robust audit processes to determine compliance. Many companies have a chief compliance officer and a small team to combat the problem. Some companies have an AML department who work with internal audit and corporate security (CS), to handle the heavy workload. Tasks assigned to different groups may include processing hundreds of suspicious transaction reports and know your client (KYC) documents per day. Deeper due diligence of potential laundering and on the clients. Higher risk and high net worth transaction teams. Investigation of suspected and/or confirmed cases. Teams to deal with clients and employees willfully violating the rules. Gap analysis conducted to see if a control was missing, missed or intentionally ignored, and remediation. All these steps and many more are subject to human error, challenged with loop holes, and evolving criminal methods.

Software to help identify fraud and money laundering became more available in the past 5 years. The process still involves teams of analysts to enter the data and review the results. Well-intended digital currencies such as bitcoin and the dark web are being used to further criminal enterprise's ability to operate with little detection. Financial intelligence services have risen with state-of-the-art investigation techniques to work with FIs to combat these adversaries. It is still not enough.

2020–30

AML business leaders have come to realize one thing. We are behind. Ask yourself. Can my team, all my team, not just one specialist, comb the deep, dark web? Do we have access and clearance to all available databases? Do we understand what blockchain, bitcoin, and similar hot button topics are? Are we manually processing piles of spread sheets in our day-to-day work? Do we invest in quick, up to date, practical training for our teams?

There are leaders in AML compliance tacking these questions and aiming to move into the next decade ahead for once. Today's software is often disparate. Often somewhere at the beginning or end of the money laundering transaction is fraud. Analytics to detect fraudulent transactions and money laundering red flags are separate systems. Automated databases for clients to enter their data for review are not always synced with the detection software. Software that helps organizations prevent money laundering and terrorist financing activities by automating KYC, profiling, and reporting features are not always synced with the company's core transaction system and therefore, a manual process is involved. Some applications are better for law firms and some for FIs. Some can handle enterprise with multiple subsidiaries and some are siloed.

In the next several years, single, intelligent applications will be developed and will handle the work of teams of analysts. By the end of this decade, these features will be a part of the company's transaction software already. Machine learning will automate millions of complicated transactions. We will still need, if not more than ever highly skilled AML/anti-terrorist financing (ATF) experts. It is hard to train machines to understand how people think, what drives us, and to know when they are certainly lying. By the end of this decade, AML experts will be university educated in financial crimes. They will be technically competent, and all be certified anti-money laundering specialists (CAMS).

2030–40

Legislation often moves slow. By 2030, we will be in an era where the penalties are severe for noncompliance, greater for launderers and crimes much more sophisticated. The principles will remain the same. Financial crimes departments in FIs will include fraud, AML, and other related specialists under one leader. AML will be an intelligence-led function. Virtual operations centers will integrate, fusion center like programs to bring public and private sector specialists side by side. Territories with little to no rules, capacity or capability will have caught up to where most leading countries were in 2010. This will help investigators stop the flow of transactions and even recover funds in a truly global environment. Many companies will be indemnified to support one another in this fight. Professionals working for large companies who are caught breaking the rules today, will have gotten the message loud and clear by then. Industries rife with money laundering (adult entertainment, small electronics, nightclubs, art, development and restaurants, etc.) today will still be a problem tomorrow. As cash becomes a thing of the past more so in 2040 than in 2020 we will be able to conduct AML surveillance much better.

Questions

We are strapped for resources, yet the tasks to meet the demands of the regulations keep multiplying, what do we do?

- Demonstrate this in a clear report to leadership. It is a cost of doing this business.
- Question why are we processing so many reports? Are our advisors, sales team, or alike doing too much high risk business and why?
- Are we operating with clients, in a service or territory beyond our AML risk tolerance?
- Are we working like its 1995?
- Should we engage a software provider, consultants, and/or outsource some of the workload?
- Have one of the largest business or accounting consultancies come conduct a review of your program and make recommendations.

Steps

- Benchmark with peers, see what they are doing and where they are headed
- Make sure your teams attend industry association events for AML/ATF professionals
- Ensure they have the accounting, computer, and criminological skills to support their AML knowledge
- Ask internal audit to review your processes from beginning to end; be transparent and accept the recommendations

Considerations

- Do not try to operate just under the regulatory radar or your own risk tolerance.
- If there is no law, regulation, or penalty related to this transaction in the country; avoid doing what would be against the rules in your most regulated areas of business. Do the right thing and you won't have to worry.
- Go digital, completely automated.

Conclusion

Money (or currency) laundering will still be an issue in 30 years from today. Keep advancing your technology and techniques. If you're not changing, you're dying.

Anti-terrorism applications

Simply put anti-terrorism works to prevent terrorism. This is the application of security procedures, reporting mechanisms, building design, hardware, and even software to deter terrorism, reduce its impact, and even stop its effects. Counterterrorism is the proactive efforts to stop the act of terrorism, the flow of its money and is usually a function of military, intelligence, and police. As a CSO you will play a role in all these applications and both the anti and counter sides of the efforts.

Additional to facility threat, risk, and vulnerability assessments (FTRVA), a company's security department or a qualified consultant may conduct an anti-terrorism review of a building, site, operation, or even excursion. An assessment of the likelihood and probability of terrorism and its impact is a good starting point. Is the area known for incidents, is the activity or the proposed operation known to have been targets, are vulnerable and susceptible? How would they be affected?

There are a few good recourses that provide minimum anti-terrorism standards for buildings. When conducting any assessment, it is good practice to have provided the premises, operations, field locations, and event planners with relevant, standard advance. Guidelines offer the internal clients of the CS department with easy to follow standards to build space, plan events, and set up remote operations without having to go back to security multiple times, which also save security significant consulting time. At times, we will review a location for general security surveys and the recipient of the report feel the recommendations are unfair or too great. As professionals we aim to provide appropriate guidance. If we have an opportunity to issue premise standards and give the facility ample time to put these into place, then we would expect future security audits measured against those guidelines to come up with what some look at as a perfect scorecard. The recipient should never feel it is a report card and the author should not treat findings as a matter of noncompliance. You are partners working for the same organization with a common goal. The premise may feel it is unfair that the consultant or CS professional who walks through the premise in a day, provides a to-do list with dollars attached to it and leaves, has the easy end of the deal. Nor should the security expert who has to spend a career keeping up to date with controls, security systems, world event, new methods to commit crime, see a gap as the premise not caring. Both parties have day jobs. If the reviewer benchmarks against new materials and is realistic about it, the premise should understand that this helps to move the needle ahead gradually. Risk increases. Volcanoes existed a million years ago, protests of 50,000 and the assault rifle did not. A band of rouge robots bent on world demonization do not, yet. When it comes to anti-terrorism audits, this may be completely new. An entire country which has seen very little in violent large-scale terror attacks suddenly sees a couple in 1 year and one directly or indirectly impacting a local enterprise. This would be grounds (and should have taken place already) for an audit of this type.

2010–20

At the beginning of this decade, attacks in the United, the United Kingdom, and France were only a few that stood out in the minds of security professionals. Walking into a hotel, mall, or office tower in Israel in 1992 to find heightened security, metal detectors, bollards, vehicle searches, and patrol dogs may have seemed routine. Introducing these across the locations listed above in 1992 (pre-World Trade Center bombing 1993) would have seemed excessive. As this decade progressed corporate social responsibility, going green, sustainability began to fall into a similar category as health and safety, and fire life safety had in years prior; as conflicting practices to security measures at times. Building structures with less material and more windows make vehicle interdiction and blast mitigation a challenge.

Window laminate, glazing, and better transparent materials were deployed at many premises that we would not have considered doing so a decade earlier. In some places or types of structures, this has just become a way of design. Passive and active vehicle barrier systems previously reserved for government, military, and high security installations began to spread to private sector commercial applications. Training courses on anti-terrorism programs seen at consulates and embassies in 2000 have become certifications to thousands of security experts by the end of this decade.

For years, frontrunners have been trying to implement security systems, biometrics, trained human screeners, and analytics to assess and alert security to behaviors observed in different crimes including terrorism. What appeared to be in its infancy a decade ago has made leaps and bounds today. Machines that can read body language to identify you, assess if your carrying weapons or explosives and about to commit violence are midway to optimal efficiency. The perfection of this technology will not be the measure of its success, but how we fairly and reasonably apply these when the time comes. How we know we have done this right is the question? The gold standard is not the ability to detect but not becoming the ominous big brother, police state so many fear. We succeed if it is done just right. A raised had clasping a weapon and the act of striking someone has a split-second decision point between them. The threat and the act are not always synonymous. Terrorism offenses and the act of terrorism have a thin line when it comes to how far we go in the name of privacy and acting against it. Do you pull the trigger early, convict someone for what they may have done? As the CSO, the systems you help build, the evidence you collect, the intelligence you share, and the action you may take, collectively have large impacts on our society. Hollywood has shown us what happens when the security apparatus, the surveillance machine, or full force of the elite counterterror team comes against the good guys.

Bollards have become cleverly hidden furniture, challenging suspiciously park trucks is routine for security and parking enforcement, observing, and reporting possible hostile surveillance has become basic training for shopping center security. Deputizing the public to report suspicious behavior and packages is completely normal. In this decade, terrorist organizations became good at recruiting online. The fortune 500 companies alone employ millions. Some of those potential recruits have day jobs, what I am implying is that not all terrorists are from far off and away place. Some are home grown, working for an everyday employer. Perhaps reading their indoctrination materials on the company network. When if someone visits sites noted for violence, terrorism, extremism, and weapons repeatedly. We now have software to detect these actions and behaviors; and report them to CS.

2020–30

In the next few years, acquiring weapons or the materials to make bombs and weapons will become harder. Controls that will trigger when multiple red flags are observed will activate a mechanism that will analyze, cross reference, and escalate concerns. The suppliers of these products should cooperate with their public partners to increase our ability for possible early detection.

Architectural design, urban planning, space consultants will have a better understanding of crime prevention, anti-terrorism, blast mitigation and impacts, cover, and concealment when they graduate. Security students at all levels will understand the basics of anti-terrorism and counterterrorism when they complete a certificate, designation, license, diploma, and/or degree.

The base (first several levels below and above grade) of any tall structure will be designed with vehicular and blast impacts in mind from the perimeter, the curtain wall and right into the core. Although there has been a trend on using less building materials, designs will emerge that provide protection and still help to curb the effects of climate change.

As we advance artificial intelligence (AI), embrace the IoT and converge security experts it will become nearly impossible to avoid detection of any monetary, online or communications activity related to terrorism in the next 7 years unless you are 100% off the grid. We are a short few years away from being able to stop and/or arrest a vehicle speeding toward a crowd or building. Easy to install, cost effective, active vehicle barriers will be deployed at most premises as part of the basic construction. Suspect vehicles will not be able to pull into any major parking lot without the plates being scanned and run against watch lists.

The authorized and licensed use of cellular/frequency jamming equipment will become a gradual tool and practice for private security to deploy when an improvised explosive device is suspected.

2030–40

As seen throughout this book is a trend of completely interconnected security systems, smart buildings, security robots, vehicles, and more. Detection and neutralization will be significantly more efficient in 20 years from today. The public will not tolerate terrorism in any form and therefore, the tactics and tools to counter it will be more widely accepted. Cyberterrorism will become a completely new, very real threat. Ensuring that our future cyber-police are equipped with the ability to proactively go after people in both the physical and virtual space will be critical. Data backup and recovery need to occur in seconds.

Not only will we see the continued development and use of nonlethal options to neutralize suicide bombers and armed terrorists; but also the issuance and authorization of trained security forces to deploy them will be in use in the most affected areas. Picture a standoff where the adversary is hit with a sticky foam cannon.

The police and sometimes security have an impossible task. When an armed attacker commits an act of terrorism or an active shooter event takes place, there is often in inquiry that looks at the actions or nonactions of the responders. If the response was not quick enough or not optimal according to a report written by someone sitting in the comfort of an office reviewing video and transcripts, which may be necessary but sometimes not fair can have severe impacts to the response team who experienced the incident first hand. If the armed assailant threatening police is shot, the question of excessive force or alternative options are raised. After four decades of significant lost lives, children and other loved ones, the first robot to taser an armed suspect, a professional protection officer who locks the suspect in a compartmentalized area of a corridor or the law enforcement drone that nets its first bad guy won't be given a second thought in 20 years from now.

Questions
Will all security be armed in the future?

Security are unlikely to be armed with firearms. Security who are not armed today are less likely to be armed with firearms tomorrow. The use of nonlethal options for security will increase globally.

How will terrorism change?

Terrorist groups, geographic locations of base operations, causes, and ideologies will change.

How will attacks be executed?

Cybersecurity (I will use the nonhyphenated version of these words here forward as we will all in the future) will become much better than it is today. Hacking systems from the outside will take the very best of human/software efforts. Insider, cyberterrorism threats will be of great concern. Persons with malevolent intentions, with trusted access to critical infrastructure systems will be a threat like nonother seen before. The control of aircraft, power, and telecommunications could have catastrophic consequences if tampered with. With a human mission to Mars likely to occur by 2040 cybersecurity may take on a whole new meaning.

Steps
- Have an antiterrorism assessment conducted of your operations
- Include terrorism as a consideration in any threat assessment you conduct (premise, product, event, etc.)
- Make sure that security is included at the beginning of any new business venture (merger, acquisition, development), the CSO should consider if terrorism is a risk and how antiterrorism measures can be implemented from the beginning
- Keep informed on how this threat changes globally, what impacts it has, and who it effects ongoing

Considerations

Like any foundation in your security program (training, staffing, tools, etc.), being well educated and informed about these threats should not stop at the ivory tower of CS but should be appropriately disseminated to all levels of security and key business partners throughout the organization.

Conclusion

Terrorism will evolve, controls and methods to curb it will too. Our understanding as security professionals needs to advance. Affiliation with a group, religion, or nation is not synonymous with terrorists. Not all safety applications have to be considered security and antiterrorism to be installed. If cars accidentally drive into banks, malls, and offices; then a curb, bollard, or berm can be used simply for safety.

Case management

Case management software (CMS) (security and investigation, not legal) refers to the use of software to store, sort, analyze, and report security, threat, investigation, subject, and enterprise security risk management (ERSM) data. It is where all the security officers enter their reports. It is where all the CS personnel log records, investigations, and occurrences. It will be one of the single most important tools for any security program in the future. From guards, to logical and physical analysts, to investigators up to management it will be the central repository for most of their written work. Videos, photos, evidence, and much more will be compiled in these sophisticated applications. In 2013, Fraud Magazine covered a two part article on CMS offering some good insight into the considerations for selection and day-to-day use.

This section is called case management as many departments are still not using software. Some small security departments are at best sending the occasional email to management following an event or possibly writing a report in Word. Some guard service providers offer the use of software for a small fee to the premise. There are some advantages and disadvantages here. If the premise is the main or only location for that company and they do not see value in the investment of such software, then this additional offering may make sense, allowing the guard provider to bear the management and investment of the systems while clients pay for their portion of use. The service provider can offer this to a handful of similar clients. The client should then make contractually sure that they can have a copy of the data should the relationship end. They will need to understand who has access to the data, what the aggregate data could be used for what recovery practices are in place, and how secure it is. If the premise is one of many owned by the same company, it would be wise for that company to procure the CMS separately and manage it separately. If that company has any form of security specialist supporting the field offices or other buildings separate from head office, that specialist's data could be managed in the same system. With support from the information technology or systems department (IT/IS), that specialist should manage the dashboards created by this data. This may work the same for field investigators.

If you're not using a CMS today, your already behind. If your CMS is not working for you, it is often not the CMS, but the internal management or lack of management of that system. Like any system you purchase security access control, video surveillance system (VSS), etc., if you do not have a service contract with the vendor, then you need a dedicated or partially dedicated internal team of software champions supporting your daily needs (access rights, backup, updates, patches, views and dashboards, etc.).

Scribbles in a notebook are of no use to anyone. Rooms full of printed incident reports or investigation report binders are useless. This is a waste and its day is over, yesteryear, done, finished. Centralized, backup, remotely accessible, shared, automated, digital case management, that is the now.

A bank robber commits robberies at six local banks branches, two belong to the same bank. The details are shared between police and bank CS. The link analysis and geographic profile of the data shows the same large, high-top red sneakers were worn on four cases, the same blue sedan seen at three. The area which appears scattered show two central locations between the branches where the circumference overlaps. A suspect is taken into custody. His girlfriend who lives at the center of one of the center points on the map drives a blue sedan. The suspect's grandmother at the other, a pair of red sneakers identical in size, look, and tread rest in the doorway. The software shows a direct correlation between the time he robs the branches and calls made moments after to a known drug dealer.

A series of retail shop thefts and break and enters in parked vehicles for merchandise occurs at a mall owned by a major realty company. As suspect and vehicle information is entered into the national database, two more malls along the same highway, owned by the same company start to identify a pattern of occurrences and details. The information is shared with police and eventually a ring is uncovered between several men working nearly a dozen malls in the greater metropolitan area along the highway corridor.

A CSO opens their CMS dashboard first thing in the morning. What were a few isolated cases are now showing a clear trend of frauds in one business unit. After entering all the security system, employee, and network log data it shows an employee who is often the first in and first out searching for client accounts with a similar profile, wealthy retires. The cameras, access, network, emails, and logs show it is that employee on that terminal during those times, making those queries. The system links a couple of recent cases from external complaints and connects the frauds on those clients to the employee's searches. Emails and printing reports show the attempts and successes at removing the data from the system. If you could automate only half of your data entry, analysis, and reporting today, you would be that much further to early detection and mitigation of losses.

2010–20

You are spoiled. Those were the words uttered by my interviewer more than a decade ago. After trying to articulate a point several times, I bluntly asked "what do you mean"? She said, "You are spoiled." We laughed, and she explained that my resume showed that I had worked for billion dollar enterprises with robust security programs and my expectations may be skewed. She was absolutely right. The fact was I actually expected more. What I thought was little to no resources was in fact at times well above what many of my peers had to work with. Years later I can honestly say that does make a difference.

I was told by more than one very experienced investigator that you could not train computers to do the work of a good investigator. I believed in this for short time. That was until someone selling software showed me a pile of disparate data and reports and a computer that seemed to mean nothing. Within a few minutes, we had a link chart, some pattern analysis, and a concerning graph. In the early 2000s, many mature security programs were using software to organize and store reports. They were still limited and siloed but miles ahead of teams using paper, with poor filing systems, relying on staff retention and good memories to connect suspects and cases. By 2010, many of these case management systems were on their second and third generation. Several companies had successfully created decent national databases for their CS operations.

One of the most well-known public sector success stories to come out of this decade was the FBIs Sentinel project. It not only drove agencies to work together, the FBI to learn, adapt, and evolve it taught the FBI about project management, agile working teams, and going green benefits such as reducing paper and storage. I am all for paper. It is a renewable resource. It can be used in art, and is a good alternative to bags, wrapping, and much more. However, security at all levels need to go paperless to be able to connect data and help CSOs make well-informed decisions. It should be recorded in one form or another on a handheld device, written on a computer, dictated, etc. It should be protected from tampering and saved in the right place. It should be free of clutter and link to other critical data. That is exactly what we have today. The top 10 case management systems offer all of this and more. Palantir is the supercar of case management, take some time to research Sentinel and Palantir, the accomplishments and success they have had today is where we all need to get to tomorrow. There are many more in fact, RSA's Archer platform, Resolver Inc.'s suite of services and others have incident specific modules which can be tailored to your departments needs. Imagine detecting fraud, cyber, AML, and security anomalies at the approach. When the first signs of reconnaissance begin a warning triggers, it kicks off an automated, silent, and steady correlation of data and deep analysis that provide a series of alerts, actions, and mitigation recommendations to beat them to the pass.

2020–30

Several of the perceived limitations of CMS from the previous decade will be nonexistent in the next. A generation of CSOs will be leading who have come up with these systems, seen their implementation and benefits. CSOs will now be able to start connecting these to other security, enterprise, and external third-party systems to pull together timely relevant data. Direct pulls from financial, accounting, human resource, client, and network databases will speed up the process. A study of how cases are put together and how threat data is compiled, processed, and disseminated will be reconstructed with the help of machine learning and virtual decision trees to automate most of the process.

Every protection officer on patrol will be carrying a handheld device that helps them report maintenance issues, record events, take photos, take notes, and start a report. Investigators will enter a report, make requests for evidence and other supporting materials. They will be able to cross-reference the data with other databases in a few keystrokes and all less than an hour's work.

Insurance reports, financial anomalies, threat assessments, maintenance logs, and investigations will connect to find building neglect, miss-management, and even sabotage. By the end of the decade, these systems will help to teach building and security systems how to report their own deficiencies and escalate matters as a human would have. The results and formatting produced by these systems for fraud and AML case will boost the investigators professionalism and save hundreds of thousands of dollars for CSOs and quite possibly millions for their employers. No longer will notes become lost, tasks forgotten, steps skipped, or details seen as too small. They will all be uploaded into a single platform with a suite of interconnected services that will illustrate results humans may have never conceived.

2030–40

Twenty years earlier CSOs were hearing complaints about CMS such as there is no spell check feature, I cannot find my report, someone edited my report, I must cut and paste to email it. Today you may here have concerns such as, we still require teams of analysts, it's not providing the results I want, I cannot seem to get the dashboard I want configured easily. By 2030, these will have seemed trivial. Versions of these software services will have long been cloud hosted, constantly updated without disruption to the client, the recovery and restoration of backup data will take a matter of seconds. The fears related to connecting other systems to it, to enhance results will have been long solved. We will no longer need custom versions for different enterprise or use case. The out of the box product will be open architecture, intelligent, and able to find trouble, create reports, and offer real intelligence with half the resources and a tenth the time we need today. Power and storage will be bigger problems than any other concern we have today. Confidentially, integrity and availability will have been engineered in from the beginning. Because everyone will be using automated software, it will be affordable.

Questions

Where do I begin?

Do you have several notebooks on the go as a CSO? Are you juggling three calendars? Do you have napkins, sticky's, and anything else that was in reach with phone numbers and notes on them? Type it, scan it, put it on the computer, and now sort it out.

Are your officers using memo books? Written shift reports?

Put this on the computer, make sure it is stored on a network drive only. Do not store anything on a personal drive or desktop where it could be lost or cannot be shared.

This all sounds complicated.

Speak to your peers, read trade periodicals, search online. Develop a chart that illustrates the features you want across the top and then place 7–10 software on the left. Now check off which features they offer or not.

Steps

1. Educate yourself on the pros, cons, and providers of CMS
2. Determine what you need
3. Determine what you want
4. Ask for some demos and include key business partners who may also benefit from this, approve it and/or help you implement it
5. Sort all your current data into a shared digital location
6. Organize the meta-data onto spread sheets
7. Work with procurement to select a CMS service that is right for you
8. Be realistic and patient, draft a project management plan and budget for it
9. Allow the provider and your IS team to guide you
10. Once set up, start to feed the machine with all your data
11. Set up your view (what the CSO can see should be a different view than what a security officer or investigator sees when they open the software), dashboard and reports
12. Test, train, test, and train
13. Use this and only this, use it everyday, play with it, read the features, talk to the provider and use every feature it offers, change it up, use different views, dashboards and analysis, continue to build onto it

Considerations

Try to avoid big design up front. Set small realistic goals to start. Go digital, share information.

Conclusion

When the head of plant operations or security manager open their dashboard in the morning, they may see newest incidents. They will be looking at everything for that location. Assuming one or two occurrences are written a day, they should see the newest for review. A CSO may be responsible for 60 locations. Their dashboard may show the newest incidents as those escalated by the individual premises or operations. Their first reports may be the most serious in nature. A single slip and fall may not make the cut. Something involving an employee who was maimed, or a fire. Other things that may come up for the CSO are trends, such as 20 slip falls at a single premise in a short time, or an incident that took 12 h to recover and had major lost production time. It takes time to learn the system, embrace it, not tolerate it, and to get your settings optimal. It is a continuous process. When it is all said and done and you're looking at the most clear and efficient dashboard, worthy of handing straight over to your leadership team and realize what it used to take your department to get these results you will appreciate the value.

Crime prevention through environmental design

I am and always have been a big fan of crime prevention through environmental design (CPTED). I have heard all side of what has become a debate. It is a necessary part of crime prevention. It is all smoke and mirrors. It is outdated. It has grown to encompass too much. I don't know if these are inherent of CPTED or those trying to convey its message. Telling property directors that you can reduce all the crime at their premise by removing spray paint and broken windows is a tad excessive. Going into significant detail about electronic security systems and deep psychological discussions in a CPTED report losses its simplistic beauty. We tend to overcomplicate things or try to use an established soft science as a vehicle for everything. We like to challenge simple principles like CPTED or the fraud triangle. These simple yet effective frameworks are no different than humans. You cannot put absolutes on people. We are layered, complicated, emotional beings. Let's keep it simple. The bushes out front are so large they have created a hiding place for attackers. They block your clear view from the window to the street. The lights are so bright in the lobby at night, the security officer cannot see the street, they only see their own reflection. Want to show your property line from the field next door and have little to now money? Cut your field, leave one strip around the perimeter growing wild. These are so simple and yet we often overlook or forget these basic principles. There are many good CPTED consultants out there who can perform audits for you, train your staff on what to look for, and help you develop a program. If we as security professionals worked hard at crime prevention and supported our law enforcement colleagues at apprehension where reasonable, we could accomplish so much.

2010–20

By this decade, there were many very good papers, studies, guides, and books on CPTED. Certified practitioner programs were available, and many courses and programs included a section on CPTED. Unfortunately, some CPTED reports looked like a threat risk assessment and vice versa. Some property owners who received an unfavorable report, the ones that say your grounds are not perfect or you may need to spend a few dollars, tried to side with the CPTED is all smoke and mirrors crowd or looked for allies, including the ill-informed security professionals who did not understand it and therefore, viewed it as a waste of time. The principles are so simple and if translated just as simple you don't need scientific proof they work. The same person who challenges these basic principles, often supports excessive patrol forces and electronic security systems blindly.

One good application of this methodology during this decade was some well-rounded TRVAs that included a section on CPTED. Some security departments implemented CPTED guidelines and sometimes a checklist for officers to use and were not solely reserved for CS specialists.

2020–30

Some of the very early principles of CPTED were observed in urban planning. These were in line with how society to some degree thought. These were wrong. By 2020, no longer will we build neighborhoods with 5000 sq/ft homes to one side and 1100 sq/ft row homes to the other. No longer will we dare to write that a bouncing basketball and the activity around a court to be negative. We will eliminate segregation of classes in new developments. We no longer need to separate the elderly and children from teenagers. In a generation of people who will know they can do anything, no matter where you began, no matter where you're from, and what difference you perceive in yourself, everyone has a shot at doing something great. No one is better than the other. CPTED will not focus on demographics and social classes; but rather it will stick to modern crime theory. Break and enters, theft and pride of ownership have not changed. A good and competent guardian of a premise is as important now as it was then.

Like most things in the logical side of security, CPTED will be built into the design, rather than an afterthought. Society is becoming more educated, connected, and civilized. Although we can learn about bad news faster and it is often over-sensationalized, our population growing, it is not deteriorating. In fact, society is improving. We are not afraid to talk about and address social issues, our voices can be heard, and we can all effect positive change. As we find ways to ensure all people have access to education, fresh water, and food sources, we will begin to eliminate certain types of theft and desperation. It will be easier to identify why certain crimes are committed and use simple principles to reduce them.

The concept of reducing isolation and placing vulnerable activities in better locations will be common sense. In this decade, we will use technology, not as a replacement but to compliment good CPTED principles.

2030–40

As we enter this decade, it will be a long way from the 1960s when the original concepts began to formulate or in the early 1970s when the term was first coined. Two generations of CSOs will have come and gone. CPTED will have taken a strong academic turn and evolved into a long used, clearly defined science that has stood the test of time.

We will have observed another two stock market crashes, a shift in the industry of the day and a new paradigm in policing. As land becomes scarcer, immigration will have mixed cultures around the world, it seems less likely we will protect borders and property as vehemently as we do today, but instead share of sense of community and a responsibility to care for what green space and public places we have left. CPTED will simply divide those who wish to live well and those who break the law. Some gray will increase while some will simply be black and white. The legalization of cannabis in various parts of the world is a good example of how something that was considered a back-alley matter 40 years ago is no longer a community problem. CPTED historically has looked at the placement or deterrence of certain activity. We will eliminate some of these perceptions. Pot in some cases will be legal while other drugs are sold in the mall and not dark alleys. This changes a lot of how we thought 30 years ago. Not a cat or dog will go unregistered, technology will play its role and if you can chip every animal and label them as property then modern ways of marking property lines will certainly prevail. Where CPTED lays clear guidelines and best practices to reduce crime, technology and society will close the gap in the physical space making it near impossible to commit crime undetected. Do not take my word for it. Think about a fist fight in the street in the middle of the night in 1970. No try that now. Security cameras, mobile phones, social media, and a 24 h society. The focus will fall into the virtual space. Imagine an app that allows you to put on augmented reality glasses and see every property line, water main, and submarine cable, little to no surveying. Imagine rolling back those glasses to see the view ahead of you a week or month ago. When the window broke, when the graffiti appeared, and when the bush was last trimmed. How many cameras were on main street in your nearest city in 1970? How many today? How many in 2040?

The challenge of clear sight lines, hard to identify property lines and feeling isolated (between campus buildings, down an alley) will be eliminated with augmented reality and the unintentional super-surveillance society we will create.

Questions

Where do I begin?

- Consider having someone in your department certified in CPTED.
- Hire a consultant to conduct an audit of one of your premises.
- Ask your land lord if they have had a CPTED audit conducted.

Steps

Conduct a CPTED audit or have it included in the next threat assessment of one of your major premises.

You may be pleasantly surprised to see the way it brings out a new way for you to look at your premise and address small gaps.

Speak with your local police service and see what they are doing in the area, in relation to CPTED and if they have a unit or officer who specializes in it.

Consider conducting an audit of each of your locations every few years.

Considerations

- Reach out to and join a CPTED organization or group.
- Pick up or search a local resource on the topic, familiarize yourself, or get a refresher.

Conclusion

Society is changing. The old mentality of this is my property stay out, no trespassing has become, help me care for this property, share the liability, and split the taxes. I don't need the headache and expense in some cases. Leasing and renting will rise with the next generation. Urban parks will take on a whole new meaning as green space diminishes. CPTED is a simple, common sense practice that helps to identify obvious solutions to age old problems. The art and science of CPTED will evolve and has a big opportunity to play a larger role soon.

Corporate counterespionage

A hundred years ago one might have hired a private detective or just any capable person and have them spy on or even go work for the competition. Dumpster diving was not just a thing of spies but early competitive intelligence. The employees who talked too much in the lounge, bar, or elevator were and are always a problem. Disgruntled employees, those who have financial issues or even those who willingly go to work for the competitor can sink ships. Protecting raw materials, finished products, and of course people by means of old fashioned access control were the greatest focus for years. The value of intellectual property was as understood by law enforcement in the 1950s as cybersecurity was in the early 2000s. It took losses, first to market competition and gray market counterfeit to realize that the research and development (R&D), marketing and legal teams needed a whole new level of protection.

2010–2020

In this decade, most major enterprise had come to understand the importance of clean desk practices, encrypted laptops and phones, locked files, and technical surveillance countermeasures (TSCM) sweeps (also known as bug sweeps). We will go into more technical detail on TSCM later in this chapter.

Many corporate security (CS) departments had become aware that the threat from other corporations was real but that state sponsored actors were at play too. Entire corporate counterespionage programs were formed. CS still struggled with getting thousands of employees worldwide to clean and lock desks, secure their laptops, file sensitive papers, and shred all materials. Enter the hacker or even the inadvertent leak. Employees accidentally sending out materials, employees working on nonapproved systems, emails, and social media blunders. Then, we came to understand the possible impacts caused by the curious or malicious computer savvy cyber-soldiers looking to gain the upper hand. An adversary who may have never stepped foot on the premise or met any employees.

Practices to monitor leaving employees especially those going to work for competition were better defined. Analytics on logical and physical access control can flag concerning behavior. What are they printing at night, trying to email themselves to private accounts and what files are they trying to access or download?

Some of the most dangerous things for a CSO to suffer from are complacency, being ill informed and assuming that old tradecraft has been forgotten. Many today think TSCM is a thing of the past and it's all about the cyberattack. Think again, surveillance equipment is inexpensive and much more sophisticated today than ever before.

2020–30

In the next decade, disparate methods of prevention and detection will come together from the background check of new hires to the sweeping of office space, the new generation of CSOs will understand this paradigm and bring together key elements to mitigate this risk. Business will move faster than ever before. The way we utilize office space, the work from home employee, the bring your own device trend, and the influx of contingent workers and offshoring will change things completely. Projects will move fast, the acquisition of apps and startups will eliminate a lot of large, slow, costly R&D programs we have today. The protection of a merger and acquisition or the confidentiality of a launch of a new product, service, or brand will be of the utmost importantance. Once something hits the market it will duplicated on a three-dimensional (3D) printer, reverse engineered or out marketed in minutes. Speed and innovation will be an enterprise's only chance for survival. The CSO must work agile, be able to turn the team's target around on a dime and use their ingenuity to outsmart those seeking to steel trade secrets. This is where former intelligence personnel will shine in the CSO seat.

2030–40

In 2005, you could by a GSM, dial activated (auto-answer) microphone device online for $40USD, throw it in a planter or behind a credenza and enjoy several hours of remote listening just by dialing a burner GSM SIM card. However, the cost of bringing in a qualified sweep team and the $200k/USD of equipment they use was more than 10-fold the cost to find the device.

The idea of working in a giant faraday cage will seem obsolete. The cost of detection and jamming equipment will be the same as a half-decent cell phone. Several years ago, it would have been easy enough to have an insider drop a cell phone on in a room and use another to listen to the incoming meeting. Another problem was bugging ourselves, such as pocket dials, using AM/FM frequency wireless microphones in meetings and opening an attachment on your phone or computer and leaking your data, audio and even video. By the time 2040 comes around the current generation who are the best at living online and the worst at protecting themselves and maintaining any form of privacy will have learned some hard lessons. These will be tomorrows business leaders who will support better protection of data in the workplace and be careful who their speaking to and will be more conscious of who is listening.

Blackmail will have a run of success. While so many young people are putting their entire lives online today, they may regret this openness tomorrow when it really counts. For example, you are being interviewed for a Supreme Court position. The video you posted in 2020 at that party may come back to haunt you. They don't even need to spy on your personal life, you handed it right to them. In some regards, matters which seemed private 40 years earlier will be streamed nonstop in 2040, taking today's adversaries power away. For example, someone brings forward a nude photo of another in 2040 with an intent to blackmail. The supposed victim may say, "Oh yes I looked great there, but I posted about 40 more myself." We are already seeing how useless it is to place a spy camera in the lives of so many when they are posting their every move for you online, to the point its lost its luster. Adversaries may very well use your WIFI router (if you still have one) to see a 3D image of your room. They will use your own smart TV to listen to you with little to no effort. Wearable devices, game stations, and audio-controlled devices will always be hackable and offer spies on any payroll access to your audio and location. CSOs will also have to keep this in mind when running an executive protection (EP) program. You could try to take your company and personal life completely analog but then again you could always go out of business and cease to live a normal life too.

Questions

Can I just buy some gear and sweep for bugs myself?

No, you do not have the right gear, you have not been training what to look for visually, how to use the complicated equipment or even want that liability.

My access control is impeccable, I have metal detectors, bag checks, and more. Do I need to worry about someone planting a device, do we still need to sweep?

The latter part of the question is best answered in the specific threat assessment, do you have secrets worth knowing, stealing, spying for? If yes than the answer should be self-explanatory.

Do you have internal investigations for violence, fraud, theft, and other matters?

If you have insider problems of those types, what makes you think you won't eventually have an insider threat in this form?

Do you vet all contractors and contingent workers the same as you do full-time employees? Do you watch every technician, contract repair and maintenance service person in close detail always? Likely not. Therefore, there is some degree of risk.

Steps

- Train a member of your team on the risks of corporate espionage.
- Train them on corporate counterespionage and information protection (all information not considered information systems).
- Draft a standard, contract, and program with the aid of key internal partners. All discussion of this program should be kept on a need to know basis.

- Tender the sweep work to a qualified third party. Preferably one with counterespionage experience.
- Have them review your program with you, make recommendations, and train a select group on what to do if a leak, bug, or other threat is discovered.
- Continuously enhance the program, this does not mean increasing the spend, but using the budget to change and keep up with evolving threats.

Considerations

- Discuss the intricacies of the program with key information security leaders in your organization. Identify gaps, opportunities, and share knowledge. You both want to know about suspect USB keys. Their team may sweep for rouge WIFI devices and know what a company device is and what is an unknown device. Without telling facilities or other departments what you are doing, you may conduct a walk and examination of the entire premise and preidentified areas of high risk. Label and seal devices you are unfamiliar with before bringing in a sweep team. Noting the brand of devices and information is important. A listening device or camera may replace the one that is there or be placed in one. Note differences, changes, and reduce access.

Conclusion

Outsiders working with insiders may be one of your greatest threats. The insider threat is real, it is too great to risk ignoring. Educate yourselves, your leadership, and sweep.

Cybersecurity

This has become the corporate plague of the past decade. The fear of being hacked keeps executives, chief information security officers (CISOs), and CSOs up at night. Unfortunately, with a shortage of qualified information security experts and fear mongering executives have allotted large sums of money to unqualified professionals to handle their cybersecurity. Cybersecurity is the protection of your data, your enterprise, and yourself in cyberspace from cyberattack. Information security discussed below is the protection of information systems. Both are challenged by the same issue above, amongst other matters.

This list of threats continues to grow and the sophistication or barrage of some of the simpler attacks is growing exponentially. As a CSO today, you should familiarize yourself with all of these. As a CSO of tomorrow, you must become an expert on every one of them. A few examples of attacks are cross-site scripting (XSS), denial-of-service (DoS), distributed denial-of-service (DDoS), drive-by, eavesdropping, man-in-the-middle (MitM), password, and phishing and spear phishing attacks to name only a few. Untrained attackers can buy kits or seek advice on the web to execute these attacks. Many physical attacks to an enterprise have a clear goal. Theft and fraud for gain. Damage to sabotage. The cyberattacker may be as hard to pin down as an extremely violent criminal. What goes on inside ones' mind is not always clear to even the threat actor. Why do people hack? You guess is as good as any. To gain, steal, disrupt, to seek attention for curiosity. Whatever the true intent the damage is done once the data are accessed by an unauthorized party.

Throughout the book, I have told you to network everything. Share and communicate more. You could go back to handwritten messages and couriers, but you would not likely stay in business as a conglomerate today. Even these traditional methods became flawed and exposed in time. You simply need to build it better, secure it, and be smart about it. Here I will not talk about the methods of attack or protection in any detail. Instead I will discuss one of the most important shifts that must occur with the help of CSOs and CISOs. A shift in the way society deals with and views cyberattacks.

2010–20

In this decade, some of the breaches reported were on a scale that would have been unimaginable a decade earlier. Often when a crime is committed by a perpetrator in the physical space, the suspects face is plastered across the news. This may bring awareness and possible investigative benefits to the case. On the other hand, it may sensationalize these crimes and bring on some negative results. Many people can name the attacker but often don't know the names of all the victims. Some online crimes are treated like kidnapping and ransom. A payment to unlock the data or servers and the attacker remains anonymous. When a company is hacked, the CEO and CISO take the brunt of it in the media. It is like being the coach and the goalie in many respects. If our solution is to keep paying the criminals, continue with the mentality that they are a magic, entity unable of being caught and we can just change the consultant, leadership, or CISO every time a breach occurs then we will not make progress. This would not fly in the physical space. Post cyberattack the CEO must step up give a speech and literally stop focusing on running the company for a point in time. Even the largest of conglomerates are not faceless, evil, money hungry, capitalist, sociopathic machines. These companies were often founded by someone who had a dream, who wanted to earn an honest living and has persevered. They employ tens if not hundreds of thousands of people. The company and staff donate to charity, volunteer for the community and are good people trying to provide for their family's and contribute to society. Bank fees are not evil, they pay for many good kind people who support a large organization. The cost of a product is the right of the producer. There are always options. When you spend time reading, listening, and even getting to know some of those opposed to capitalism or the hacker elite they make some sense. There may be a better way, a better system and I hope one of them figures that out. However, you will also find those on the extreme end of the spectrum, some miss-guided who simply think they want anarchy, who do not understand the reality of their crimes.

Every country should have laws and every citizen should understand that curiously poking around the private network of another is no different than walking up to the front door of their home or private office, picking the door lock, in some cases kicking the door in and looking around. Some intentionally or unintentionally even damage property, cause unlawful mischief and in some cases steal. When someone breaks into a building, jumps the turnstiles, and sneaks into the office, they have trespassed or even committed a crime. Everyone without authorization who does this in the cyberspace has just done the same thing and should face similar if not greater consequences. No one glorifies this criminal who physically trespasses and yet they could walk out with computers, boxes of files, harm employees, and much more. The CEO is not often in front of the camera apologizing for this and the suspect if caught is detained by security and taken away by police. When an active shooter enters a premise, we support the victims. When a hacker spends day and night trying to steal your data (not the companies data) your data held by that company we shame the enterprise and not those responsible. We the people whose data that may have been leaked, the company unless negligent (most are not at all), the executives and security professionals employed by them are all in this together, all victims in one form or another.

In this decade, our law enforcement partners began to catch up, in the sense that a few services designated an individual or unit to cybercrime. Police began to respond to calls for service of this type and laws began to gain some strength in more forward-thinking places.

2020–30

In this decade, user controls will be implemented. Not to monitor our every move, censor or stunt creativity but to empower CS to take proactive measures against attack or to cyberattackers. Cyber-police of some form will enter the global space and laws allowing them to cross borders virtually and physically to take real action in identifying and apprehending these criminals. We will see a generation of crime fighters who will team with security experts to identity early warnings of an attempted breach and will be able to track the source and shut it down. The public will be made aware through public and private campaigns and training on how to protect themselves as common as it is now to keep your wits about you in a dark parking lot. Remaining anonymous online when trying to commit a crime will become harder. Some of the most famous hackers have been punished with standard criminal penalties and had their rights to access technology taken away. CISOs should be empowered to take affirmative action against unlawful hackers. The public and private partnerships to combat cybercrime in the previous decade should be made much more formal, expanded to proactively support victims and corporations; and duplicated worldwide.

We will begin to identify resources spent in the previous 20 years educating students on less important risks and integrate cybersecurity into the lives of youth from the time they enter school. They will understand what not to do (do not click on everything that pops up), to be careful about who they are speaking to online and what to do if they are cyberbullied.

2030–40

Allowing CS experts to fry an attacker's computer remotely would be nice, but when the servers are being slaved by another for nefarious purposes the victim may be in shock to find their computer or system terminated. Still offense is a good defense. In physical security, professional protection officers (PPOs) and now even robots are proactively patrolling, challenging people, and coordinating with law enforcement. Since the days of castles, to red force/blue force modeling, whenever defenders must sit and wait for the attackers to continuously try new methods of attack the attackers will eventually get in. Unless you have proactive defenses such as an army who are actively be seeking the threat and destroying it, todays defenses will eventually be defeated. By this decade, we will have developed systems that will take an active stance against attack. We will see security experts who will be resourced and empowered to hunt for threats and take reasonable action. We will not just send the threat away, we will share the information on the event and attacker with our key public and private sector partners through formal means.

Cyber-police will be a highly sought-after position by only the best. Corporate systems will have been developed in a way that allows for freedom of movement and access but limits exposure to accidental breaches caused by employee ignorance.

Questions

What can I do today to help better prepare my organization?

Bring in a consultant or hire a qualified expert. Do not put them at the helm or in operations in anyway. Have them strategically develop a plan for you ranging from risk assessments to ongoing programs. Never consider security an afterthought. Train your people, devote resources to this.

Steps

- Get an unbiased assessment of your state of cyber-preparedness
- Even if you're focus is corporate or physical security join cybersecurity groups, associations, and committees
- Keep up to date on recent breaches, ongoing threats, their cause, defense, and solutions
- Educate your security team, executives, and employees at all levels with the right level of awareness suited for them
- Have response, continuity, and recovery plans
- Have a third-party conduct cyberattack drills, include communications, public relations (PR), and legal
- Repeat

Considerations

If your CS department does not have a seat at the cybersecurity committee already, then do so. If you do not have an advocate or person knowledgeable in this area in your department, then make it so. Consider internal job shadowing and secondments. Whoever is responsible for your physical security systems and building systems in the coming years should have a strong grasp on this subject.

Conclusion

Security experts, true security experts of any kind need to stop questioning one another's credentials, thinking that their way to the top was the only way. Law enforcement, security, army, business, or academic we have brought value. When an incident occurs physical or cyber we need to avoid the armchair commentary and rally behind one another. You have been or will be hacked. I am as certain of that as an unwanted party has been and will be asked to leave the premise. All security professionals in the next 20 years must become familiar with and in many cases, experts in the cyber arena.

Executive and employee protection

Both employees and executives need protection. In most cases, however, a line employee does not layoff a few hundred employees, speak to the media or make tough decisions on behalf of the company that impact millions or billions of dollars. The executives are often blamed for many problems, are the face of the organization, and are, therefore, sometimes at greater risk. Employees facing personal matters, workplace violence, domestic issues are sometimes assessed as high risk. All employees are more vulnerable away from home on company travel than in the office or a familiar place. We will examine this in more detail later under travel risk management (duty of care). Nearly every resource in CS can be used in executive and employee protection (EEP), protection officers, security specialists, threat assessment, investigations, intelligence and more. The function can be divided into two main areas when being facilitated by CS. The first is operational, some departments employee both the manager of the program and those who will execute tactically. The protection personnel, security specialists, or manager who will escort the principal or group to and from the event, excursion, etc. Sometimes this is a one person show, someone who manages, facilitates, and executes the protection services for the enterprise on behalf of the CSO. Some departments conduct the assessments, planning, and governance behind the program and outsource the groundwork, which may include driving, close protection, and event security. There are many different models, the one that works for your organization will often differ from another. This is a service that can be ramped up and down with the needs of the organization. Sending a couple hundred top-producing employees, their plus ones (spouses, etc.), and several company leaders on an international trip takes a team to plan and execute effective security. The image and knowledge of today's close protection professional and the skills and resources of today's EEP Manager have risen in the past 20 years.

2010–20

In this past decade, we have come away from the bodyguard mentality and moved into the protection professional space. Close protection professionals are often associated with full-time personnel assigned to protecting celebrities. Corporate EP professionals have become skilled at conducting detailed threat risk assessments, operational plans, logistics, and more. Their knowledge of the world and world events gained from monitoring operations, business deals, travelers, and premises plays a large role in their day-to-day protection work. Employees benefit from this everyday in the office. Some large corporate protection teams diminished in this decade and were replaced by educated, trained professionals who were strong in the administration and management of the program. Global risk consultancies became more involved in providing on the ground support to these programs. Some programs protecting the top executives of fortune 100 companies and sometimes board members remained the same in the number of personnel assigned, however, shifted to an intelligence-driven model of ongoing assessment and protection.

2020–30

In the next decade, all employees will have gone through basic active shooter training, been briefed before business travel on the risks associated with business travel in general and the destination itself. Executives will require special protection of the data they take with them and changing laws as much as they require physical protection today. Compliance and legal departments will play a large role as will information systems in this area. Providing executives with burner equipment to travel with, advising what paperwork to take and not to take and how to avoid trouble. Chewing gum, lithium batteries, and satellite phones are already under scrutiny or even restricted in some international business and technology hubs.

Remote file sharing applications like Qnext will become more important. Even when using a VPN service, the executive must often travel with a company imaged device. If using another remote service from a hotel computer, you run the risk of keystroke loggers and screen recording software. With products like Qnext, a file can be brought up from around the world in seconds, opened on a mobile device, and will not leave a trace on the device. The app can even be temporarily deleted from the temporary device or the device remote wiped if the executive runs into trouble or must turn over the phone.

Corporate travel will continue to reduce, however, large enterprise will need to explore new markets continuously in the years ahead. CS will need to have contacts, service providers, and understand these locales.

2030–40

Predictions of future society are always interesting. Some cast us in a futuristic, retro dystopian era where society has completely crumbled. Others depict the future as a completely civilized tech driven all seemly well dystopia. The freedom fighters or rebels or terrorist often still seem to make it into the plot. If it is a degraded society, killer robots or a rebel siege there will always be a need for protection. As fast as start-ups become conglomerates today, empires will fall just as fast. In-house protection teams will be reduced to a director or VP lead part of CS with a couple of specialists. Specialty companies will be outsourced to handle the ground work and kidnapping, ransom, and extortion insurance, packaged with risk services will be the new norm for every major enterprise.

Health monitoring of key senior officials, residential security system monitoring, and social media trending will be commonplace, and all handled by the security operations center (SOC). Protection professionals will less likely carry a tactical pen, flashlight, and knife. They will be educated beyond defensive tactics and need no more than a mobile phone. A corporate EEP specialist will be able to locate an employees lost device from the road, wipe it and issue them a new one in minutes. CSOs will be just as interested in travel experience and trusted traveler enrollment of their protection professionals than they are of security experience. The future protection professional will understand the importance of protecting image and reputation is as important as the rest of their mandate. They will have PR on speed dial and know how to initiate a business continuity event. Kidnap and ransom response training (this is not extracting persons tactically but negotiating a business deal) will be a part of their basic training.

Questions

I am a CSO of a CS department, what kind of training should my EEP team have. Tactical, self-defense, driving, and similar training are nice to haves. Threat assessments for targeted violence, domestic and workplace violence assessment training, international landscape (political sciences), and technical skills (computer savvy) are much more valuable. Many entry level protection specialists are great at self-defense and shooting a pistol and often have never booked a flight on their own, facilitated a TSCM sweep, or coordinated with heads of security for airports, airlines, resorts, and hotels.

Steps

- Benchmark similar companies to gauge where your program sits with respect to full-time employees, contracted resources, mandate, training, and qualifications.
- Determine if the specialists in your department are aligned properly. EEP, travel risk management, event security, and operations often work well together.

Considerations

Before developing, enhancing or abandoning your program assess the needs of the enterprise. Educate and speak to leadership and implement a program that suits your needs. You can have a best in class program with good governance and service providers without building your own militia.

Conclusion

Like most things CS today, organizational resilience of tomorrow will be intelligence driven, technologically proficient and agile. Stick to these principals as you forge ahead.

Facilities security

One of the bedrock of physical security is the protection of facilities. This has been one of the first forms of physical security and will be one of the last. Security has a long and interesting history. Many publications have taken the reader through the origins of military, law enforcement, investigations, and security. In the past several decades, it could have been as simple as guards, gates, and locks. Imagine explaining today's world of premise security to the night watchman in 1960. Many things have not changed, simply the benefit of technology has made things easier or at least provided us more reliable records. Patrols have been and still are conducted. Sentry duty is still a common cornerstone of the security function. We have tried to replaced guards or at least enhance their capabilities with the addition of alarms, cameras, electronic access control, and now robots.

Facilities can come in many different forms and the security of them. Large office towers, shopping centers, factories, business, medical or educational campuses, data centers, and much more. For years, a large department store may have employed a store detective now known as loss prevention to catch thieves by day and a watchman (an old term, now a professional protection officer) by night to watch the premise. To this day, many large organizations employ a CS department at head office, some of their mandate and duties are related to the facilities security often from a strategic or leadership point of view. They employ security officers often from a third-party service provider to facilitate premise security 24/7.

If we can learn anything about people and the future of cybersecurity from facilities security is that since the beginning of mankind trespassing to one's cave may have gotten you ridicule amongst the tribe or even a club to the head. To this day, there are penalties for trespassing and yet thousands of years later people still trespass for many reasons, some continuously as a career criminal or free shelter. This goes the same for break and enters crimes. If the penalty is a ticket, arrest, jail, or even the risk of being shot people still do this daily nearly everywhere there are facilities, dwelling, or grounds. I do not predict this will change much, other than the enhancement of premises access control and the tracking of criminals.

2010–20

In the past decade, we have been shifting away from trying to design a better key and lock and focused more on electronic access control. As many new small private security service providers have popped up, the merger and acquisition of medium to large companies has been observed globally. Large guard providers have entered the technology service arena as seen in decades past and then stepped back out again in a few instances.

We have observed a continuous shift away from in-house security officers at facilities and the use of contract security officer services. In places where security plays multiple roles such as security, investigator, health, and fire life safety such as hotels, critical infrastructure, and retail loss prevention; many teams have not only remained in-house but also enhanced their talent pool, resources, and staffing to meet greater demands.

The first robots began to patrol alongside their human coworkers and security officers have started to learn about smart buildings. Terrorist attacks in or directly targeted at facilities have continued. Active shooter events in nightclubs, schools, and offices have taught us that security is there for a lot more than patrols and locking doors. The observe and report model in a major premise has also shown that it does not work. Employees and the public expect a rapid, trained, and confident responder. Having a team of security onsite who can respond much faster than law enforcement, who in many cases are mandated not to engage and/or are not equipped and trained appropriately to if they can engage or choose to, is still an issue up for debate.

Not only do we have systems to track threats to travelers, but also we can now enter building addresses, geofence them, and have our security control rooms offer greater situational awareness to leadership. Building security control rooms which will be discussed in detail later in this chapter have evolved significantly. Protecting asset worth hundreds of millions of dollars, it contents, and occupants has become a duty of care to property owners. The commercial real estate market is competitive. If one landlord is known for providing commercially reasonable security and the other for a lackadaisical or haphazard attitude about risk and security, potential and existing tenants are likely to discover this by reputation, experience or due diligence and choose the former.

2020–30

In the next decade, we will expect to see hyperconnected buildings. Buildings that are highly automated, networked, alive, and well on the internet. These building, security, and even company network systems will be remotely operated, provide health status and change staffing and operations forever. IT skills for building operators, security, and management will be paramount. Adversity to technology will make the employee obsolete the moment the switch is flipped. Buildings and security systems will be hacked, servers held for ransom payable by bitcoin and building managers will have to understand terms like blockchain or its successors.

The balance between bullet-proof access control and complete camera coverage versus privacy and overly restricting employee/visitor movement will still be contemplated between security professionals and occupants.

2030–40

By the point, we are halfway through this decade security control room personnel will be information systems, information security, and electronic security systems specialists. The amount of data, the number of systems, and increased risk of being hacked will call for an entirely new paradigm of security specialist. Building materials, suppression systems, and automation will reduce the chance of a significant fire in new premises. The increase in power, heat, cooling systems, closed-loop water, and wiring will bring an increase to existing hazards. Professional protection officers in facilities will be focused more on customer service and response.

There are environmental benefits of building vertical to avoid sprawl that are equally important as the risks of tall buildings. Tall buildings will get taller and shopping centers in many places where the climate permits will be replaced with more outdoor shopping complexes comprised of many stores in one property connected center (outdoor shopping centers). Medical response to the top of a high-rise facility will remain a challenge, as will securing and patrolling a widespread shopping grounds.

The use of third-party hosted security systems, cameras, and even operations centers will increase. By large many of the principles and practices throughout this chapter including security personnel, robots, CPTED, and systems will create an entirely new look for how security is provided to premises.

Imagine a mall with grand hallways and corridors. Now instead of an officer patrolling this massive facility at night alone, add a few cameras in entrances and exits. Add a few more to those long corridors and wings. Picture those cameras being fitted with the best analytics, the camera, scanners, and alarms know if it is a cleaner or security officer. This intelligence system can detect, analyze, and escalate to a remote operations center all anomalies. Imagine a mobile patrol team arriving in minutes trained to deal with the matter at hand in a professional and swift manner. A robot on patrol and a voice over an enunciator direct the party to identify themselves. The intelligent building fitted with state-of-the-art technology that cost a fraction of today's basic security system.

We have all of that. Maybe, but in 2040 an intruder without the right mobile device, credential or biometric who enters unauthorized after hours will be assessed by several scanners feet from the door, verified or rejected by facial recognition and a team alerted for further assessment.

Questions

As a CSO who works for a company that leases our premises, how does this apply to me?

Conducting TRVAs of the office, operations and premises even where it is leased it just as important. You may not be responsible for the property and may not lead the security operations, but you are qualified to ensure that is suits the company's needs.

The landlord and their security do not work for me, how do I influence them?

By building good relationships with your peers at those entities, by your security managers working with theirs, by building language into the lease to provide commercially reasonable security and to comply with inquiries, investigations, and security reviews you may achieve better results. Think of them as a partner in security and life safety, manage as a vendor and trust but verify.

Steps
- Work with your internal premises department to understand trends in premises, smart buildings, and smart cities.
- Make sure your department has a role in site selection (leased, owned, and developed).
- Provide due diligence, threat assessments, and minimum design specifications.
- Conduct ongoing assessments on existing locations.
- Actively participate with counterparts to look at where facilities security is headed, what you can do to support this and stay current.

Considerations

It is not hard to be allured by EP, major fraud investigations, or the rush of crisis management. Often good foundational building security takes a back seat. Make sure you still employ facilities security experts on your team and help support them to remain up to date.

Conclusion

If there are properties, there will be property owners. Those owners will need security experts to lead their security programs, provide consulting, and assess risks. There will still be a need for physical security in this industry for as long as those premises exist, it will simply evolve, take on new practices, and require the addition of cybersecurity skills.

Fraud investigations

Corporate fraud is one of the most long-standing atrocities that has plagued companies big and small for nearly as long as there have been businesses. Fraud committed by insiders, outsider, and/or a combination of both. Annual fraud losses among the largest companies in the world collectively total billions upon billions of lost dollars. Unlike cybercrime and money laundering, there are clearly defined laws in countries around the world, long-established means of investigation and a successful history in place of fraud deterrence and recoveries. From 1990 to the end of 2009, we not only observed corporations being victimized with larger and larger frauds, we also witnessed large frauds committed by leaders of companies. Some of these were not as simple as taking money directly from clients but miss-leading shareholders, owners, and clients about the financial state of the enterprise and/or the capability of the products which had been falsified. Mass corruption and greed from this era were turned into numerous movies and documentaries.

Today, several committees and associations government, joint, private and not-for-profit offer support, membership, communication, education, and training. The most recognized is the Association of Certified Fraud Examiners (ACFE) and the Certified Fraud Examiner (CFE) designation.

There are and will be good fraud detection, investigation, analysis, and forensic careers with FIs, business and accounting consultancies, and private companies to name only a few. The internet age has been one contributing factors which made fraud more sophisticated, global, and on a scale that seems to keep breaking its own infamous record. As far back as the Enron scandal in 2001, frauds have sometimes been followed by new guidelines and laws such as the Sarbanes-Oxely Act of 2002 to help establish controls that will reduce future losses of the same kind on the same scale.

White-collar criminals were marched out in front of the cameras and sentenced to prison time, fines, future career restrictions, and public shame. Looking at the past few years, time and time again we still see more people committing large-scale fraud. The ACFE's 2018 Report to the Nations lists further staggering and blatant corporate frauds.

2010–20

By 2010, there were tens of thousands of professional fraud fighters. Forensic accountants, professionals certified in fraud examination, financial crimes, AML. Colleges and universities offering certificates, diplomas, degrees at all levels in the field and law enforcement and federal agencies devoted to the fight. Is has become a sought-after career for intelligent, inquisitive, hardworking career-minded people interested in making a difference.

Knowledge of accounting principles, laws related to frauds, governance and controls, and now computer crimes have been a good foundation during this decade. Old frauds done by mail or in person became telephone scams in the 1990s and then internet facilitated frauds in the past 20 years. Many cybercrimes result in frauds and extortion today. Educational programs in fraud are beginning to include web research, financial and computer forensics, and new and more complex frauds as part of the basic curriculum.

2020–30

In the next decade, the controls in place, corporate code of ethics, public awareness, and business schools addressing these matter to graduates will eliminate ignorance. Those leaders caught for committing fraud will have blatantly set out to do so. Motivators such as pressure will be a lame excuse, ego and greed will continue to be top causes of this behavior. Anti-fraud professionals will be able to categorize, detect, and act on frauds much more easily with the digital revolution and the improved fraud education. The CFE designation will become the most commonly earned designation for CS professionals in FIs. More fraud fighters will have a degree in accounting or financial crime-related disciplines than the previous decade. This is a good, long, and steady career for the patient professional. Departments will have those who investigate frauds, those who detect frauds, and those who audit, develop, and implement controls working on highly skilled teams for compliance and CS.

2030–40

Fraud detection applications and features built right into the systems used for client transactions, accounting and finance will be required by 2040 and not just a nice to have. Unlike physical and information security controls, frauds controls do very little to inhibit or slow down business if implemented correctly. Corporate transparency and good practices will be judged by social media so many times by 2040 it will change the way companies report information, the culture and tone from the top.

Foreign corruption will still exist. Some nations will take another 50 years to get caught up to where the United States is today in its governance over public officials. The pressure for companies to explore new markets and break into them will lead some to fall into this slippery slope. As a CSO you will need to support the business, while steering them away from unlawful risks and criminal activity. This is another reason why CSOs in many organizations will report to the top of the company, the board of directors, legal, compliance, and/or audit.

In FIs, the rise of financial crimes departments will bring on new career opportunities for anti-fraud professionals and pave the way for greater public/private partnerships.

Questions

What are some of the challenges in the near future for fraud investigations?

- Biometrics used to access banking and other services such as voice and fingerprint will come under greater security and evidentiary challenges.
- Methods of hiding your tracks online will be ahead of tracking criminals until the future "cyber-police" rise.
- The nondigital generation will continue to be victim for another decade, which will keep case volumes on victim client/retirees busy.

How do we get to the level of automation and integration discussed here?
- The best way is from day 0. Design the systems with the controls, alerts, and analytics into the applications used for business, accounting, finance, etc., when you start, refresh, renew, or replace those systems is where to begin.

Steps

- Create a list of all the software used to process financial data for the enterprise (client, accounts payable, account receivable, inventory, invoices, cheques, etc.).
- Develop of matrix of frauds, how they are committed, how they are mitigated (common controls) and red flags.
- Connect with the Information Systems, application owners and evergreening or strategic teams who review and update these systems.
- Make sure that when the next major changes occur with the system that your department is included in the upgrades and that they budget for these features.
- Work with these teams and the vendors, convey your objectives up front (these project teams often include end users, avoid providing all details to end users on the controls and alert systems).
- Have someone from your team (more than one) licensed on the software, trained and able to pull down their own reports for investigations.
- Where the software is limited, a fraud specific application may need to be purchased and integrated with the enterprise software as part of the same project.
- Simply automate, go paperless, go digital, and build the controls right into the book of record.

Considerations

The fraud profession will grow and demand qualified applicants who are up to the challenge. Every business, even the most nontechnical, nonfinancial of businesses should engage a fraud expert to review their most basic transactions, the business they conduct with vendors and clients, and provide recommendations.

Conclusion

As a CSO, your department may lead, support, or work parallel to the company's fraud investigators. Make sure that they are appropriately resourced, remain in touch with technology and acknowledged for the positive impact they have.

Fusion centers

There are some good definitions of fusions centers and cyber fusion centers online. The core objective is to place interagency, interdepartmental, or both personnel in one place to collaborate, share intelligence, and apprehend criminals and terrorists.

If done right, these can be very successful. Where an enterprise does not want to create one large team (investigations, physical security, AML, fraud, cybersecurity, crisis and business continuity) they can consider fusion centers. By assigning one to three people from each team to work in and rotate through the center an agile working unit can be formed to enhance situational awareness and response capabilities.

2010–20

Post 9/11 a number of government agencies became very good at working together and creating fusions centers. Most flourished. Some partnerships were challenged in the beginning of this decade. Most of these were based on partners not funding or resourcing their part of the partnership. Other relationships were strained with the pre-9/11 challenges of partners who shared very well and those who shared nothing. Government operations have found their niche today and can be very effective. It has still been a challenge to get complete private sector fusion centers in full operation. Centers funded in cooperation between public and private sector with the sole purpose of providing tailored, real-time intelligence, especially those in the cyber discipline have been successful. The establishment of clear guidelines on how to share information while respecting the rules of evidence, privacy and need to know controls have matured through the past 10 years.

2020–30

In the next decade, large enterprise who do not have a consolidated CS department or those who have not practiced convergence may still cooperate by assembling small agile teams made up of employees from similar departments to handle crisis, investigations, and intelligence gathering. Some may proceed by formalizing this in the form of an internal fusion center. This can take the form of a group of employees from each team, segregated in a workspace where they can both work individually and collaboratively. Another model will be work areas similar to the security operations centers (SOCs) staffed and functioning like a SOC. This is where live ongoing work occurs, on a more tactical and operational level.

The inclusion of more private security partners into publicly lead fusions centers will increase as budgets and skills become harder to acquire.

2030–40

By 2035, the lines between corporate operations center, fusion centers, and agile working teams will be blurred. This will simply be the way work is completed. Some enterprise will merge all like departments in one and have agile teams working on projects and investigations while others may split all forms of security under the ESRM model and the remainder under the Special Investigations Unit (SIU) or financial crimes. These departments will have many different sections and specialists. Their agile work will reflect what is done in designated fusion centers today.

Steps

- Speak to public sector and private peers to learn more about active fusion centers today.
- Many large data center/data management and large professional consulting firms offer fusion center services, these may be worth exploring as an outsourcing option.
- Do not rush off to form the super elite team of crime fighters if your organization does not need one. Educate yourself first on the topic and make an informed, cost effective, and results driven decision.

Considerations

Outline your goals and objectives, take a project management approach to assessing your needs. Determine who should be involved in the assessment committee, how the program will be funded, and what the alternatives are.

Conclusion

Fusion centers can be a very effective method of enhancing collaboration for both public and private sector teams. Analysts are critical to the success of any intelligence-based operation. Don't start by designing a fusion center by today's standards, look at where automation and department structures are headed, understand your company's long-term strategy for organizational hierarchy and make forward thinking decisions.

Global security operations centers

A Global Security Operations Center (GSOC) may take on different meanings in premises security, corporate security (CS), and cybersecurity. When the GSOC is focused on premises, the enterprise often occupies a lot of real estate (or even owns it but leases it to third-party tenants). This GSOC manages a centralized access control, alarm, and video system monitoring for facilities around the world. They deal with building emergencies, call emergency services, patrol services, and managed automated call trees to escalate matters to leadership, occupants, and tenants.

CS GSOCs may also cover these and additionally or only monitor global world events and travelers, manage how political, security, and environmental factors impact premises, operations, vendors, data centers, and personnel. They retrieve records, video, and logs for investigations. They may monitor employee and executive events, travel, and select key senior official residential security. They can track company vehicles, executive vehicles, and handle communications.

Global Network SOCs may monitor external trending cyber threats, internal threat hunting, network health, business continuity and crisis events.

2010–20

At the beginning of this decade, many GSOCs servicing CS operations were intended to provide a global view of the world. In some cases they may have been oversold and may have been expected to provide ambitious intelligence which would be shared with operations. Much of what was in place was a semi-regional operations center for building security systems, alarm monitoring and very little in the way of real-time intelligence, needed by parties outside of the security department. Many organizations subscribing to services such as NC4, International SOS, or Stratfor gained more insight than some GSOC personnel who were limited to watching the news.

Within the past several years those using global mapping and positioning systems to track travelers, began to expand these evolving services to monitor assets and operations. As these tools allowed operators to geo-fence areas and assets on a map, the services offered real time, actionable threat intelligence and leaders developed processes to escalate concerns; the return on investment became apparent. Still many of these proprietary centers are expensive to staff 24/7. Businesses have also found that they still need on-premise security desks, control rooms, and even regional SOCs. While some duplication creates redundancy and the ability to better manage large-scale crisis, it is often brought into question when the enterprise needs to scale down expenses.

2020–30

In the next decade, the ERSM model will see a shift where many like departments currently measured in the operational risk practices begin to unify. The entire systems component of physical security will move to the information systems or information security GSOC in larger enterprise, this will occur faster where a facilities or real estate department does not already own this service.

Outsourcing of global threat monitoring to third-party GSOCs will also work best for many mid-sized organizations that are global in scope, but do not necessarily work in high risk locations or have many corporate travelers.

The consolidation of physical security systems will bring a need to centrally monitor these. One location can pull reports, logs, review video, program access credentials, and handle communications. One of the challenges of local in-house GSOCs is languages. If the enterprise is a large global one, the GSOC may not have personnel on duty 24/7 who can speak every language with native proficiency.

2030–40

Often when a security practitioner thinks about a GSOC they picture a large room with many security cameras on display, some alarm panels and TV's off to one side, phones ringing off the hook and radios chiming. A very good example of where government operations centers were yesterday and where CS GSOCs will be in 20 years is the Everbridge, Visual Command Center. Third-party services who tie in the enterprise mass notification, travelers and assets into a map that offers different views, real-time threat information and easy to understand dashboards. This is the direction that large digital centric, risk conscious organizations are headed.

Many organizations will focus less on the space or room and more on the data. Analysts sitting side by side of other employees with their laptop and two extended monitors will replace many large operations centers. There are a few examples of why smart leaders will create a separate area for security matters to be managed. These may include the following. When they work in a cube farm with no privacy. When they work at the reception desk and are interrupted constantly. When they are trying to deal with highly confidential matters or crisis in the open. When the security control center can be compromised due to lack of protection, from sitting out in the public view. Open-concept environments do not work for everyone. Placing these teams and departments on one restricted floor makes sense and will be a good working alternate in the future.

Questions

I am having trouble convincing my leaders that we need a GSOC, what can I do?

There are a few resources including business cases online, many good articles and books. Speaking to your peers and a qualified consultant is a good start. Do you pay for separate rooms at multiple sites now? Do you pay for separate alarm systems, have too many vendors to manage and/or have little to no monitoring at other locations? Consolidation, improved quality, and a global view by experts may be the business case here. What you should ask is does my organization need one? Do you have similar operations now that could be improved by the design of a GSOC? Do you have a card administrator in the security office who are fine where they are? Do you already have a basic security control room for head office that simply needs a refresh and not a major upgrade? Are you hung up on the grand design of the room rather than practical functionality and technological enhancements?

Steps

- Develop a business case
- Conduct a needs analysis and feasibility study
- Tour other GSOCs and issue a questionnaire to peers
- Seek funding, approval, and buy in
- Select a project team, integrator, and consultant
- Select a location
- Look ahead, how will day-to-day operations work?
- Clearly define what your trying to achieve, who are your clients, how will this benefit them, keep revisiting this as you progress

Considerations

Make sure the space and design are not too grand, however, ensure it has room to grow or evolve in time. Make sure to include all locations, departments, or department members who would benefit from a GSOC in the early discussions. See where you can leverage existing resources.

Conclusion

A GSOC can be a force multiplier and a good example of how consolidation and centralization of resources with the right level of redundancy can enhance an enterprises organizational resilience.

Industry standards and guidelines

Security is often thought of as an entry level, low-level career. For many years, security executives were not seen as many other career professionals. Yet almost nowhere else will you find an industry around the globe like it. Security officers have step-by-step procedures on what to do throughout their shift, how to respond to emergencies, collect evidence, write reports, take breaks, lock and unlock doors, etc. Security specialists develop company standards on how to assess risk, how to organize a protection assignment, respond to crisis, crisis communications, and design specifications to name only a few. Most people security will report to in the private sector and their peer departments do not have such clearly defined and organized standards, guidelines, operating procedures, and policies.

CS professionals are often required to reference their work. In addition to the many books written by leading industry experts and text books; associations such as ASIS International have spent decades publishing guidelines and standards developed specifically as practical study and reference materials. Twenty years ago one could find very few peer reviewed, committee written, practical reference documents. Today, there are volumes of guidelines, standards, how to documents, and research papers for most aspects of security and most industries. Today's CSO can network and research online and access a global community to solve problems they may have faced alone 40 years ago.

2010–20

In this past decade, the number of CSOs with a higher education, board certified, and working in a global environment has been larger than in years past. Many security leaders and academics have volunteered on working groups to help produce new and updated versions to helpful resource documents. Society benefits from these practices. As workplaces become safer, methods of protection and response improve, and employers better protected the cycle have gained positive momentum. The importance of CSOs taking the time to give back to the community to help share their experiences and knowledge is important to continuing this achievement for the industry.

2020–30

In the next decade, access to the second and third generation of these documents for professionals internationally will be easier than when they were first conceived. Websites, applications, online share sites, and more will allow even the most remote locations to access cutting-edge standards. No more will a CSO have to keep a bookcase or even fill a network folder with this data. Access and storage improvements will allow for better document management.

2030–40

Toward the end of this decade, existing standards will have become the basis in laws, government best practices, and used in legal context numerous times. Standards reflecting new departments, ones based on convergence and ESRM will be written for a new generation, new department structures, and ways of measuring the success of the program.

Questions

There is so much online, how do I know which is the best?

You don't. Find a reputable source, compare the same standard from a couple producers. Often the best will sound similar and complement one another. Make sure they are current, relevant, and remember they are guidelines, not must do documents. Each enterprise and situation are a little different.

Steps

- Conduct some online research
- Start a library of good standards and guidelines
- Share them with your department
- Use them as an aid to develop documents that are tailored to your company's needs

Considerations

Look into how you can contribute. Read up on the most current documents. Ask yourself, do you have an expertise, interest, or passion? Can you join the next working committee, submit a proposal for a new standard? Get involved, actively participate, and continue doing so.

Conclusion

Industry standards and guidelines have elevated this profession and will continue to do so. These help to form the base study material for certifications, they provide guidance to new CSOs and allow nonsecurity professionals to reference important information in the protection of people, assets, and information.

Information security

Information security provides confidentiality, integrity, and availability of information and information systems from unauthorized access, use, disclosure, disruption, modification, or destruction. Over the past 20 years, the roles of both CSO and CISO have become more prevalent. Physical security systems which have been integrated and networked to create system redundancy have a greater risk of compromise than older, disparate systems. Now that video management systems, access controls and alarm data moves across the internet and can be managed from mobile devices, we need to start to understand the criticality of information security. The world is changing rapidly. Autonomous vehicles, smart buildings, smart cities, and robot security personnel will need highly skilled professionals to design and maintain systems to protect them. Cybersecurity focuses more on protecting the system and yourself online. Cybersecurity deals more with the live system, that is already in use. Information security starts at the concept stages. Information security professionals have been around since before it was a career or computers were invented. It has become one of the most rapidly growing professions in the past 30 years. It was almost unheard of to expect a corporate or physical security professional (PSP) to understand network or systems security 20 years ago.

2010–20

In this past decade, the job postings for the role of director security and CSO were surpassed by the rise of the director, information security, and CISO. In 2010, I observed numerous job descriptions in job ads where employers were seeking information security professionals with a background in information systems and a degree. At that time a designation was noted as a nice to have. Now you can find employers looking for CISOs with 20 years of experience in information security, a graduate degree in the field and a designation or two as must have credentials. There are CSOs in commercial real estate and industrial settings who now have responsibility for information and/or cybersecurity as well as physical. These are industries that would have seemed to be last to converge these practices a decade ago. Large enterprise have developed departments of experts who assess information risk to business, vendors, applications, data hosting services, and much more. CS leaders can now rely on the expertise of their information security colleagues to help with major technology decisions and assessments.

Information security professionals have several specializations to work toward or move through. The number of professional development programs, certifications, and degree options have quadrupled in this decade.

In early 2010, surprisingly many company's treated information security as a burden expense, an afterthought and CISOs struggled to change this perception. Today, leading companies are developing their systems, programs, and products with security top of mind, designed right into the process, software, and corporate culture.

2020–30

In the next few years, information security will need to be almost completely synonymous with information systems. When tomorrow's toaster has the technology of yesterday's smartwatch, security will need to be engineered into everything from the moment it is designed. No longer can it be an addition. We will have to rethink firewalls completely. No CSO will graduate with a degree in security management without having learned and completed an exam on information security.

A decade earlier if you were to ask a security manager about the security of their building security systems, they may have directed you to the lock on the door to the equipment racks and the conduit protecting the wires. In 10 years from now, a security manager in the most industrial of work environments will understand the importance and concepts behind securing physical security systems from intrusion and compromised by hackers. It will not simply be about them understanding not to click on links, but that they will need security for their security.

A large challenge for information security experts is to please all parties. Make it secure, don't impede business, do it for little to no dollars, and make sure it's easy for all the employees and customers to use and access, but not the bad guys. Please have that done by this afternoon. Unlike physical security you cannot take down the access control and leave some security officers at the door for the day while you perform tests, inspections, and upgrades. These experts will find ways to move mountains of digital data securely to a new location in order to replace old infrastructure. They will be educated in both the why and the how. Experts will be both strategists and practitioners. It is critical for CISOs to understand business. Tomorrow they will manage very large budgets, be critical to every business decision and need to align with the corporate strategy in their own work.

2030–40

In the next 20 years, we will see a complete convergence of certain aspect of the security function. Business technology, security technology, and security operations will cross over so close in numerous touch points that only experts will be able to ensure the risk to the enterprise is sufficiently addressed. Information security engineers and architects will be some of the most sought-after experts.

Information security professionals will become expert witnesses in technology-related death investigations, lawsuits, postbreach commissions, senate committees, and congressional hearings.

Some large enterprise will roll both security departments, corporate and information into one department where business continuity and crisis management will roll up underneath one CSO. Some will branch financial crimes or investigations under legal and compliance and premises security will be split. The systems will go under the former mentioned security department and the officers will fall under premises or real estate. Security specialists who conduct threat assessments will split, one group focusing on technology will move to security while those assessing geopolitical, criminal, violence, and other related types of risk will move under compliance or investigations depending on the enterprise. Educational programs will begin to reflect this upward shift. Information security departments will have evolved and taken on an entirely new name and place in the enterprise.

Questions

There are so many information security designations and certifications, which one should I take?

Is not uncommon to see experts in this space with several. A short certification course on a specific application is not a professional designation. You can go three general routes. You can be a career expert. For example, you may graduate from university, take a penetration testing certification and become the world's most leading authority on pen testing throughout your career. You can graduate, gain experience, remain a generalist, take a management specific designation, and work your way up the department over a career. You can also start as a specialist and then work toward management later. You do not need the alphabet behind your name, you need to know what you're doing and how to do it. In information security staying current and in fact ahead is more important than knowing everything. It's a team sport, learn to rely on the different skills of your teammates.

Steps

- Hire a consultant to assess the state of your program.
- Recognize that patching is not a long-term solution.
- As a CSO today, accept that some level of convergence is going to happen tomorrow.
- Hire people who know their way around a computer, who embrace digital, and can think out of the box.

Considerations

No matter what type of CSO you are, one with a team of two working for a large consumer goods producer focused on physical and CS or one with a team of 200 in a bank focused on financial crimes and security risk, a director or vice. Information security must become second nature, not a concept for other people. Make sure to partner with your tech savvy colleagues today as much as possible, leverage each other's strengths and foster a positive relationship with all level of both departments.

Conclusion

No department will take over the other, no role will become redundant, a simple shift is coming. Information security is more critical than the public, executives, and employees have yet to understand. Make sure you are a leader and not left behind.

Major events security

Corporations host and sponsor many events. This may be on or off-premise, company specific, or community involvement. A company may host their annual general meeting (AGM) onsite or offsite. A locally hosted political or sporting event may indirectly impact the site with road closures and increased crowds in the city or may be invited to set up a tent or media center on a part of the premise. The company may sponsor the Olympics or similar event and offer volunteers. In any case, a risk assessment should be conducted. A plan to manage, comanage, or work with event organizers and security should be laid out with a series of contingencies. The chance of protest, violence against large gatherings of people and crimes of opportunity lost in the anonymity of the excitement, are often prevalent challenges in major events.

2010–20

Today, large CS departments often have a specialist, manager, and/or director who leads events, major events, and similar services from a security perspective for the enterprise. They work with internal partners, seconded colleagues, risk consultants, and many other professionals in a committee to bring the planning and execution together. Security officer service providers often play a role in major events and are a critical partner to CS. Smaller enterprise may rely on their CSO to play this role too with the assistance of consultants and other providers.

The ability to meet virtually, maintain lines of communication, share intelligence has changed in the past 10 years to security's benefit. Public and private partnerships have proven valuable during these occasions. The ability to use other security technologies, service providers, and operations centers to support these events have added to the return on investment for those services. Duty of care (travel risk management) and other crime and risk intelligence services can be homed in on the event specifically. Online posts and chatter offers greater situational awareness. The security, planning, and intelligence at major public events such as New Year's Eve in New York City, the Super Bowl, and the World Cup have prevented, thwarted, and/or discouraged attacks. Gatherings of protestors, large weddings, religious ceremonies, night clubs, and other less secured gatherings of people have seen vehicle ramming, suicide bombings and other terror or criminal attacks around the world.

2020–30

As a CSO or future CSO, you will likely be expected to secure events in ways thought to be too expensive and intrusive in years past. There may no alternatives, aside from canceling the event or lowering its risk by changing locations, attendees, or the level of publicity. Society is, however, being conditioned to expect checkpoints, screening, biometrics, baggage checks/restrictions, and pat downs at more and more venues. Temporary vehicle barriers are becoming normal for community events where crowds will fill the streets and parks this could be a simple as parking city owned operations and construction vehicles to block roadways. There are service providers who specializes in event security and the wise CSO will rely on their experience and the transfer of some risk.

The ability to leverage the information, skills, and tools from other experts who will converge in future CS departments, the ability to track all company devices in the operations center for safety purposes and the increasing number of security personnel cleared to participate in public sector security briefings will enhance our ability to keep people safe.

More CSOs will have developed standards, assessment tools and automated these to take some of the burden off security and allow the event planner some independence in the planning stages.

2030–40

In the next 20 years, converged security operations will be able to provide preevent information, monitor the event in the physical world and cyberspace, and control systems to enhance the work of professional protection officers. Automated check points, robot security personnel, and augmented reality will all be normal tools for any event. Security specialists imbedded in CS (protection services, organizational resilience, global security) or corporate investigations (financial crimes) will be experts in event, terror, and violence (behavioral) threat assessments.

The use of armed police will increase. Companies will hire armed police for major events to transfer risk and increase response force capability. The arming of security in many locations is not likely to happen. The increase in terror and active shooter events will demand armed, on scene, rapid responders.

Questions

Should I develop a special event security team?

As a CSO you will need to determine what is best for your company. Having a couple of generalists trained in major event security and related subjects is one option. Having a lead for protection matters, including events that have regular service providers to provide the people resources allows you to ramp up and down as required. Remember policing the streets or securing venues is not your responsibility when you are just a sponsor and have a single booth or tent.

Steps

- Connect with any departments or personnel who host corporate events (marketing, corporate secretary, events, sponsorship, and/or government relations, etc.)
- Make a list of all events hosted on and off-premise, sponsorships, etc.
- List all upcoming major events occurring near offices, operations, travelers, and other critical assets to the enterprise (upcoming Olympic Games for example)
- Develop a scoring method to assess how this may or will impact the enterprise, threats, risks, and outline levels of security for each risk level (static officers, event specialists, high risk protection professionals, etc.)
- Develop an event summary or profile sheet (attendees, location, dates, excursions, reasons, etc.)
- Post these in an automated database, on the intranet, or other location and train event planners and organizers how and when to complete them; and send them to CS in the earliest planning stages.

Considerations

- In many cases, a well-briefed group, who you can monitor remotely, who are with a travel destination service provider who can translate and knows the environment is sufficient. Do not be afraid to ask for money to secure the group and do not recommend a security detail that outnumbers the attendees and cost more than the excursion itself when not necessary.

Conclusion

When people leave their surroundings, gather in numbers, participate in a variety of activities these and several other factors will increase the chances of a security event occurring. Being prepared in advance, documenting your plans and sharing them appropriately is very important to a successful event.

National security operations centers

A simple difference between a security control room and SOC is that the SOC includes a "war room," offices, canteen, latrine, etc. The control room is a room where officers watch cameras, maps, and the news. A GSOC discussed above is exactly what it sets out to be global. A National Security Operations Center (NSOC) is essentially a corporate center servicing a national region (country region). This may mean that the large global company has local SOCs who are supported by NSOCs in each major operating country that in turn is supported by a global security operations center (GSOC). This may be a perfect level of redundancy or/and an excessive waste of money. It depends, are they doing the exact same tasks, providing the same services? Some mid-sized organizations operate across one single country but in every state or province and major city. The NSOC may be the only or overarching control room to many nationwide. The local control rooms could handle the bulk of premise security systems while major incidents, investigations, fusion center work, redundant support, travel tracking, and other CS duties are managed from the NSOC with little overlap unless required.

2010–20

One challenge to GSOCs is time zones and languages. NSOCs can service their own countries reducing the need for complicated control rooms at multiple premises and still being able to provide good services with an understanding of local laws, customs, languages, and events. A few commercial real estate, telecommunications, and industrial enterprise with a large footprint built successful alarm certified NSOCs in this past decade. These companies are now simply upgrading components as they need replacing and as technology and services advance. Many proprietary and third-party NSOCs hire people who will be permanently situated in the NSOC and are trained for this. Rotating patrol officers off the floor to come in and cover the console for periods of time is becoming less feasible as the technology in the NSOC increases and emergency communications and alarm acknowledgement takes a certain temperament and level of skill. This environment can be filled with long stretches of quiet monitoring, hours of monotonous entry, or hours of high intensity response and dispatching.

2020–30

Companies who have a handful of campuses with control rooms and many locations with none will start to build or upgrade an existing operation to an NSOC and will consolidate monitoring, credentialing, and communications from a single high quality, purpose-built center.

Large enterprise who have security control rooms, cyber and information security monitoring staff and/or centers and crisis teams will start to create fusion centers with a few highly skilled operators all situated in one highly advanced control room where the health of the entire organization physical and digital can be observed and where investigations and crisis can be managed or supported from. Separate desks or rooms for each of these functions will be eliminated. A university graduate certified in threat hunting, incident response, network monitoring, and cyber security can easily be trained to program an access credential and watch a camera.

2030–40

As those enterprise who are large enough or have the need for an NSOC in previous years continue to operate one, the skills of the workers and the technology within will only advance. However, in 20 years, an NSOC will still be an NSOC. There are a few companies today whose leaders cannot justify an NSOC or GSOC. In time, they still not build the physical environment, however, the outsourcing of these services to offsite professionals or the implementation of an in-house, proprietary set of desks staffed by skilled analysts using applications will be able to do the same tasks as their peers in larger robust centers. Distraction, compromise, or anonymity may still be issues to work around in this model.

Questions

What are some of the advantages and disadvantages to outsourcing the NSOC?

If you have on-premise control rooms, desks, or security personnel in the office who can still monitor alarms and cameras, then the third-party NSOC is an alternative to having your own. It may or may not save your money. Like most things in CS, once you start a project to save money, get return on investment or pretend security is a revenue center you have already lost. Improve quality, transfer risk, enhance services, and redundancy. These third-party centers are often secure, professional, supervised 24/7, and can split costs. You can build and pay for the level of service and priority you need.

What if another client tours through and sees my operations?

If the CSO from the hospital down the street happens to see a camera in your hallway will your operations come to a halt? Address these up front with the service provider and be reasonable.

How do I know my data are secure?

Always include your information security risk assessment team in these projects.

Steps

- Conduct a needs analysis (Do I need another layer? Can it back up my SOCs? Will it do something my GSOC cannot handle?)
- Benchmark with peers and consider engaging a consultant
- Consider all options (not building one, building one, creating a fusion center, using two desks in the office instead of an entire center etc.)

Considerations

Speak with other departments who may need an environment like this. Seriously explore both managing your own center and outsourcing. See if one can be built to house and service more than one program (cyber, business continuity, and physical).

Conclusion

As an enterprise grows they should only remain so agile. They need to grow their protection and resiliency capabilities along with it. If the enterprise is overdue for an NSOC, the executives should take the time to review the business case and provide feedback or accept the risk.

Network security operations centers

The term network security operations center may refer to the room where the health, threat management, and investigations pertaining to the network are performed. Sometimes it is simply a couple of analysts in the office observing three screens each.

2010–20

In the early part of the decade, a network security operations center sometimes followed the footsteps of physical NSOCs where a few companies set up prestigious rooms, filled with many screens. A robust simple version of these could be seen in few data centers by larger providers. Some technology companies had already combined the NSOC (physical security) and network security operations center functions into one space.

2020–30

In the next decade, the physical space of the network security operations center will be less important, rather than the applications the specialists have at their disposal to hunt for threats, detect anomalies, and manage crisis. Outsourcing the network security operations center function to major providers including Accenture, IBM, HP, and the Herjavec Group to name a few, will likley service more half the fortune 100s.

2030–40

In 20 years from today, the ability to proactively hunt threats and neutralize them before they impact the enterprise will be a reality. Many network security operations centers started out dealing with incidents after the threat had impacted the network. Later the ability to detect threats attempting to bypass security became an early alert system which has allowed us to react sooner. When the IoT hits its peak, we can no longer stand by waiting for a pacemaker to get hacked. As soon as this becomes chatter, or someone actually sets out to cause serious offences in the future hyper-connected world, the NSOC of the future will be able to detect and act upon these threats before they become a reality.

Questions

What are the career prospects for this area of expertise?

Currently finding experts certified in the most up-to-date applications and software in the environment is a challenge. Finding such experts built for working in these environments and sometimes under high pressure is harder yet. Soon the rapid changes to the threat landscape, the applications to combat them, and the need for operators who understand cyber, information, physical, and crisis response systems will be very limited. With a global shortage of experts, jobs prospects for those with the ability to do the job well and with the right resumewill be excellent.

Steps

- As a CSO today you should be working with your existing CISO to support the development of a network security operations center program, cooperate with the exiting one, and leverage the resources.
- Benchmark peers to see who has a combined center and learn what they have done right and may do over if they were to begin again.

Considerations

The NSOC function is nonnegotiable. You need this capability for your enterprise in one form or another, and have these services protecting your company today.

Conclusion

Leaping forward and embracing change so freely sounds scary. Being completely unprepared is worse yet. Make sure that you get out of your comfort zone, admit when you don't know and ask questions. Network security can make or break an enterprise. Helping to instill client and shareholder confidence by reducing and avoiding breaches, losses and disruption is a good way for a CSO to contribute. A network security operations center is not a new resource but one with a lot of potential to protect the enterprise.

Nonfinancial investigations

Corporate security (CS) conducts investigations. If there is a designated investigations department CS may or may not own the investigations function. Historically, many banks have included physical security, fraud risk management, and investigations in one department. The investigators have handled both financial investigations such as frauds and other nonfinancial investigations such as violations of the corporate code of conduct. The physical security team may conduct a portion the nonfinancial investigations such as bank robbery response, workplace violence, office theft, etc. Physical security may also take a threat assessment approach to these events instead or as well as an investigation. In some FIs, these departments may be separate but still work closely, physical security and information security can provide logs, record, and other evidence. When there is a separate investigations department from CS, CS may still conduct investigations including the occasional minor internal theft or fraud. Many organizations do not have a designated Investigations department. The security experts who oversee the security strategy that is executed by facilities security teams may conduct or facilitate all investigations with partners such as Legal and HR. There are many models, scenarios, and styles. These can be based on the enterprise, risk appetite, and experience of the leaders to name a few variables.

As discussed earlier, investigators reporting to legal may conduct the investigations while AML and fraud risk experts reporting to compliance or audit may develop controls and then conduct audits to look for gaps during and postinvestigation. Similarly, the operational security managers may conduct the nonfinancial investigations while the strategic security managers develop governance and controls. They may also take an incident of workplace violence, for example. The operational security managers brief security at the premise on what steps to take during the incident, what to do immediately after (enhance security, be extra vigilant, retrieve video and call the police as needed, etc.). These managers may also conduct small investigations, which may include lost property. The strategic security managers on the other side of the same team may review the policy, work with the assessment team, and provide a behavioral analysis or threat assessment.

Conducting investigations into shrinkage including theft and abuse can take a lot of time for security. Access logs, video, witness statements, and other data are often used. If the departments are separate, then clear training and understanding between them at all levels is important. You can often gain more from a consolidated team, cover more ground quickly and avoid too many gaps. This works if each team is seen as equals.

2010–20

In the past decade, nonfinancial Investigations conducted by CS could range from theft of materials to incidents related to terrorism. Surprisingly, in the begging of this decade, many large departments were still not using case management or using what they had to its full potential. In the past several years the rise of the forensic investigator has been significant. These investigators can support any investigation. They specialize in reviewing logs, drives, and anything related to the employee's computer, applications, and transactions.

Investigators are not only coming from law enforcement, but also academia, career professionals (accountants and lawyers), and within the business itself. A former bank branch manager members of internal audit and other inside professionals can also make great investigators. Outsourcing of investigations has become more common. The outsourcing of investigations from the employee ethics hotline has become standard.

The rise of employees using and getting into trouble over social media abuse, cyber bullying and for actions outside of the office but still considered the workplace (at meetings, company trips, etc.) has changed the skills needed for many of the investigators, and the policies of many enterprises. Employees may post inappropriate information online and have found themselves in violation of the code of conduct. Using the internet to bully others by posting harmful statements or trying to anonymously damage the reputation of others are just a few examples. Investigators have had to learn how to master web searches and all forms of social media accounts.

2020–30

Theft of goods and materials stolen from outsiders will still be a very real issue in the years to come. Global competition is placing a lot of pressure on these companies to produce goods for and sell them for less than competitors. Many consumers do not concern themselves with the difference in quality of small household items such as a dish sponge. The sponge from a dollar priced store versus one from a major big box retailer is inconsequential to many buyers. Therefore, the challenges of internal theft, gray market counterfeit, or supply chain theft cannot always be met with all the security resources available. Placing a global positioning system (GPS) tag on every sponge in a shipping container would lead to one less sponge producer quite rapidly. This is an extreme, however, simple illustration. Building materials including copper and reinforcing bar (rebar) are taken from construction sites, completed sites, and even attempted at live transformer stations. When materials are stolen from a project, not only does the company suffer the replacement costs, but also often increase site security and project delays while the materials are recovered or replaced.

Asset loss prevention and recovery will become more important than apprehension. When offenders are apprehended recovery of assets or products becomes possible. Disrupting the criminal distribution chain and locking up offenders and reducing their ability to repeat offend in the short term all benefit the process. Companies who can support their public partners with these investigations in the next decade, will need to find ways to accomplish this with innovative solutions. The common theft of personal effects from office space will still be a challenge. Employees do have some expectation (perceived) in their workspace, while adding cameras to all work areas and office space is too expensive and always will be. These and other obstacles will continue to limit deterrence and forensic tools needed to reduce and investigate these minor offenses.

2030–40

In 20 years from now, security professionals will be trained to conduct these investigations from the time they start their careers. The software they use to conduct investigations will offer checklists of scenarios and steps to be taken. CSOs will make sure that all their CS personnel have this training and these resources. The thought of spending days investigating on a stolen computer will be long gone. All corporate laptops will be equipped with wipe and kill apps and/or tracking software. The fusion center will be able to pull all logs and records pertaining to the space, occupants, and access transactions in minutes. The case management application will lead the investigator through the report and investigation in a day. Security, HR, and legal will be able to host an impromptu Skype meeting to review evidence and nest steps by day end. Witnesses will be sent and invitation to a meeting room where a Skype video interview will be conducted by HR and investigators saving travel and meeting arrangements that lagged investigations years past. An employee who is working from home that day, will be interviewed within the hour of analyzing the data.

The cost of tracking materials will be significantly less than years earlier and tracking assets will be conducted from the SOC. The introduction to autonomous freighter ships, trains, and transport trucks will bring new challenges for physical and cyber-hijacking. According to Jason Caissie, PSP, CISSP, CPP, vice president, Operations of Profile Investigation Inc. "Many investigators today would count interview and interrogation ability among their top skills, while relying on technical experts for aspects like digital forensics, deep web searching or even social media scans. With the importance of digital evidence increasing exponentially each year, the investigator of the future—both police and private—will be required to perform these tasks themselves. A well-rounded investigator will be expected to follow all evidence, from the interview room right into the digital world."

Questions

What is the value in using skilled investigators to investigate office thefts?

If you are suffering office thefts some principles often hold true. You have a weakness in your processes such as contractor escorts, screening, and employee background checks. This is not their first time and won't be their last. The thefts will become more frequent and in greater value. A sweater today, a laptop tomorrow. A lost laptop can mean lost data. By investigating you show the victims you care, theft is not tolerated and allows them to focus on work. By apprehending the thief, you remove the chance of future losses by this person.

Steps

- Encourage your team to keep their investigative skills up to date, bring in group trainers and order related periodicals for the department reading compendium.
- Update job postings, when you hire to look for investigative, forensic, case management, and modern skills.
- Attend some courses and conferences to get back in touch with where things are today and where they are headed, even if you're a CSO today, learning is a lifelong privilege.

Considerations

- If you are in a field or industry benchmark with peers to see what nonfinancial investigations, they are most often conducting. Compile methods and lessons learned. Consider forming a committee and writing a professional standard for your industry. When faced with your next loss, network with peers to see if they are currently impacted by the same issue and how they are approaching it.

Conclusion

Theft and workplace violence will still be here in the next 20 years. Make every effort to develop a security program that can provide best in class preventative, investigative, and responsive solutions to your enterprise.

Physical security personnel

Earlier we discussed staff who are managing physical security systems for premises, executive protection (EP) and the future (security guard) professional protection officers. In global security, CS or sometimes embedded in investigations or financial crimes departments are experienced security specialists, managers, or investigators who focus on the physical security arena.

2010–20

At the beginning of this decade, many companies experimented with different models. Having a team of 10–20 physical security specialists supporting the organization was not uncommon. These roles may have ranged from analyst, operator, coordinator, specialist, manager, director, and AVP. In scenario 1, CSOs have hired and trained generalists. These members could review security layouts for new premises and offices, provide EP, respond to emergencies, assess risk of operations, premises, incidence of violence, and facilitate travel and event risk management to name only a few tasks. A group of 10 may work under one leader at corporate headquarters while the remainder were in other global field offices or local country headquarters. They may be divided by geography, which means team members trained to do any task, however, only focus on one country or region. A second scenario is where some teams are split by those who produce governance and analysis (strategic), and those who focus on operational and tactical tasks or groundwork (execution). In this model, you can either make all members global or divide each member to a region. For example, one strategist for the United States and one operations specialist for the United States. In some cases, location or geographical separation allows you to have local experts who know the territory, customs, laws, and contacts. A third of many scenarios is to hire and train experts who can do it all. A lead for workplace violence, a lead for EP, and so on. Challenges in the geographical model depend on how well a team situated abroad can be managed and how deep you go. If you expect them to speak the local language, you now need an EP specialist who speaks (Spanish), for example. If the team is all located at headquarters this may be a challenge, if some of them are based in the field you may be able to hire a local expert. On occasion, the regional team feels secluded or begins to attempt to branch away from the CSO and work more with local leaders. When you have absolute experts working in silos, you lose some of the redundancy. If you only have one EP expert, who covers them in their absence? If you have generalists, you may find that you need to send them to more training when new projects and technologies arise.

Currently, some teams are moving away from the generalist and moving to specialists. Others are moving in the opposite direction. Some are becoming more global and removing the geographical separation.

A common certification for the career level is the ASIS International, PSP, certification. Many organizations also send their people to courses on EP, behavioral threat management and kidnap, ransom, and extortion training.

2020–30

Now that there is a large pool of long-term CS professionals who are college educated, already have 15–20 years in the field and have earned key designations, the hiring pool for security leadership and CSOs will be much richer. The availability of educational program and the online delivery will help to produce security specialists at a much earlier stage in one's career. The PSP of the next decade will not need to be classed as a generalist or expert. They will be experts in most areas of corporate physical security much earlier on in their careers. They will understand more about the world and have access to real-time world events their predecessors could only see in the headlines a day later. They will be computer savvy and do everything on a computer, phone, or tablet.

Compensation for a senior security specialist will be quite reasonable. With the options to do internal secondments or rotates desks, many will see this role as a long-term career. The specialist spends a year or two on protection and then rotates to major events and so on.

2030–40

In 20 years from now, corporate PSPs will be employed by the corporation or a risk consultancy. They will almost all have university education, professional certifications, and focus on prevention, risk, and resiliency. They may have never worked a day as a professional protection officer or in the military, etc. Many of these professionals will have gone to a program of higher learning with the goal of this specific career in mind.

The evolution of educational programs and department structures will dictate the skills and duties of these personnel. If the company has moved the experts who handle all matters related to physical security systems to the information or cyber security group than they may see specialists from different educational backgrounds applying.

Because life safety and the prevention of loss including physical data is part of core responsibilities of this role, future physical security personnel will be required to have a designation or even a license. Not necessarily what is known today as a security guard license but rather a professional standing like what the CSOs may earn before entering their role.

Questions

What is the difference between a professional protection officer and physical security personnel?

Most professional protection officers will be the new generation of today's security guard who may work for contract service providers outside of industries such as hotels, casinos, cruise ships, and critical infrastructure. Physical security personnel refer to those CS experts who focus on physical security programs. Even the operational and tactical of these team members would more likely facilitate and lead EP experts rather than provide the protection themselves.

Steps

Develop a long-term view of your security program. When developing a 3–5 year strategy be certain to look ahead at the needs of the enterprise. Look at college and university programs focused on law, security, and investigations or risk and security. Develop relationships with these schools and consider job placements, job shadowing, and recruitment from these programs. Guest lecture and share CS as a career option for these students.

Considerations

By hiring the best suited candidates to help the needs of your organization now and in the future will set your team up for success. Consider sharing what your departments do today, instead of what people assume CS did yesterday. Share this with educational institutions, professional associations, and committees who can help to shape and influence the future.

Conclusion

CS is a career and the role of CSO is a profession. CS professionals of the future at all levels will be formally educated, tasked with significant responsibility, and will face some of the largest challenges to face private enterprise in decades. It will take a motivated high caliber candidate to meet this challenge.

The professional protection officer

Many educational programs are focused on law, justice, and criminal sciences. Some of these do not always align with practical applications and knowledge for security officers. A security officer protecting a workplace is a very important role. The officer who finds the lost child at a mall or amusement park, the officer who performs first aid when a desperate family stands by, or the officer who patrol large parking facilities at night, so workers can go home safe. Many college programs are well in line with this career but are still out of reach for many students leaving secondary (high) school. The certified protection officer (CPO) program from the International Foundation for Protection Officers should be shared with many of these youths and even career officers who do not have the time or means to enroll in college. This course has evolved over the years to introduce the learner to topics that every security professional must know. Even an experienced CSO who did not come from the world of security would benefit greatly from the foundation this provides.

Security Resource Officers (in school settings)

This role is one of the hardest to fill and yet one of the most important roles in this changing field. A school resource officer needs to be of high moral character, integrity, and have a great temperament with today's youth. They must exercise patients, tact, and civility. It is always a challenge in some countries to think about arming security. Having a shootout in a school is never a good thing. However, having responders who are not prepared and equipped to deal with on-premise and on-campus active shooters and other life-threatening situations is of little to no use. More and more schools will see the temporary or permanent use of these officers. Soon the program will include behavior threat analysis training, enhanced response authorization (SROs authorized to use deadly force when lives depend on it), updated protocol and entire training and education programs to develop this as a career path.

Physical security processes

Earlier we discussed governance including policies and procedures. A process is a series of actions that lead to an end and produce a result. Processes are important to any line of business. In some cases, they can be critical to safety and security. Engineers are excellent at developing flow charts and processes that link an input to a series of options along a linear path to get to a close or specified result. These can be quite simple, such as steps in a task, or they can be entire matrices that cover several options and anomalies.

2010–20

In the past decade, CS departments have done a good job at developing various processes. A TRVA methodology may be accompanied by a process document. This may explain the several reasons a TRVA gets initiated. Due to a review cycle, following a major change to the operation and security or even after a loss event. It will then provide steps of how to initiate the project, how to conduct the review, develop a report, issue the report and recommendations, and follow them through until closure. A few CSOs have engaged consultants who specialize in audit and process development to review all the tasks managed by CS and refined them. Continuous review of the process based on the results it produces, things missed, or changes in law, policy, or best practices is necessary.

Some departments record the results in a database. Some have communications systems to initiate an event. Not many have completely automated their processes.

2020–30

In the next decade, entire processes will be situated on cloud hosted software that allows for partners, employees, and others outside of the department to initiate a request for service. The steps taken, logs completed, and reports written will all be entered into these systems. A series of actions, escalations, and controls will enhance quality, make certain steps are not missed, and verify that tasks are complete within the expected service-level agreement (SLA).

2030–40

In this decade, single systems will handle the entire event, automate some of the steps completely and send emails, and generate reports without the user going to another system or manually entering the input. All these rules will be engineered in from the beginning. Machine learning will tell the system what to ask, remind, connect, and produce all of this just from the first few entries. This does not mean that these detailed processes developed by security experts and managed by supercomputers will eliminate CS personnel. On the contrary as enterprise become more global, the population grows and demand for fast results increases we will need teams of specialists generating these results with these automated process machines.

Questions

What are some of the processes CS may manage?

- Clean desk inspections
- TSCM sweeps
- Security review programs, etc.
- Traveler incident management
- Major event risk assessment, scoring and security arrangements
- Reviewing security for new corporate locations (selection, design, and commissioning)
- Workplace violence behavioral assessments and security arrangements
- Contracts and procurement of systems and services

Steps

- Make a list of all the programs your department manages
- See if there is a clear written, accurate, up-to-date process for each task, one worthy of withstanding an audit or to be used as a training document
- Draft or update these where needed

- Make the entire process digital
- Engage business partners to review the process for input and see how they would automate some of these steps.

Considerations

People often worry about developing processes that are too prescriptive and hard to live up to or could become a legal matter later if a step is not adhered to. A process is not a policy, some deviation is logically expected if it is a smart decision. It is not a procedure followed by protection officers who are administering first aid or responding to fire alarms. It is a common business practice.

Conclusion

Having published, comprehensive, automated processes are good governance; it will reduce time and errors.

Physical security technology and hardware

I have covered a lot about specific technologies, how they will advance, how and where they are controlled, and who controls them. Here, I will speak generally about the importance of them and why they are a good investment in general.

2010–20

It is not uncommon for the head of security to request new or upgrades to security systems today and to be met with challenges, including leaders who question the value of the investment. It is sometimes the same leaders who ask why security spends so much time on certain tasks. Computer, pen, paper, desk, briefcase, office, accounting department, sales department, etc. Try running most business without some or all of these. Now try running a business without any form of safety, security, data protection, etc. If you are managing a business, security is almost always necessary and to do this job or to provide this protection some form of investment must be made continuously.

The headlines this past decade about workers being assaulted or killed in the workplace, traveling employees finding themselves in trouble, law suits against employers on safety and security-related matters and cyber-breaches still have not resonated with some leaders.

Today, there are many cost-effective options, technology, and hardware that can be deployed to protect a business. Often people are the most expensive asset. What about an agile, highly skilled team equipped with the right tools, instead of a large department who are the only form of protection? I have seen premises with little to no systems and hardware, however employing a dozen security personnel per shift.

Even the small shop, stores cash and files out of reach of customers and uses a half-decent lock to close for the night. It is amazing how a local corner store has an alarm system and couple of cameras while many large offices, from much larger organizations have no alarm or camera for a 10,000 sq/ft office. The assumption that the landlord will protect my assets, people, and information is absurd. CSOs must be very knowledgeable about many technologies and hardware choices and understand the level of interest and appetite their leaders have. This will help the CSO gauge the appropriate solution to request and deploy. Selling managers on the idea of more security by fear is not a good solution. What happens when there is no history of incidents for years? If a risk assessment deems the location low risk? Fundamentals such as door locks should still be a baseline requirement.

Many CSOs do not dictate a specific product but rather a performance and minim standard specification. The door must be locked at night. The lock must not be easy to defeat. The locking system must show an audit trail of entries. Security should have the ability to review the entries when required.

2020–30

We are entering a world where office doors must be able to open with no mechanical interaction during an emergency and with only a few pounds of force. A time when the less building materials the better. The design of hardware that still allows for the same level of protection will become harder to come by. In the earlier part of the past decade, security managers became much more educated on locking and storage containers, locks, and doors. This was previously a locksmith or facilities specialty. By the end of the decade, the number of courses related to security that cover these topics had increased, however, the increased use in electronic access control has most senior security leaders forgetting about the fundamentals of locks as we move into this decade.

The need for security professionals to deeply understand technology and hardware will be more important than ever. With the increasing perils that will come from occupantless data centers, autonomous methods of transportation, shipping and the cost cutting companies will need to do to survive in the next 10 years, it will be back to the basics of securing goods and assets from theft and tampering.

2030–40

In 20 years, the software that manages integrated security systems will be a single platform. One easy to navigate interface. Protection barriers using sound, nature, science, and energy will become the hot button topics. Nanotechnology will make its way into production and building materials with the pressure to find new building resources and where the military and aerospace industries will seek lightweight, high intensity materials, commercial security will later benefit. When all of these become common technologies and affordable, they will find use in physical security applications.

Questions

Will CS professionals of the future need to understand technology and hardware for physical security?

In theory and earlier on in their careers, yes. However, as all professionals are advancing some of this will become the sole responsibility of the information security and facilities professional to use and deploy.

Steps

Think about the last time as a CSO you walked the trade floor to really understand what is available for tech and hardware. When was the last time you picked up a hardware and systems periodical, had a demonstration or assessed how current the skills of your people are in this area? Do you have a hardware list that is up to date with your suppliers? Take the time to review these and document a game plan to remain current.

Considerations

Hardware that works or is building code compliant may not be at all company locations. Engage local licensed, certified professionals to help design these systems.

Conclusion

A CSO will have employees who are passionate and understand technology. They will also have employees who would rather not spend a career selecting locks, safes, and cameras. Interest can often outweigh intelligence when it comes to being successful at many things including school, work, and life. Make sure you have the right people and the right people doing the right things.

Security operations centers

A security control room often refers to the room where the monitoring of cameras happens. A SOC often refers to the entire working area for the control room, offices, security meeting room, canteen, and change rooms. In the large campus, industrial, mall, or office complex setting this is a great resource. An area where security can work through crisis without outside disruption, with lower chances of being compromised and a central operation for the security manager to manage the team, events, and control room.

2010–20

The dispersity between SOCs in this decade has occasionally been large. I have worked in, helped design and visited centers with the best of design, technology, and amenities. Officer safety, comfort, and health go a long way to producing good results. Room with stale air, no washroom nearby, nowhere to store a lunch or access food 24/7, and always the wrong temperature can lead to a series of unfortunate events. Add poor design, bad ergonomics, uncomfortable seats and constant distraction; and you may find that the lost morale can lead to turnover, great operators opting out of the role and fatigued workers.

2020–30

As we move into the next decade, there are so many SOCs to tour, consultants and designers with plentiful experience and open source documents, designing SOCs will be much easier. Security leaders will need to be able to clearly produce documentation to support a strong business case while also remaining reasonable.

2030–40

Like the fusion centers discussed earlier there will be little to no SOCs left in the future that do not double for other similar centers that look for cyber events, support business continuity, and crisis matters. SOCs will become more open concept, be fitted with technology that needs less room. Technology equipment such as servers will be hosted offsite and therefore, less room needed and less heat from equipment produced. As more bodies are hired to look at more systems and locations, the furniture and equipment will become more space efficient and therefore, companies may not need to seek a new and larger space but instead upgrade what they have already.

Questions

I work in an enterprise who do not own their premises or manage their security systems, is there still value in a SOC?

Yes, a SOC can be a central area for CS to work and monitor other systems that track events, travelers, and bring resources (security specialists, analysts, and investigators) together.

Steps

- It is valuable for all security leaders to understand if a SOC is a benefit or unnecessary cost to your enterprise.
- Conduct a feasibility study, what would a proof of concept look like, what if we do not do it, what will we accomplish if we do, alternatives, risks, benefits, and costs.

Considerations

If your company has moved to an open concept, officeless, work from home environment, make sure a SOC is not counter to this strategy. If you have a team that performs little monitoring, however, works in an agile setting, consider other models.

Conclusion

The entire security operations of a major premise should not be managed from a desk out in the open of the facility, nor should the head of security work at the same desk or an office that doubles for a storage room. Making a long-term investment in the protection strategy for your operations will only serve you better when the company needs it most.

Technical surveillance countermeasures

Bug sweeping may be a part of a larger corporate counterespionage program, a full TSCM program or a one time or occasional service. Sometimes these programs and services are not used by companies because of a lack of awareness, costs, or interest. Few large CS programs have invested in the equipment and training to conduct these sweeps in house while others transfer the risk and outsource this to a local specialist. Engaging in a global risk consultancy or security firm who can offer a single point of contact for contracting, facilitating, scheduling, and billing is another choice. These companies may carry out the work or outsource it globally. When trying to outsource a global program to a sole provider, you will have to weigh the benefits such as the quality and consistency with the cost of flying them around, how many jobs can they handle at once and can they get their equipment across all borders where you will need them and at a cost that fits your budget.

When implementing or managing a program, it should be kept as discreet as possible, centrally managed, and based on some criteria and process. There are some reasonable government documents online that outline some specifications for running such a program. You can also engage experienced peers to see what they may suggest.

2010–20

At the beginning of this decade, many large enterprises with a CS program were familiar with these services and often had them carried out. Many providers had become good at not only providing a report on their findings, but also recommending ways to proactively protect the business from these threats, how to protect your critical data and offered other ways to protect your business based on their observations.

As technology used by companies has changed including audiovisual equipment, wireless devices, and portable electronics the risk of leaking data or being intercepted and the importance of sweeps has changed. Now searching for hostile USB keys and rouge WIFI devices has become an issue. Some TSCM professionals are using the physical sweep of computers and special software to examine computers in their work. Often TSCM tools require a license and special equipment. The training to ensure the team is technically proficient is critical. Clients became educated at what to do if a threat or suspicion was a concern and what to make sure the provider did while sweeping.

CS departments became good at where and when a sweep should be conducted, how to keep this a secret, and how to secure the area afterwards as needed.

2020–30

In the next decade, we will see the need for the team currently responsible for this program coordinating with the information and cyber security departments. These departments often have assessments and sweeps of similar types done in the same premises. Identifying what is legitimate and what is not will require multiple stakeholders. It is likely that this will become a service under the technology and operations or information security departments in a few years.

The ability to secure hidden surveillance equipment online has become as easy as buying a loaf of bread. In the next 10 years, the risk of someone commandeering your computer or phone to spy on you will be as dangerous as clicking on the wrong link. It will take a lot to prevent these vulnerabilities and more to detect them.

TSCM sweep providers should be able to show they are evolving with the threat and can provide solutions to the changing technologies. Threats and criminal methods from 20 years earlier will have evolved to a point where the TSCM experts must refresh their tools and approach.

2030–40

One major concern today is security systems that spy on the owner (the premise or company that has purchased and is using the equipment) for state actors. This means that your security cameras may have been commandeered (hacked) by or tempered with (knowingly or unknowingly to the manufacturer) foreign governments or even sophisticated competitors.

It will take the thinking and technology of both the companies' information security team and a TSCM expert to help prevent and detect these threats. Software analysis as a detection tool and anomalous network activity will need to be examined by qualified people to determine if there is a problem. When we become aware of the possibility, existence, and loss caused by the first such future threat, we will need to be prepared to react. We must also not get so focused on cyber-threats and technologically advanced threats that we completely forget about bad old-fashioned bugging gadgets.

Questions

Do they ever actually find anything?

There have been few publicized cases. One interesting read online are the articles associated with the former Nortel headquarters in Ottawa, Canada and the bug that may or may not have been found. The FBI has provided videos, docudramas, and important information on actual cases, protection methods and charges laid. These are all available online and describe state sponsored actors attempting or even committing corporate/state-sponsored espionage. Cyberattacks have been increasing for years. Dumpster diving is an old practice and hidden cameras have been found in homes, businesses, washrooms, and other establishments as reported many times in the past decade on the news. Numerous private citizens have been victimized, stalked, and harassed by parties taking over their cell phones.

This is a real threat and it is not going away anytime soon.

Steps

Have an independent assessment conducted by a risk consultant to determine if you need a program, what it may look like or how to enhance the existing one.

Considerations

Employee training and education go a long way. Employee and contractor screening, access control and locking down sensitive areas and computer ports are also good ways to reduce the risk.

Conclusion

This is a real niche in the security field. It is important to understand the threats, but also depend on a qualified expert to execute on the program. A CSO is to be knowledgeable but should never worry about not having intricate knowledge of these specialties.

Travel risk management (duty of care)

Every decade I hear someone say the world is changing. It's not the way it used to be. They are in fact right. But as we become a more socially conscious and sensitive society who are improving on many social and human rights issues we have seen greater and greater mass shootings, acts of terror, and natural catastrophe. When employees go on short or long-term work assignments and are expatriates, travel alone or in a small group on business; or attend larger events on conferences or retreats, they are often at greater risk than in the familiarity of their home environment. An employee traveling from their home country to another may end up in a location where crime is lower than home. That same employee may now for the first time be without complete medical coverage or in a place where natural disasters are common. When companies send employees away on business new responsibilities emerge. The home country has their own laws, the company may have its own set of rules these may be the only state of operation the employee understands. If they act a certain way, conduct business a certain way and get hurt, injured or in trouble with the law in a foreign place it can come back to haunt their employer. Following law suits from victim employees, legal precedents have paved the way for new expectations. Duty of care comes in many forms. Travel risk management is one-way employers need to fulfill their obligations to protect their people. They should be proactive and provide some level of travel risk management, in the form of awareness, preparedness, and/or security.

2010–20

At the beginning of this decade, few companies had specifically developed a travel risk or security program for all employees and fewer yet had staffed a specific role or even department. Some places (states, provinces, and territories) required the employer to file that the employee was leaving the home location as government coverage or private coverage did not extend beyond that region. Executive travel briefings and protection during trips was already a common practice for established CS departments.

By the middle of this decade, companies who specialized in providing security, extraction, medical services, and event monitoring became a normal course of action for CSOs to add to their arsenal of services. Application-based tracking software that could provide the location of travelers, track itineraries and the state of risk in the region leaped forward. International SOS is one example of a firm who specializes in global medical and security services. They are one of the pioneers to offer traveling employees a mobile application to get country reports, locate medical assistance, and report a crisis.

Companies providing global risk management and K&R support including Control Risks a global consulting firm, based in London, UK offered specialized support to events abroad amongst a range of other important services. These providers allow a CSO to ramp up and down the security detail based on the risk profile of each event. These companies have established networks of global contacts and employee leading experts. They have been using technology as a force multiplier long before many of their peers.

I have observed many companies in the past 10 years elevate their programs from travel briefing and insurance to small teams of in-house experts who follow clear policies and guidelines, supported by specialist firms.

2020–30

In the next 10 years, two things will occur. More large companies will develop programs for travel risks management and hire experts to run them. The use of live mapping platforms to track travelers and receive real time intelligence will be in place at many enterprises. Some companies are now offering several ways to track the travelers and now include corporate assets, premises, and critical vendors on the interactive maps. GardaWorld's, Crisis24 is a system that does just this. A platform that can be tailored to the specific needs of the client. When clients can monitor several areas of risks, hundreds of potential threats across the globe from one center and on one platform the return on investment and improvement to CS's service offering will entice more CSOs to explore these solutions.

When we close on one war, a political situation between nations creates another challenge for travelers. Border crossing, denied entry, and even detention are always a concern. CS will need to work with their legal and government relations partners to know how to react to these matters as they arise.

Medical surveillance from both the World Health Organization and private providers is important to understand. Know what places some employees need avoid, what shots they need before going, and what to do if they exhibit symptoms upon return is important to document and plan for.

Travel briefings no longer simply inform you what neighborhoods to avoid, they include the reviewing and discussions around your use of social medial and customs. Opinions expressed by employees at home could get them arrested or worse in some countries.

2030–40

In 15–20 years from now, employees will know their rights and expect some form of protection even when abroad. Many companies will have reduced travel that can be done by email or video, while they will increase travel to compete for business in the global market. CSOs will need to learn about new operating territories, engage providers strong in these regions, and even establish new networks abroad.

As more companies engage these services, those providers will be able to expand and have home offices on the ground in most destinations which will benefit everyone. Many employees will leave behind the big brother concerns and embrace the fact that cool technology may very well save their lives. Mobile tracking will be down to the square yard in 20 years. If an employee enters a taxi in many countries that cab will be tracked based on the technology that was included during manufacturing. The data available from autonomous vehicles will allow for better knowledge of where a person is and where they may have last been seen.

Cybersecurity teams will play an important role in the monitoring, training, and protection of employees. Creative ways to protect data abroad will be a top concern.

Questions

How do I know if I need a travel risk management program?

Nearly, every business has someone who must leave the office at some point during their work. A factory may have all its operations and offices in one location. All deliveries and shipping are handled by third parties. Do your sales people go out to see clients, attend conferences, tour supplier locations? Are employees sent away for school or training? Does the leadership take the occasional trip to look at other parts of the operations, to consider investments or expansion?

A program could be someone in HR making sure the employees personal or company fleet vehicle is insured, that they have coverage from their government, benefits or travel insurance. It could be as simple as a memorandum to employees to check a government website for travel advice when planning and prebooking of trips. All companies should have a program of one form or another.

Steps

- Investigate the use of a travel security application that can show travelers, the world and a current state of events.
- Consider designating or hiring someone to manage policies, procedures, briefings, and monitoring for you.
- Determine who should do monitoring (24/7 coverage and languages should be considered). Is it the SOC, NSOC, GSOC?
- Provide advanced communications with the assistance of departments such as HR, communications, privacy, compliance, and legal to let employees know what you monitor and why. They should also know how to find information on their trip and how to request a briefing.

Considerations

Having an automated system to track flights, travelers, security, political, and environmental threats is important. Explore how this system pulls data, where from, and compare it to that of competitors.

Conclusion

Our ability to share helpful information to thousands of employees in today's world through many different communications mediums available to us has made this a much easier process. We have access to so much information and now automated, online systems to provide us with refined information. There is little reason not to develop a strong program to protect your travelers. People are our most important asset.

VSSs (formerly CCTV)

In the past decade, we have moved away from CCTV as a name for our security cameras. Video management systems (VMS) and video surveillance systems (VSSs) appear to be the dominating market names.

In the early part of the decade, nearly everyone had caught up to using digital video recorders (DVRs), by 2015 many were into intelligent video and using network video recorders (NVR).

We are now seeing companies who have created stand-alone VSS networks which allow them to backup data offsite, creating redundancy and in some cases increasing storage. Other models may include having a private network hosted and managed by the integrator and/or a on the enterprise infrastructure of the company but on separate servers. Another trend is service providers who are not only cloud hosting your video for you but also are applying advanced analytics. Ten years ago, alarming features, facial recognition, and analytics were choppy to say the least. Today, we are seeing a true intelligent video. Both cameras and software are beginning to offer features that allow for a very accurate picture. The colors, lighting, brightness, and clarity are generations ahead of where we were at the beginning of the decade. Where we will finish in the next year has a lot to do with codecs.

How much to spend on a camera, what type of camera, the features, and where it was sold from continue to be up for debate. Much of this debate is understandably with the people providing the technology and/or heavily invested in these markets. The move to the next-generation video compression, that can significantly reduce file size, but still provides high-quality images is still up in the air today. Knowing which video codec will dominate the industry does not seem too clear. The race for an industry wide successor to the H.264 (MPEG-4 AVC) has been slow in terms of IT progress.

When cloud hosting was introduced, it was misused by many as a marketing term. Many of those account personnel who were driving the excitement were not able to articulate what their inherent differences were with managed, hosted, and cloud services. How is my data hosted, secured, and what about preservation or collection of evidence? Can we still go in and pick up the server for that data? It took a few years, but they have gotten it right and it has become a great way to store and access your data.

For those mired down in regulation, privacy and security concerns companies like the Qnext corporation (developer of FileFlex) offer a breakthrough alternative to the cloud agenda. Understanding the options will help you make quick decisions when investing in security system upgrades and the corporate systems they must work with. As a CSO, you should run through a few scenarios. The security control room needs to send evidence to the police, insurance, and/or you. See how secure, fast, and complex this is for each scenario. Now see if there is a better way of doing this. You can look outside of security for most solutions. Ask marketing or IT how they share large files. Review and share video with third parties. Ever proof a company ad? How?

2010–20

If you are reading this and have recently entered security management or are a CSO from a fortune 500 company, you may be thinking that you are not even here yet or many years past. I have tried to look at where the average user is today and hope that we can all surpass this tomorrow.

Many premises are equipped with a stand-alone, on-premise series of DVRs, a few dozen low light, color cameras, and few are using the alarm or point of sale integration. Video analytics are seldom used to their full potential and often senior security executives of today are not aware of all the features they already have and are not using.

Clearly documented minimum specifications for equipment, standards and performance are a nice to have. As-built, riser diagrams, and hardware schedules are rare to find as written by the CS department and integrator; and provided to the on-premise security manager. Site maps for camera locations, numbers, positions, and the marked out viewing area of each camera are often only found in the more established departments. Master service agreements and clearly defined SLAs that outline what is in and out of scope for the integrator and response times are not always in place. A business plan which includes the evergreening of this equipment is not usually published until the system needs desperate replacement. Detailed records of installation, repairs, and replacements in line with invoicing records are not something most premises heads of security are trained on keeping. Using the cameras for active patrol, logging camera operation (are they still recording), aligning video retention time with published guidelines [e.g., payment card industry (PCI) standards], and setting up remote access. If we go back to our security audit checklist and our ESRM reporting, you may see that capturing the handful of examples of good VSS governance provided here are below average. They were implemented only in part. Known by the senior CS staff, however, too detailed for the new site security manager. Implemented but forgotten, lost on the CSO who does not have a long-standing security background and/or were to granular for CS to have even considered. Call the people running your VSSs across the portfolio tomorrow, benchmark your peers and see how long it takes them to answer these questions.

- When was the systems installed?
- What software platform is it managed by?
- Do you have an evidence process and procedure?
- How many images per second (IPS) or frames per second (FPS) are we capturing?
- How is it backed up?
- What is the retention period?
- Can we remotely access the data?

If you are not impressed with the answers and you are the CSO, look inward, and then lead outward.

2020–30

After reading the state of VSS across small enterprises and the average premise above, I know that in the next 5 years CSOs will invest in making sure their security specialists receive VSS specific training, obtain a few books on the latest and greatest in VSS technology and practices, and look beyond the integrator for advice on what should be done to manage a best in class system.

Currently, AVC (H.264) codec is the leader in video compression. HEVC (H.265) is intended to be the long-awaited souped-up version of its reliable predecessor. In the next decade, I am confident that the market will decide who the winner is in the HEVC versus VP9 versus AV1 battle for market penetration supremacy. We are spoiled. As easy as it is to research how great algorithms will reduce files size and help us digest bandwidth hogs, we have come too far in high-quality video to accept anything that will degrade what we have today. It is possible that H.265 will be abandoned. Unless security-specific applications are military funded, born from intelligence or have a monopoly they do not have a chance against mass market application funding. Thirty years ago the only one watching videos at work were for the most part the security guards. Now everyone is streaming nonproprietary, high quality (in some cases license free), video software backed or supported by the world's largest social media and search engine providers.

By the early half of this decade, off-premise hosted video will be common. VSS which are fully integrated to other security systems, CSOs who understand and maximize the available analytics and portable cameras for special events will be old news. As the US government has moved to block the use of certain foreign surveillance equipment used in government facilities, by 2025 we will stop wondering what data cameras are sending and will be certain before they are deployed. We will understand endpoint protection and make sure that if our cameras are all IP, power over Ethernet, cat6, or Wi-Fi connected that they will not be a vulnerability to the network or vulnerable to attack.

2030–40

By this decade, the future will have arrived. The ability for the head of the GSOC or the premise security manager to pull up any camera on their mobile device with full functionality and to send the stream to the CSO during a crisis will be an easy and common feature. What we will have learned from machine learning and applied to intelligent video will have shifted us a generation ahead. The ability for the system to spot, analyze, track, and alert the operators to hazards, suspicious items and persons will be completely automated.

The high-end radar and thermal features of today will be found at nearly every premise in the exterior cameras. By the end of this decade, we may never run a cable to connect video again.

In the next 20 years, fewer CSOs will come from areas outside of security and intelligence. Almost none will come from law enforcement and other fields. The CSO of tomorrow will speak fluent PPS. They will be able to instruct the integrators on what they want and expect with confidence. Before graduation of any entry level security program, the CSO of tomorrow will have written an exam on the inner working of the VSS technology.

Violence in the workplace prevention, response and investigation

One of the most important functions of a CS department is the workplace violence prevention and intervention program. You cannot put a price on the preservation of life. In today's world, we are afraid of being sued, complained about, shamed on social media, judged by hashtag, and hurting anyone's feelings. We are worried about making any decision. We are too concerned about someone questioning our credentials, even when our gut tells us something is not right. Security professionals complaining about the expertise of their colleagues is too common. The policeman turned CSO questions the field experience of the career security leader and the career security leader questions the academic credentials of the former policeman. Shame on us.

A CSO needs to step up and know when someone is being a jerk and when they are exhibiting behaviors systemic of workplace violence. Overzealous is a better way for a CSO to be described than apathetic. When we look at the statistics on workplace violence, domestic terrorism, and active shooter events, we see a troubling history that is not going away anytime soon. The numbers in the past decade are staggering. To be told to step down off the soapbox occasionally is better than looking back at an event and asking, "could I have done more"?

If you're a CSO and you haven't ruffled some feathers, then you may not have been doing your job. Employees *must* know when to call for emergency services and when they need to inform human resources and security about concerning behaviors no matter how insignificant or trivial they seem. We must be professional, listen and have a process to deal with these things.

2010–20

In the past decade, many police and government agencies have produced workplace violence and threat assessment tools, resources, and white papers. Most major corporations have included workplace violence, harassment and bullying prevention and intervention as a part of the training all new employees receive, and policies they must follow. CS professionals have not only been receiving training from providers including Gavin de Becker and Associates but also have began using tools to help form risks assessments specific to workplace, domestic, and targeted violence.

For many years most, employers have implemented zero tolerance policies. Unfortunately, there continue to be employee on employee and even employee on nonemployee incidents. Violence committed by outsider on or toward employees in the workplace, while working on or off-premise has led to grievous bodily harm and even death. Training the employee population to be aware of their surroundings, how to protect themselves and call for help has become a common practice for CSOs with best in class programs.

The Center for Aggression Management offers the critical aggression prevention system (CAPS), this is one example of a system that helps the security practitioner to start to connect the dots and identify red flags before they become an incident when applied by a trained professional. It was no more than 20 years ago that security specialists had to have an advanced education and sometimes their gut instinct. Today, there are assessment tools provided by public and private sector to help nonsecurity professionals determine if a problem exists and/or is in fact a predicate behavior to violence.

Toxic workplace behavior is now being addressed. Employees no longer must tolerate the passive aggressive, sarcastic, or even outright temper tantrums of people in the workplace, systems are in place to address these matters.

2020–30

In the next decade, we will see features built into security systems that can enhance our ability to go on lockdown and send alerts, access control analytics that can send alerts when behaviors synonymous with crime are detected, and violence assessment alerts built into case management systems. The advancements in video analytics will help us to read body language, detect weapons, and provide a warning sometimes earlier than the human officer can. Professional protection officers will be able to deal with reports of violent behavior more effectively. Their education, initial training, and on-premise training will all include modules and lessons on the prevention, detection, and intervention of violence. Many more companies will have access to qualified mental health professionals they can engage to assess these matters and to support postincident counseling for employees and even clients.

Where laws may not be as established with respect to harassment, stalking, bullying, and violence the enforcement of strict corporate policies in the regions by the expatriate operations will positively influence the progress these regions will eventually make. ASIS International and key partners will continue to provide updated national standards to assist businesses in developing programs, assessing, responding to, and investigating these incidents.

2030–40

By the time we enter this decade, duty of care legislation, best practices, and the likelihood and probability factors found in risk assessments will lead many enterprises to have qualified behavioral assessment experts on staff to deal with workplace violence. The corporate investigations, financial crimes, security, and human resource departments to name only a few will send people for annual training and be able to address the earliest warning signs immediately. Something as simple as dismissive and callous behaviors will be noted.

Wearable technologies and portable devices will be used to verify the history of body temperatures, heart rates, perspiration, online behavior, location, and much more in the investigation of incidents. Cyber-investigators will be able to provide their colleagues with the user's network, email, social media, and other important data to predict, identify, and respond to incidents.

Employee background checks will screen for these past behaviors more stringently. We will have moved past outdated inappropriate stereotypes. Security specialists will be trained to understand that anyone can find themselves unexpectedly in a condition, series of events or a situation that lead them to do things they would have never thought possible or have been possible by the people closest to them. The education from millions of case studies will teach investigators to look at things from an entirely new perspective and the responder to keep their guard up when they are dealing with any person.

Questions

Where do I start when developing a program?

Engage a qualified consultant or service provider. Form a workplace committee, obtain good materials, standards, and develop a project team. Gather the guidelines and obligations from legal counsel and mental health experts. Speak to peer organizations. Contact your local law enforcement liaison, domestic violence outreach center, and other community partners.

Steps

- Designate a team to develop policies and training programs.
- Have the team trained to assess concerns, develop response plans, and conduct investigations.
- Speak to leadership and address how matters will be handled and by whom.
- Continue to develop your program with the help of others.

Considerations

Make the investment to have your security and investigators trained and retrained. Implement procedures and acquire tools to conduct, record, and report assessments.

Conclusion

Workplace violence is one of the most harmful situations for a company to experience. The employees impacted by these events are often changed forever. It is one of the most important things for any CSO to address as a top priority.

Corporate security tomorrow

Possible future corporate security department structures

As we have progressed through the past five chapters we have learned about some of the fundamentals of leading a corporate security department. I have outlined where components of these programs are headed and how advancements are going to re-shape how we work. We have an idea of the evolution of the tools we use to execute our tasks. The very title of this chapter is deceiving. As we have seen, CSOs, professors, and professionals have tried to re-brand their departments and staff titles with little success in this past decade, in time we may see a complete shift. The future protective services group also known as the classic physical security programs will remain quite active at the tactical and operational level, possibly even as a group in the head office offering exactly what it says, protective services. As we near 2030–40 corporate security as we understand it will nearly cease to exist. The highly educated, licensed risk mitigation, and threat response experts of tomorrow will be business savvy, subject matter experts working in converged departments of one form or an-other. They may be embedded with other key partners or under the direct manage-ment of the chief security officer (CSO). The CSO will likely be a member of the executive committee. These professionals will only know a world where they can speak fluent business, organizational resilience and have a strong grasp of informa-tion systems. In Fig. 6.1 I have used organizational resiliency as one possible depart-ment title.

Along with the debate on what defines a CSO (it's your head of security plain and simple) is where should corporate security reside and to whom should the CSO report to? One thing not to get confused with. Physical and information security do not have to merge because that is what you believe ESRM is about. Not at all. ESRM could be as simple as reporting metrics together. In the next few years some of the security systems will go to IT. Where the enterprise owns their own real estate, some of the premises security and security systems will remain with facilities. In the totality of large financial institutions or the financial services industry the security experts and their directors may branch off to a larger financial crimes or investiga-tions departments. The FBI can provide an interesting comparison, and therefore it is a good background for many corporate security-related positions. Many federal investigators are trained and do their time on security matters such as protective intel-ligence, bug sweeping (TSCM), threat assessment (of anything), workplace violence, corruption (code of ethics), and major events. Security coordination at the super bowl

The Chief Security Officer's Handbook. https://doi.org/10.1016/B978-0-12-818384-7.00006-9

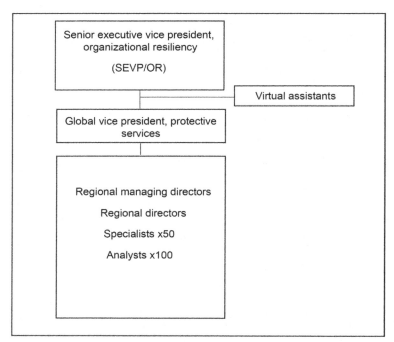

The numbers here represent full time employees (FTE)

FIG. 6.1

Example Group A: Organizational chart (2030–40).

was handled with great security coordination and planning by support of the FBI, the word security is not found in the acronym FBI, and special agents are often thought of as investigators, yet they can still assess risk and identify threats very well. The physical systems and control room experts who move with INFOSEC will report under Global IT, while the investigations or financial crimes department may very well bring the security specialist under their fold as investigators, who will report best to legal and compliance. Toward 2040 when the SEVP of security or CSO report into the C-Suite those departments will merge under an organizational resilience program with other like departments. Another idea is to place operational physical security (protective services) at the corporate level (not the security officers protecting the building who work for facilities or operations) who manage the security systems, provide protection, secure events on the ground, and place them in the financial crimes department along with fraud services and cybersecurity. This way all the systems can be managed under one umbrella and as the technology and fusion center advances the leader of the financial crimes department can see the patterns form. They will be able to monitor travelers and events from the global security operations center (GSOC) too. The physical security experts who assess risk of operations, premises, workplace violence, develop governance, and have a more strategic role will either be integrated with corporate investigations under compliance or become members of operational risk. They will simply be senior investigators (or similar title for example manager or director investigations) or one level of manager of another in risk.

Team structures, how we work and where we are situated within the office or premise will completely change over the next 20 years. Agile teams are highly effective. Some business professionals are confusing agile for smaller departments, doing more. It should mean working agile. Not having unproductive meetings but rather quick effective working sessions. The corporate security departments of tomorrow will have to grow to some extent if the enterprise does. The senior official who cuts these programs down to the bare minimum while driving for greater corporate results is being shortsighted. I do not mean that you need to build a security program that is an expense problem. The executive must face the fact that there will be public and shareholder accountability when breaches occur. A review that demonstrates that the CSO is poorly equipped by the employer with little to no resources would look unfavorable.

In Chapter 1 we looked at two examples to simplify department structures. Here we will look at two more examples. Fig. 6.1 also known as Group A and Fig. 6.2 known as Group B. These figures have been further simplified. Where the corporate security function is large, global, and focuses on an all risk, all hazards approach through a corporate lens, they will fall into Group A. Where corporate security is a smaller department with a stronger emphasis on core physical security, who support or lead large security teams who are comprised of (security officers) professional protection officers, and the security of premises, vessels, parks, and other large, important assets and or high occupancy entities, will fall under Group B.

You will see I have used the years 2030–40 for these figures. That is because some aspects of security take a long time to change across each industry they support globally. You will notice that lead is at least an SEVP. I anticipate as these leaders become more educated and more capable than the average CSOs 25 and 30 years earlier (myself included), they will report to the C-Suite or be one of the C-Suite members. A large section of middle management will have disappeared, and instead highly skilled career analysts and specialists will emerge. These roles will not necessarily be stepping stone positions for many. The number of these people will not grow much. This is because as the enterprise and demands grow, the technology supporting the business and the security program will automate significant portions of their work that is manually processed by large teams today. In some enterprise in the Group A category the physical security program will cease to be a subcomponent of another similar department (cyber, INFOSEC, financial crimes, business continuity, or investigations) and will be a newer, larger protective services department. This will occur in more cases in Group B enterprise. As more and more people attend college and university in the future a greater number of security management and similar programs will emerge at more of these institutions globally. Employers will demand this level education and the candidate market will be rich with it. It is possible that today's top certifications may evolve into licenses. Employees will achieve security director roles following years of higher learning, job placements, summer work, and

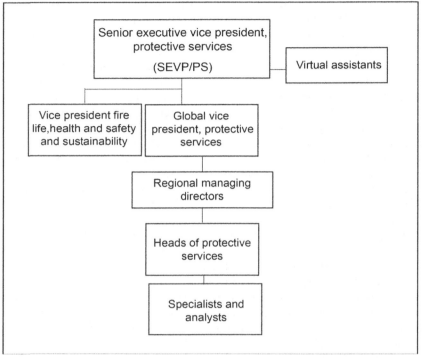

FIG. 6.2

Example Group B: Organizational chart (2030–40).

certifications instead of waiting 7–10 years of progressive working experience. The employee career and education backgrounds for senior security leaders will vary less, titles of departments, leaders, and other security staff will be streamlined. Like we refer to some social networks and search engines today as a verb we will see some technology as a coworker or another almost invisible tool that blends into our everyday life in the office, like today's laptop, just a seamless part of our vocabulary.

In Fig. 6.2, Group B we once again look at what a possible structure will be from 2030 to 2040. This type of department is where the largest entity is physical security, unlike corporate security departments that are only a small percentage of actual security personnel. This can be a combination of premises security in some cases, operational and strategic security leadership comprising most or all the protective services team. If this were a fleet of ships, factories around the world or office towers the current heads of security (manager, director, etc.) may be referred to as the director, protective services, leading the specialists, analysts, and professional protection officers. These professionals and leaders will more often come into the field with higher education and more credentials. They may have majored in more tactical and operations areas of elective studies, however still have the overall same alma mater as their peers in Group A. In both figures, the head of department have a virtual assistant. The ability to narrate commands to have emails sent, presentations drafted, expenses filed, and calls arranged will be accessible to everyone in 2040.

A lot of departments will embed security risk consultants for periods of time within their departments. Outsourcing of security in operations will be much more common. However, more organizations will employ a CSO as a member of senior leadership. Companies with no security lead today will more likely have put one in place in the future to address these risks, better service their employees, and avoid litigation. The very title chief may be gone from many organizations and simply replaced with global head or even simpler some variation or level of president.

We will see more equality in the workplace and less wage disparity of any kind. Physical security roles have been around for decades. Heads of security who lead departments heavily embedded in the physical space, protection and facilities have rarely been elevated to senior company management. Yet today we find information risk and information security departments lead by senior vice presidents (SVPs) more often. Their counterpart in physical security is often an assistant vice president (AVP), managing director, or senior director at best, on rare occasion a VP. More often when they are a VP, they have a small cyber department, investigations, or crisis team as well. For many mid-sized enterprise, funding a large corporate security program is not feasible. Keen professionals however often show their worth and acquire other program to form a larger department where each unit can share pooled resources. It is not uncommon for physical security professionals to seek to understand their level of authority, see their public counterparts more as partners than their own internal colleagues. IT-based security roles are often lead by people who have a formal education, immediately align with the business strategy and focus on the love of the technology.

The head of security in a facility should report to the head of the facility like any other department head. The head of protection services should report to a senior leader. When the head of corporate security reports too far down or to an operational department in the organization, they may lose independence from influence over their mandate. It would be difficult to investigate internal theft, workplace violence, and perform audits on the very people and the departments report to while remaining transparent and effective. There needs to be a channel or line of oversight. Accountability and transparency are important to have a program that looks out for the best interest of the entire company with an ounce of fairness. Often when a company employs a contract head of guards who report to their building operations department or a facility supervisor, they make the same mistake by placing their CSO in the wrong environment. It is also the responsibility of the CSO who reports their metrics, large risks with solutions, and areas of improvement to the top. The CSO who briefs the CEO on day-to-day security work is doing the enterprise, the role of the CSO, and themselves a disservice.

When the company is medium sized, and one leader manages all of security and like programs, they should report to the top people in the company and be a part of the executive leadership team. However, the chief operating officer (COO), chief financial officer

(CFO), and CEO only have so much span of control. In a fortune 100 conglomerate where there are heads of fraud, AML, security, investigations then reporting to a chief technology officer (CTO) or chief compliance officer (CCO) makes sense. In 20 years this may change, but we are not there today. We need to help elevate our industry (security) ourselves (development) and work with our companies to evolve our departments in a way that makes sense and improves our service offering to our employers.

Sometimes we are afraid of giving up a piece of our empire even when we are overloaded or don't even want all the pieces. I don't know a CSO who loves to talk about the day-to-day operations of access control card programming and entry logs. I do know cybersecurity leaders who are right at home in front of a wall of screens, discussing data analytics. Sometimes those colleagues could care little about what goes on behind the scene during a fire alarm or who is threatening who. If everything that is systems based in security is best managed by information systems or systems-related security experts, then it is time to let go of that piece of the equation. If that is what your entire program is founded upon then you may need to rethink your department mandate. CSOs at some point need to stop worrying about where they report, the size of their team, and what they do. When you set a goal, achieve it, set another goal and achieve that and then you have well developed a program and department that has the adequate resources, does not break the corporate budget and provides great service; spend more time maintaining it and less time trying to build empires. Do a great job, not more jobs. Work very smart and reasonably hard. The wrong attitude, ego, and a habit of looking over the fence often leads to disappointment and large, inefficient teams that over promise and under deliver. When times get tough for the company the responsible CSO will have to find ways to help reduce costs, and if the security budget is all tied up in large teams, who have less to do as business slows and travel is cut the CSO will have hard decisions to make. CSOs should be strategic, not busy.

Many CSOs are great leaders and modest business people because they truly care. They care about people, the work they do and the state of their employer's operations. If achieving the ideal department and reporting structure means that they will lose their way, then that is a great loss to the enterprise.

Some CSOs find themselves reporting to a department who does not want them, a leader who does not understand them and internal clients who very much need them. To voice this, present this or do other than what is asked is a dangerous game. The CSO must develop the best program they can, be as professional as possible always and wait patiently for those right moments to shine and share their insights with the right leaders, while never undermining or forgetting the people who lead them and who hired them.

Today's security officers are better off reporting to the operations or facilities department. Where the risk is higher, the premise higher profile and the security program of a building department, there should be an in-house head of security reporting to the head of the facilities, general manager, or head of operations (the most senior person leading the premise). Where the facility is smaller a contracted head of security reporting to one of the premise leads may be sufficient. Unless corporate security has the staffing and owns the security budget for the premise, they should not manage the security department. Special agents sent to help a local sheriff's office do not manage the department. They support it, provide advice, work together, and if needed conduct independent investigations when there is an internal problem.

In some cases, the head of security could spend years waiting for the company to develop a world class program. When the event occurs that triggers this initiative they may be surprised that they are a part of it, but perhaps not leading it. Look inside, ask yourself, am I ready for those very large ambitions? Am I the best suited for the job or do I have a lot to learn and should support the new global CSO and wait for my time (if that is meant to be). If you're looking out for the best interest of the company and the company is doing the right thing, then your job is to support that.

Here are a few simple examples of possible future reporting structures.

Example 1
Department
Technology and Operations
Business Unit 1
Information Security
Units
Engineering
Vendor Risk Management
Architecture
Information Risk (Assessments and Testing)
Business Continuity and Crisis Management
Business Unit 2
Financial Crimes
Units
Protective Services (security systems, operators in the fusion center, protection)
Cyber Security
Fraud Analytics and Response

Example 2
Department
Legal
Business Unit
Compliance
Units
AML
Fraud Risk Management
Investigations (including threat assessment, workplace violence, corporate-counterintelligence, security governance)

Example 3
Department
Organizational Resilience
Business Units
Information Security
Cyber Security
Global Security Operations
Information Security
Units (shared resources)
Analysis
Forensics
Fusion Center

Example 4
Department
Legal
Business Unit
Compliance
Units
AML
Fraud Risk Management
Investigations and Protective Services (including threat assessment, workplace violence, corporate-counterintelligence, security governance)

Example 5
Department
Global Security
Business Units
Global Security Operations
Protective Services
Threat Assessment Center
Security Strategy and Governance
Units (shared resources)
Analysis
GSOC

Example 6
Department
Technology and Engineering
Business Units
Information Security
Cyber Security
Unit
Network Security Operations Center (NSOC)
Business Continuity
Crisis Management

Example 7
Department
Legal
Business Unit
Compliance
Units
Investigations
AML

Example 8
Fraud
Department
Risk
Business Unit
Operational Risk
Units
Protective Services

In this model a GSOC/fusion center can be built to service all these partners.

In some cases, financial intelligence encompasses fraud investigations and AML. Human resources may employ investigators who investigate code of conduct and workplace violence matters. Some companies will keep information and cybersecurity together. They will place global security under operations and connect all physical security both corporate, physical and premises under one CSO.

I believe that core security practitioners will be working in a standalone department with its own budget and mandate called protection services. This department will report to the COO. Professionally they will be protection professionals. Their leaders will be compensated at a managing director or vice president level. They may be the global head of security or CSO. The baseline employees will be security specialists and the team leads will be directors. In the next 10 years all the pieces will fall into place like a puzzle. The educational programs, licensing, and careers will come together to make this happen. It will make the interaction between public partners a little clearer. This will allow hiring managers and human resource professionals to know what they are looking for. A managing director, protection services will lead a team of specialists and experts who will provide key people and asset protection programs across the entire company, no matter if it is national or global.

Corporate security departments are not formed just because. The structure needs to make sense. They will not evolve unless everything else moves forward and comes together. What works for one department may not work for another. Look at how your program is funded, who it makes the most sense to be integrated with and where the actual need is. Sometimes working better with other departments is a more efficient solution then moving reporting lines and forming large amalgamated departments. No team should take a back seat to another when they merge. If you remain separate, your leader will need to allow you to collaborate equally. It is a give and take process to solve problems for your enterprise.

There is also a large opportunity for global risk consultancies to continue to provide embedded contract security experts in smaller protection services departments. Where leadership see the big picture and it does not perhaps allow for a larger global security program, they can consider the use of integrating experts into the team for a term of a year or more for example. A major advantage to the sourcing employer is that they can continue the relationship with that employee or severe ties and move on after that time. The embedded consultant can reach back to the consulting firm and leverage the vast global knowledge of their peers on the work they are currently trying to find solutions for. Many CSOs in the future will be educated about how these embedded services work in school and may even, at some stage of their career may have been one of these consultants themselves.

For the past two decades, corporate security department structures have not changed much. I am now seeing significant changes and do not think it will stop anytime soon. Like any change you can be a voice in what happens or sit by on the sidelines waiting to see what will happen. I want to follow the footsteps of some of my peers who have seized the opportunities to develop these new organizational structures for their departments, in their vision and are making it work.

How day-to-day work will take place

All too often today large companies with traditional hierarchies, strong governance, and long-standing traditions try to migrate to a flattened, matrix, agile machine like the startups we see having great success. Some things to keep in mind. The slow, multistep processes are often in place because of regulation, size, and complexity. When a tech giant tries to enter the finance space they will eventually be subject to the same regulation and will need to grow their support teams and implement oversight functions and controls. When they have their first breach they will put controls in place very similar to those seen in companies traditionally working in that space today. When the market crashes will they last for over 100 years like their banking peers have? Flattening the top three layers is a great idea. It does not often work several layers below. When entry level roles need to please multiple managers, conflicts may surface. Today many people spend 9 a.m. to 5 p.m. in meetings and work everywhere in between. We are a hyper-connected, hyper-mobile work force. We work from home, work on the road, work flex hours, and deal with operations around the world. To try to expect people with little to no supervision to work from home 100% of the time and still produce the same results is not possible in most cases. In reverse to expect people to attend meetings all day, go home complete their work, clear the tasks they received in the last meeting, prepare for tomorrows meetings, and take calls to the regional offices who are located in different times zones, we are looking at a short-term situation at best. People will burn out and operate with half the efficiency they normally would.

An example of challenges facing many of us is as follows. In the classic corporate office, the legal team books a meeting with the CSO. The CSO heads across the complex to the meeting, running from the last. The very busy CSO takes calls between offices, checks email on the run and has probably not prepared for the meeting or read the pre-meeting notes in detail. The meeting runs the entire period with most time being spent by the hosts explaining the reason for gathering in detail. Each party leaves with action items only to be pushed off for the next meeting and actioned some time later. This cycle perpetuates itself.

Modern forward-thinking chief executive officers (CEOs), and their leadership teams are bringing a balance to the equation. Flexible working hours where responsible employees alter traditional office hours to accommodate a global mandate, while avoiding burn out and still putting in the hours they rightfully owe to the company. Meetings that start 15 min after the hour allow people to move from the last call or meeting and arrive to the next one on time and better focused. Keeping meetings to less than five people, no more than a half hour is more efficient. Agenda, minutes, and action items are often helpful. Agile working sessions are an even more effective way of meeting. If you are hosting meetings to present your objective and to ask for help, then you need to narrow down your statement to a simple call or written communication. Example, no one needs to sit in a meeting for an hour to be asked for one simple task. I am building a house. Can you please bring me a hammer? Senior managers do not always have to be in a meeting. One lead from the meeting can have a brief touch base with the leader to present the results.

Email overload? If you are the CSO and still receiving hundreds of alerts and email assess what they are. Can professional association and magazine emails go to your personal email account for later reading? Can alerts go to a SOC, NSOC,

GSOC, or fusion center with escalation protocol? Can you have people tell you what folder a file has been placed in or send a link via SharePoint instead of large attachments that may cost you to download or crash your email? Does your team need to print everything to show you or can they place it in a drive and present it to you on the display in a meeting space or via Skype?

Still reacting to every small emergency, attending the scene, gathering the team? Gauge what a CSO should be involved in and what they should not. You should almost never attend the scene. You are to lead strategically; your deputies should have people, or the premise security should be boots on the ground with first responders. CSOs are to be there with the leadership team in the war room during actual corporate crisis.

In the future when you are working from the office you will arrive and, in a few clicks, or a swipe of your mobile phone, you will have pre-reserved a seat for the day. You will use a biometric to login and review your agenda for the day, managers dashboard on staffing and department matters and your case management dashboard. The morning report will be in your inbox highlighting the most critical matters on the horizon and those with a direct or indirect impact to the enterprise and the current actions taken or decisions needed.

If the departments are merged or not, the key players will be situated on the same restricted office floor. On that or the other floor occupied by these teams will be the fusion center. Teams will have almost moved past formal meetings and even agile working groups. Instead they will already be working together. Since systems will all be tied into one or two platforms, on one GUI. They will have similar skill sets no matter if they are assigned to investigations, business continuity, security (cyber, information, physical), fraud, and AML and therefore will already be using the same platforms, to share, store, and work on data. Nearly 90% of what they do will be on the highly advanced, A.I. driven application. There will be almost little to no storage folders on the network, except for what the leader and administration use to store non-record work. All budgets, expense, travel, and other admin work will be on their own respective apps. If the investigator is working on a file and needs video they will click a few radio dials on the screen and the fusion center will load the video into that case file in minutes. If fraud need to add supplemental information a pop up will appear to that investigator who will click allow and there will be no meeting, discussing, or emails. No saving to folders, searching through folders, and retrieving. The minute data goes in, the CSO will be able to see it. When a loss occurs, the protection services or investigation "specialist" will no longer request third parties to pull large logs and sort it on spread sheets for hours. Intelligence software with built in parameters will see the direction the specialist is headed and run, sort, analyze, and provide a full report and conclusion in a few key strokes from one screen.

In 20 years from now formal brainstorming between groups will be rare. A quick touch base will instead be done from feet away. Careful programming of most security and investigation controls, and solutions will have been built in for every assessment, file or loss. Once the data comes in, the filed opened and the specialist completes the basics, the system will generate options and recommendations. It will show pattern, trends, and outright answers. As they read through the document, sheer eye movement will scroll to the next page. The sound of clatter of keyboards and clicking of mice will be something you heard in the old days. There will be no cords, not even to charge a phone. Wireless, contactless, and paperless technology will have reduced storage and clutter. Phones will be virtual, headsets just wireless earbuds, and devices that can run for days on a single charge. In time no one will be lugging around much in a tote bag to work. Data will be securely accessible from any screen in a few swipes of a hand anywhere. Laptops will be few and far between. All glass tablets, with on display keyboards will be used and even those will be considered old fashioned.

For the busy CSO cellular data, connectivity and reception will be improved. On the subway, in the car the CSO will be able to use a voice command to listen to their voicemails from any phone line, have their emails read to them, and pull down departmental statistics from their mobile device to a discreet wireless earpiece while commuting to work, travelling, on a treadmill or on a beach. Unplugging will be harder, but accessing data, multitasking, and saving time will be much more achievable. Imagine the time you will save when there is no longer fumbling for a pass card, when you are scanned and enter parking and the office. You come to a desk made of glass and place you hand on it, you have now reserved the seat and logged in. You walk in a room and use your phone as a PC on the private screens or overhead display for a presentation, no wires, not second login. Just a yes or no on a prompt.

There is a saying that goes something like this. "Know what you don't know." Security experts love to hoard files, data, and information like squirrels (scavengers). (I will find it more interesting that one of my colleagues from around the world will need to search what a squirrel is, we learn something new every day.) Security experts have felt the need to know everything for a long time. I believe that we need to know, only what is needed, that is, less data and only high-quality intelligence. This will also change the way we work and what we can possibly accomplish.

Many of us need to help support, embrace, and use these concepts to move the rest of us ahead, and some of us will help to make these workplaces and technologies secure and easy to access for the authorized parties. The technology will be the easy part. Adopting it, using it most efficiently, understanding, and taking advantage of all the features will take a generation of security professionals to appreciate.

The predictive strategy

If someone told you to duck, most of us wouldn't. We would look around, look puzzled, or stare blankly. If you walked into the meeting room today and simply said "don't buy it," the context, credibility, and question of authority would be in doubt. Twenty years ago if a CSO presented the CEO with an ominous warning on a major decision perhaps based on an informal piece of information they had gathered from an old police contact; the CEO would dig deeper. Post 9/11 as public and private partnerships became formal, security clearances were extended to corporate citizens and executive briefed into national security matters things began to change. A CSO walking in to the executive office and saying "don't get on the plane" may have a little more credibility and be able to express why much easier and with credibility. Today we have come a long way. A CSO no longer has people opening mail, reading the daily delivered newspaper, and asking what the corporate strategy is blindly to provide some information. Most CSOs today subscribe to several services that can provide alerts, they provide news and the status of security, geopolitical, medial, and environmental events around the world. Some of these services offer an analysis that may help predict events. For example, there is an election taking place this coming Tuesday in "Everything is Wonderful Land." Candidate A and B are running. If candidate A's party wins we expect violence and rioting in disappointment from the supporters of party B. This has occurred every other year for the past 30 years when A wins. If party B wins we expect violence and rioting in celebration from party B. This has occurred every other year for 30 years when they win. This is good to be aware of but still just information. Intelligence may be that we have a source who says either way, party B plans to start their riot in the town square following the election results at 2:00 p.m. If the CSO has set this up right their systems will tell them that they have operations or people there, what the expected impacts will be and what advanced preventative measures should be taken. Now, what if the future alerts to the CSO that can be cascaded in one click says. "Have all personnel work from home in 'Everything is Wonderful Land' next Tuesday. Starting this weekend move anything movable inside and board up the windows, riots expected on Tuesday." Today you may find yourself not only manually doing a lot of this but drafting a full report and moving it slowly up the chain. Some CSOs in fact may simply not have known at all and are blindsided by the entire event.

As I pointed out earlier our threat management, case management super systems of the future will anticipate our entries, actions, and needs. They will start processes and offer controls and recommendations as soon as we begin. What if these were all in one system, with A.I. running the show. What if we had run thousands of threat modeling scenarios, provided our best steps to deal with all of them, made detailed decisions trees and process flow charts. All connected, all intelligent. What if we could predict the next cyber-attack or riot in advance, have them actioned and preparations made before they occur. What if this happens with little input, actions, communications, or decisions from the team after the system is set up and activated? What if this system continued to run scenarios in the background? What if it continued to read media, law suits, workplace accident, reports, insurance logs and more. What if it continued to learn from each event in the world and events experienced by the enterprise and develop deeper, more relevant intelligence and set improvements in place long before a threat was even conceived by the threat actors or the storm began. We are heading there. But it will take the volunteering, boldness, and commitment of CSOs and their (internal, counterpart, public sector, and vendor) partners.

CSOs will need to find clear, concise ways to educate leadership and the entire staff population on what to do in most critical situations. During a few building emergencies (fire alarms, active shooter, power failure and floods, etc.) there are hundreds of possible options and outcomes. In most cases you can break it down to two very basic responses. Shelter in place or evacuate. Those are the two most simple and logical options. When the CSO knows their company well. Where operations are located, who the big players are. What roles people play. What operations and vendors are critical. They will be in a better position to know the impact potential of different events to different things. Layer this with good information, refined action plans and training and you will often be ahead of the problem. You should be predicting and preventing much more than you are reacting. Reactions should not be the beginning of your efforts, these should be small actions, because you already have controls in place.

A CSO should be completely connected with the corporation. They are the face of the department, a figure head. The deputy chief security officers (DCSOs) will handle administration, operations, and strategy looking downward and outward. They focus on the security program. The CSO will bridge the gap between the two and ensure both the department and the company leaders understand the company's strategy and the capability and capacity of the department. Smaller teams will need to plan and execute. They will need to be very creative with limited resources. A head of protective services who can leverage the building head of security or one of the company investigators to solve problems should always see them as equals and partners. Instead of telling, they should ask. They must respect the expertise of those professionals. In today's day-to-day work the head of protection services may spend hours trying to gather information and evidence on thefts and then try to conduct interviews and analysis on their own. There is simply too much work to be done. By trusting and sharing your needs with your partners, the future CSO will be able to work much more efficiently. Each team will share in the credit of a job well done for playing an important but compartmentalized role in addressing loss and other tasks.

What if the CSO followed what many of their colleagues do today and applied this to their business strategy? What if you looked at major events a year out and made sure you were staffed, budgeted, and plan to deal with it as much as possible now rather than later? What if this was automated to some degree as well? CSOs should start placing all of this into systems today, brainstorming, recording, and documenting. When the technology catches up you do not want to be the last one to be able to capitalize on its benefits.

Agile teams

Earlier in this chapter I touched on agile teams. Here I hope to go a little deeper. As smaller teams seem to be remaining small and larger teams are sometimes shrinking, we need to find more modern and efficient ways to handle the increasing workloads until automation advances. I also want to emphasize that as you research further and picture a bunch of grads standing in front of a whiteboard looking whimsically at a great idea, the security team do not have to be confined to a cube farm and their collaboration board to be an effective agile team. For 30 years there have been great television shows and movies about some force of five experts all working to save the world in 5 min. The team can still collaborate virtual from around the world, on the move while in play or in theatre and set out to execute tasks in real-time operations, while coming back to huddle to determine their next move. I hope I have made agile sound interesting, because it can be.

The workplace is changing. For some enterprise those changes have all run their course, and either come back full circle or landed on a new way of doing things. Some companies have aimed to accommodate a new, tech savvy generation with flexible work hours, interesting seating options and amenities to make the workplace more convenient and enjoyable. Others have swapped the large offices for modern open concept workspace and work from home programs. With enhanced audio-visual tools many are trying to go paperless. All of these create new opportunities and challenges for security.

In the corporate office it is common to see a shift away from massive cube farms of data entry specialists and top-heavy structures of general managers. Organizational flattening of the top few layers, small high impact teams of subject matter experts, and the push for a digital workforce are on the rise.

Agile teams are just that. These are teams of similar or complimentary experts. They are relatively small, sit with their manager and are changing the way we work. Departments who have similar functions and objectives are being brought under the same executives and sitting in the same space. Agile teams can quickly assemble, assess an opportunity and begin developing a solution in minutes. Each member goes back to their desk and make things start happening immediately. The manager calls for a scrum, they conduct a review, work together in real time, and close it out. What used to take days of emails, meetings, getting buy-in, and realigning now takes a matter of hours. Fusion centers offer a variation of this.

Picture an investigation department in a bank in the year 2000. The investigators receive a call about internal misconduct. They call a contact in physical security or even building security, a member of human resources and information technology. Through a series of briefings, calls, emails, and hand delivered records they compile a picture of the events, evidence, and write a report. Within a month the process is complete beginning to end.

Now let's picture this process today. Many of the similar departments are seated together. Their respective program heads report to the same CSO. Members of the investigation team have access to most records and systems already. They borrow one specialist from each team, physical security, the control room, digital forensics, and jump into a brainstorm area (an open concept meeting area). They open their case file and work around the table making each request. Some working group members today go back to their teams and work on the requests. Other teams stay right there and using their laptop complete the work in minutes. All the records and logs are now in the hands of the investigator within an hour, any questions answered, and an analysis and interview will commence within 48 hours. The file will be closed within 4–5 business days.

Highly efficient teams are already working as follows. The investigators host a quick Skype call. Forensics and the global security operations center upload their data to the case management software immediately and what used to take 2 weeks is complete within a few hours.

The director of physical security (enterprise security, protective services, global security, etc.) gather their specialists and managers together in one room for a morning. A four-part proposal in the form of a deck, which will form a business case for a travel risk management program needs to be created. All four members are told there is a template sitting in a new folder on their SharePoint. They are all given a research, benchmarking, pricing, and recommendation assignments and 2 hours to enter their results in the deck. The director gathers the team back together to collaborate, follow-up on the outstanding items, and edit together. Less than an hour later the deck is complete and ready before day end.

One final example is as follows. In some classic project management models, members of different departments, levels and specialties form steering committees, working committees, and working groups, meet, take calls, and contribute to a corporate project. These groups work individually back at their own departments and work toward goals or stages often called milestones. If the project is estimated to take 4 months the end of each month and stage of a project could be lined up. Once that stage is complete the first milestone is done. Some members of the team are devoted to the project completely while others return to their office to face day-to-day tasks. The project sponsor and project manager are accessible but not there with each working member. Some projects and stages cannot be rushed; however, the project can be shifted. If documentation, governance, memorandums, and other components can be done while parts are shipped, an agile team can gather for quick working sessions. The team can also leave their respective departments for days and meet in a common corporate hoteling or meeting space. Working parallel to one another allows them to check if they are on track, following the vision of the sponsor and avoid distraction. The head of compliance leads the AML, Fraud, and corporate security departments. They want to update the employee compliance training spanning across expertise from each team. One expert from each team, a designated scrum master and members of the communications and human resources training team are assembled in agile seating and working sessions. The collaboration, shared resources, and cross expertise help the team to complete each task and overcome obstacles. The face-to-face interaction allows them to solve problems together and leverage one another's experiences. I suggest you review a recent project or working group situation in the traditional sense. Then I suggest you try this approach a few times on similar work. See if the agile approach is for you.

I believe that stand-alone protection services departments will be a better model and survival strategy of corporate security professionals. In this smaller, lean, high functioning design, they will need to embrace technology, work agile, and be at the top of their game. Only extremely high performers will fit this model. You can have both strong academic minds and great responders. Approaching all security situations with a logical approach may be disastrous. Anyone with an animal instinct and street smarts know that just because the world should work a certain way, that there are laws and logic should prevail, does not always mean the enemy thinks this way.

There are some excellent resources online that offer roles for the members on an agile team both large and small. A few business management and leadership training centers are offering courses on leading agile teams. I highly recommend taking the opportunity to learn more about how you can become the next great scrum master.

Intelligence-led decisions

Since there were castles there was physical security, guards, and all. Approach the castle and there are two people standing in front on guard, controlling access. Maybe a moat, a drawbridge and gate for access control. A guard patrolling inside, one in a watch tower. So far it could very easily be compared to any large facility and their security officers, barriers, gates, and doors of today. An army of soldiers could be defending the kingdom. There were spies and informants. Can you imagine a century after the medieval ages when the first telescope came along? What a remarkable breakthrough. In one sense you could think that physically people have not changed much, and we act more civilized (most of the time). Really, outside of technology security has changed little. Professional protection officers of today are assigned to posts, conduct patrols or are sent out on protection details, no different than a thousand years ago. If you look at access control in 1995 and access control today to the non-security practitioner, it has not changed much. Now let's look at a cell phone from 1995 and one from today. In financial institutions our partners in fraud analytics, money laundering, business continuity, investigations, information security, and cybersecurity have grown in some cases much larger and more sophisticated in just the past 20 years. In many other industries security still plays an important role, however our technology security partners are growing and advancing exponentially. Talk to any corporate or global security expert and they can inform you about all the world events, politics, and situations which may impact operations. They can perform risk assessments on nearly anything and are very strong in areas of compliance, privacy, and risk. So how is it that we seem to be lagging? Often downsized and pushed around from department to department.

These security experts have access to a lot of data. Those who take the time to analyze and present that data often reap the rewards. We are however sometimes slow or show the wrong data. If you can determine what data is important to the enterprise, be able to remain fluid and change the information based on the fast-moving strategy of the organization and keep the data you simply find interesting on the back burner then this will be a good first step. A new security manager is informed about a protest downtown in a days' time. They standby the next day waiting for the event to pass by and may even hope to see some action. A CSO has years of data on the same or similar events. They know who is targeted by which groups, compare that to their business, building occupants, or industry. They will reach out to security and police contacts for more information. They will have a search conducted online and assemble a quick assessment. A note will be crafted with help to staff and occupants. Extra security may be arranged, valuables secured, and a dry run conducted for rolling, soft, and total lockdowns. A line of communication will be established to get word from each direction down the street of any key observations. A scout may be designated to surveil the groups' initial meeting place. In the morning all systems will be checked, doors and gates double checked, and management briefed. Teams will be on high vigilance and the CSO may pop down to the operations center and this is as close as they will get. In some cases, this will all have been documented along with alert levels and levels of lockdown. Like a playbook a code green, yellow, or red may immediately tell everyone what to do. Like a coach, quarterback, and team the playbook will have been rehearsed a many times and there will be little to no need for discussion.

Every global security department needs a designated leader for an intelligence program or at the very least a culture of intelligence by design built into the way smaller protection services teams work. If you are hiring and supporting people to remain current with ongoing training and courses, then they can react on real intelligence alone, you can say duck, and without giving them terabytes of data to assess first, this new generation will know to simply duck. It takes experienced police officers and field agents years of training and working together to give a simple nod to one another and then to spring into action and to be exactly on the same page. That is a glamorous example, but the future security team needs to be just as effective. They will know you mean duck and follow through, saving time and their own neck. This may apply to much less life on the line situations but could impact business and operational decisions. You need to tell a child what to do in the event of a fire alarm. You do not need to explain each step to the director security at a skyscraper. You just say fire. The protection professional will know what to do in few words.

The less you must process a bunch of information before you can react, the more you know in advance, can anticipate and are already prepared for the events, the better you will serve your employer. If your program produces rapid, relevant, and real time intelligence that has already been planned for, then you are making intelligence-led decisions rather than always trying to catch up. Soon technology will make this much easier. It is up to you to use that technology and make sure your team has the right tools.

Doing more with more

Often, we hear companies asking security leaders to do more with less, budget crunches, hiring freezes, smart sizing, and reductions in existing services. All the while the work load and demands increase and along with them, risks. What if we change the way we work. The work we produce and the technology we use. An old but good practice is to question why you still do things a certain way. What happens if that report does not get completed? We started that report for the old CEO. No one has asked for it in a while and we just keep making them. What if we completed tasks critical to operations and not urgent requests with no indication of urgency. What if we work agile, apply robotic process automation (RPA) to tasks? What if we suddenly have several global risks to report on? Why do we need to produce 20-page reports to show one conclusion and a few recommendations? What if all the data and references were centrally located, easy to access and noted in a one-page brief. What if processes were shortened, automated, and decisions made easier?

Department heads do not need to do more with less. Can you hire seven specialists instead of three AVPs? Can you hire the three AVPs often working professionals with a direct report each, instead of a department of 20? Can you remove all the clutter and complication from day one? Provide them with the tools and databases available today. Remove most other options.

Look at the work each team member is doing, look at what they can be doing simpler or eliminate. Look at the tools they use. The corporate security committee assembles all metrics each quarter from several departments. Each department produces a detailed five-slide deck. The second slide covers all the required key risk indicators (KRIs), key performance indicators (KPIs), security and risk statements. The deck is reviewed several times and a final draft is sent to the committee. The committee removes the other pages, take the statistics and place them onto one page in another deck for the executives, the board, and regulators. What if the next step was to tell the departments you only need two of those metrics for that audience? What if the committee secretary created a single dashboard, one-page slide, and placed it in a SharePoint file? Each quarter the committee secretary updated the slide dates, sent a reminder and everyone. Each department would click the link, open the document, enter their numbers, and save it. That would save a lot of time. Why don't we take that one step further? The CSO migrates the work to the corporate software application that is the risk, compliance, investigation, business continuity, etc., book of record (for context this could be something similar to the RSA Archer suite of services). All the reports are entered into this system and all the metrics are populated in real time. The head of compliance or risk simply import their live dashboard for that quarter into their deck. A dozen steps each for several departments is now three in total for everyone.

There are many resources available to protection departments. Take someone who is new to Microsoft Word or Excel. They initially start off just typing. In time they will learn many shortcuts, helpful features and understand what automation is already available to them. Do you have a travel tracking program or service? Do they have a mobile app? Have you simply read the manual or played with it to take advantage of the many different options? You may be able to accomplish a lot more than you know with your case management and risk/mapping services then you realized. Try to use less applications, but instead use good quality services to their full potential. No executive wants to hear that you are using half of what you're paying for. I have mistakenly asked for new services or resources, only to find out that existing ones already offered the solutions I needed. I have also found duplications of applications or services across departments during my career. The opportunities to get more done with what you have or to eliminate tools and bring everyone together on the best platform you already have is usually right in front of you. Some CSOs will join an new organization and bring the benefit and hindrance of knowledge from their last employer. They really didn't know their last systems that well but knew what results their team provided them with it. Instead of replacing everything, sit down with your new employer's service providers, your technology people supporting it, and your team who are using it. Tell them what you had, what it did, and what your needs and expectations are. Then listen. You may have that and more.

These new ways of collaborating, automating processes, and reducing steps are force multipliers. One application can do the work of a few manual entry analysts. Remember doing expenses a few years ago? Standing at a copier scanning receipts, opening every email, saving them by name into a folder and then opening the software, and attaching each one to the right expense. What about today when you can snap a photo of a receipt the moment it is received or save it from an email on your phone by taking a picture of it on the screen. Open and app from your phone and complete the report before your even back from your trip. It takes some getting used to but if you embrace it, you keep using it and stop using archaic methods, and then you will realize you're doing more with more.

A society of sharing not surveillance

In our world we develop a tool, machine, resource, application, and occasionally it becomes weaponized, militarized, and or used for criminal acts. Drones are a great example. If teleportation or time travel is ever invented, it should have been outlawed, before it was ever tested. Soon drones will be equipped with weak A.I. and then one day they will be completely autonomous. As we look to implement guidelines or "laws of A.I." we know drones in theory have already broken the "laws of robotics." We are coming into a digital age of great advancements. We can now share and collaborate better than ever. We can collect interesting data on the office, workers, and systems to help us make the quality of life, tools, and customer experience better. This data can be used for so much good, one such purpose is to keep people safer, more aware, and improve security. Many of these tools are designed to or can residually allow us to monitor and track employees. These need to be used responsibly. There will always be an investigative need or business reason for the use of the data. Security is not there to police the staff but to protect them. They need to be known as a department that employees proactively turn to, to feel safe. That is why we must use these technologies to track employees to keep them safe, notify them of danger, and locate them in a crisis. A transparent and clear difference between the responsible use of the data and who should control it, should be clear to employees, and well defined to the users. Oversight is very important.

Some of what I am about to say contradicts itself. But it will help you to see the dilemma and to try to strike an appropriate level of balance as a responsible CSO. Privacy is necessary. Total forced transparency can stunt creativity, remove healthy competition, and cause people and corporations to behave contrary to the nature of things.

Scenario 1

There is an attack in a shopping center. In the aftermath of the event the investigation reveals that the signs were there. Lack of communication between parties is in part to blame. Those close to the matter passionately wish more could have been done. When the police want your information, we expect they will need a warrant. When we are facing the ticking time bomb scenario, most people would expect them to get the data forthwith. When a robbery occurred yesterday, and you may have the video, processes should be followed to retrieve, sign over and share that video responsibly and in line with legal, corporate and evidentiary practices. When the robbery has just occurred on your premise and the robbers are on the run, the images can often be handed over to get into the hands of patrol cars immediately. If we said it was alright to watch everything we are doing all the time in hopes that it will thwart the next shopping center attack, those whom have never been impacted by such an even would likely not agree. If we said that special investigators, investigating terrorism could conduct reasonable warrantless searches in pursuit of a criminal mastermind, based on established law and rules, some of us could agree to this and some healthy oversight.

Scenario 2

Access control can be used to let people in and out. We can review logs, alarms, and alerts. If security were to give out these details freely to investigators without rules, oversight, or helping them understand the importance of cross-referencing with witnesses, computer logs, video, and attendance records; the investigator may blame the staffer for something done by someone who was using a cloned credential. When managers are freely given these records, they could use it as a form of time and attendance, sometimes without having established guidelines with their employees, spoken to them or having used less intrusive means. They may be playing favorites, on a witch hunt or power trip. Imagine using access data as one source of several to look at corporate occupancy and space usage. Imagine using the analytics to help with life safety and fire evacuation or work alone program to check in on the wellbeing of staff. It can be used to track missing workers who could be ill or injured in mechanical areas. It can be used along with other important business data on staff mobility, high and low times for lunch areas, head counts of staff, contractors, and contingent workers. To make decisions on seating, parking, and how weather may affect attendance.

Sharing information between leaders, corporate departments, and external agencies to make the business better, safer, and help society are great reasons to collaborate. To use business software to monitor people to track the change new tools make, how the office environment or new coffee machine impacts the bottom line are reasonable business practices. A certain level of monitoring is corporate responsibility. To hand over a client's entire private financial or media records to an employee without controls and oversight would be careless. To implement technologies to monitor everyone, just in case can sometimes go too far. The head of security who gets the "I know everything that goes on" complex or a "God" complex is failing to do the right thing and is playing into their own ego. This only leads to bad things. The CSO must also be a voice of reason and know how to guide business leaders on where lines must be drawn, and privacy must be respected. Just because you can monitor, does not mean you always have to. The watchers and rule makers almost never like when the tables turn. If CSOs could see nearly everything employees and occupants do in the workplace and this information were freely given to intelligence services and police who could now close the gap to a state of total surveillance, then without controls this could become a problem for society. We need to make sure we don't miss the next attack where possible, but not become the thought police. When emails are read, and logs reviewed, we must remember we too are human. We do not write and speak like robots and shouldn't be judged for it either nor should others.

Hackathons are one of the coolest events going. The chance to bring a room full of great minds together, team them up, solve problems, and let their imaginations run wild is very interesting to watch or even participate in. What they can accomplish together is quite fascinating. Sharing can be a very positive thing. Getting together with peers from both the public and private sector does not have to be a long running formal committee or about a crisis. It can be brief and about team building, exchanging ideas, information, and tackling day-to-day problems. Academics are very good at this. We need to look outside of security and see what others are doing. Who simply does it best and how we can all achieve the same things.

When we set out to spy on people for the sake of power or gain we have lost. When we can activate a series of events to help find a missing person, locate an adversary to enhance police response or find a root cause, and stop ongoing loss then we have created something positive.

Going green and the return on investment

Companies who practice good corporate social responsibility will often have a sustainability program. As technology consumes many aspects of security, we should be conscientious about our energy consumption. Often when we use the words savings or return on investment in relation to security you have already lost. Start with trying to improve the organizational resiliency of the enterprise. Improve the service you offer to stakeholders, be a business enabler. You may not necessarily be saving money as you plug new systems into the network, however you may be practicing cost avoidance and changing to responsible consumption resources when you are selective. Ask yourself how many times you have put a request for proposal or similar document together and asked the following:

- Does your company have a formal sustainability program?
- Does this product consume less energy than its' closest competitors?
- Are your manufactures environmentally conscious?

A workplace sustainability or environmental expert can probably provide you with an appropriate list. Do you have a security operations center, fusion center, or corporate security department office? Most likely you have one or more of these and most of what you do is highly confidential. What about going paperless? This enhances security, saves paper, and transfers the electricity usages to the use of monitors you already use. Twenty years ago it was not uncommon to see a patrol system throughout stairs making sure they were thoroughly patrolled. Now, it is not uncommon to see security using the elevators more often. What about the benefits of using both to reduce elevator usage, promote fitness, and ensure the stairwells are in good order?

Window film can add a layer of protection to a premise, the right film can help to reduce overheating and solar wear (for those readers familiar with blast engineering, this a simplified example looking at the benefits of the film). Determine what security lighting can be placed onto motion activation. Reduce lighting in the control room. Remove trash receptacles. All paper goes into the shredding bins. Recycle bins for cans, bottles, and similar objects. See if the building has a compost program. Use recycled materials. Use metal cutlery in the kitchenette. Unless someone needs a straw specifically, remove straws. One metal spoon can equal hundreds of stir sticks.

As you can see there are many things you can do to save energy and reduce waste. This is an important investment for your company and the environment. Take the opportunity to conduct an audit on how you can do your part and build this into the culture of your security program.

Lean and broad security functions

In this section I will look at an example future protection services and global security programs, and we will examine a version of each function in a lean model and a broad model. We will be looking at industries where security is a standalone department, where it is not a partner or subcomponent to investigations, business continuity or information security. This is a view of the near future. I will use protective services as an example where the security program is a lean department who outsources most services and focus more on risk, provide advice, and conduct audits. I will refer to larger departments who handle most functions in house, manage the operations of those functions themselves as global security (in large financial institutions or service providers this is often corporate security). Essentially these two departments will both look at:

- Electronic Security Systems
- Physical Security Consulting

- Threat, Risk, and Vulnerability Assessments (TRVAs)
- Security Governance
- Crime Prevention
- Travel Security
- Employee and Executive Protection
- Event Security
- Workplace Violence Prevention and Investigation
- Security Intelligence (situational awareness, insider threat)

Global security may additionally have a security strategy section, global security operations center, and pre-employment screening. The names of these functions may differ from company to company.

Electronic security systems
Protective services

In a protective services model, the team can provide consulting to the business for new projects. If the company is building a new headquarters, leasing an office or elevating their security systems the team can review the project and provide advice. In this model the team is smaller and therefore capacity may be limited. Having developed standards and specifications to expedite the security systems design process is important in this model. The team will have to limit their engagement as resources are limited. They can provide input for tender documents, drawings, and how the system will work once completed. This model does not allow the team to manage the project or operate the system once complete.

Global security

In the global security model, the department is often a full-service department with a much larger staffing compliment. This allows the team to rely less on service providers and consultants and to deep dive on projects related to systems. The team may project manage entire security systems from conception to commissioning. The team will be able to assign access control administrators or even use their GSOC to manage the system after completion.

Physical security consulting
Protective services

In the protective services model the team is quick, lean, and agile. They can triage requests to lend subject matter expertise to a few emergent or proactive matters. They will use predefined standards to address most situations. They will provide the company with tools to be completed by the internal client to be reviewed later by the team. If needed to can scale up or down with the use of consultants. If the demands stay reasonable this works out better financially for the enterprise. Some years the consulting fees, service contracts, and project managers may cost significantly more than a full staffing compliment. One danger of sticking with a small protective services function, is when the organization has a history of high demands for security expertise, faces a crisis to operations or even the wellbeing of employees; and the enterprise cannot demonstrate any enhancements to staffing levels for security in those years, despite corporate size and profit growth.

Global security

In the global security model, the department can embed someone to tackle these requests until they are seen through. They can assign a member to each region, division etc., and for each specialization. In the protective services model the team is required to be generalists. In the global security department, you can develop small teams who are experts in their focus area. This closes many gap, avoid burnout and allows the CSO to think and work strategically. The downside is like any large department, if the demands decrease for a long period of time, the company is carrying full time employees with less work to do and still has the salaries to pay.

Threat risk and vulnerability assessments
Protective services

In the protective services model the team may conduct threat, risk and vulnerability (TRVAs) on behalf of new ventures, new office locations, existing operations, events, executive travel, workplace violence, and more. To effectively conduct global TRVAs with a handful of staff will require the business to be more independent. Following the issuance and explaining (debrief) of the report and recommendations; the tracking and closure of recommendations by other business leaders will be required. The business can use guidelines and checklists from protection services to guide them. In many cases the use of consultants will be required to conduct the reports. Protective services will instead facilitate the process. An advantage of the third-party reports is to ensure that the report has little influence or bias from the inside. If company security conducts the report and are also responsible in part for the state of security, then it is to their benefit to indicate that the premise improve year over year no matter the actual state. Other advantage of the risk consultants is the fresh perspective, risk transfer, and ability to engage or not as the needs and budgets permit. An advantage of the internal team conducting the occasional assessment is that they know the needs of the enterprise, familiarizes them with the internal client, venture or premise, and keeps them in practice.

Global security

In the global security model, the same practices can be conducted as earlier. However, the team once again can employ TRVA experts, who are not distracted with too many other duties. They can manage the entire process and all recommendations through. They can also pass some of the findings off to the project and strategy teams in security to lead to completion.

Security governance
Protective services

Security governance can include policies, procedures, administration, guidelines, standard operating procedures, emergency response plans, and more. Security may be the sole contributor and policy owner or may work on a committee and contribute to polices owned by others. Often in the protection services model the team produces some documents, often reactionary, to needs. Scheduled reviews and updates to these are occasionally a challenge. If the team is generalists, it is hard to assign a permanent content owner. If a team member leaves, the learning curve is another factor to keeping up with this part of strategy and administration. The team are often forced to work agile, work smarter, and provide only what is needed, nothing more. This can also be an advantage to an enterprise that is conscious of resource management. These teams must be both operational and strategic and therefore their ability to consult, audit, and triage problems are their strengths.

Global security

In the global security model, the security leaders often handle a lot of the administration and governance. They may have a small unit and an administrator to help keep up with these. They can produce a compendium of resources for the enterprise. With so much available online today and so much networking between CSOs, there is no need for a very large team to handle this. There is little value in reinventing the wheel. It is also hard to do something completely innovative in this space. If a policy is in response to changes in local laws or customs, then most of the industry will have to conform in a similar way.

Crime prevention
Protective services

Crime prevention can come in many forms. By reaching out and speaking to schools, the community, and police to curb mischief, vandalism, and graffiti. It can come in the form of conducting crime prevention through environmental design (CPTED) audits. A department can host theft and robbery prevention training and provide resources.

Staff personal safety campaigns are another good method of prevention. Target hardening and controls are often deployed as deterrents or preventative measures.

Protection services is often good at conducting audits, responding to trouble areas, providing solutions, and offering staff presentations as needed. If something is to be rolled out globally, in a short-time frame or an ongoing deeper dive or program is needed consultant will need to be placed on retainer or some of the work is pushed out to departments to use the tools from protection services to execute themselves.

Global security

In the global security model a crime prevention specialist or manager is occasionally a full-time member of the department. This member or team often has strong connections to liaison police officers in the communities the company operates. They will network to keep in touch with specific types of crimes, share these with their internal peers, keep premises briefed, and provide awareness training. They will also develop programs to proactively address these matters. They can tailor presentations to each department, facility, and crime type.

Travel security

Protective services

In the protective services model the team will rely on third-party services providers to provide, monitor, and escalate traveler elevated threat and emergent matters. They will reply of employees to use the country reports from the provider. They will give briefings to parties travelling to high-risk destinations and executive events. They will advise on related policies and join the crisis team as required.

Global security

In the global security model, the department often owns the program. They will have a third-party tool to see global risks and track travelers. The GSOC can handle most of the operational work in-house. This will include watching traveler locations live, monitoring alerts, escalating the calls, and managing a portion of crisis. The manager or director of travel risk management and their analyst will coordinate the monitoring provider, ground security, medical service, and other support services. There will be a comprehensive program for training, briefings, threat assessments, and ongoing crisis drills. The company intranet site will have a dedicated page for travelers, with tips, pre-trip briefings, links to downloadable apps, and helpful resources. The travel policy will have details concentration limits and cover all forms of transport.

Employee and executive protection
Protective services

When a small security compliment is found in an organization it can be for several reasons. Two of those could be the company itself is small or the perceived risk is low.

In the protective services model the team may have one member who escorts large groups of employees attending foreign destinations for business, company retreats and award events. They will also be responsible for executive protection abroad. They will supplement with hotel security, hire event security, or close protection professionals.

Global security

In the global security model most of the work is handled by the team. They will have the bodies to send enough people for the task. Some of these people may have other functions when not on assignment. There is usually a dedicated leader of the program.

Event security
Protective services

In the protective services model the team often works with local officials or contract security hired by the company for company events such as the annual general meeting, company picnics, or holiday events. When the city and company are cosponsors or major events take place near the company, someone is seconded to this temporarily as a liaison or project manager.

Global security

In the global security model there will be dedicated resource. They will have a playbook, specific suppliers, and contacts on a roster. The team may often have a dedicated group for protection, events, and travel. Most support functions including threat assessment, security intelligence, and the GSOC may all support these events.

Workplace violence prevention and investigation
Protective services

Protective services are often lean. They will rely on human resources to own the workplace anti-harassment, bullying, and workplace violence programs. The team can provide subject matter expertise to assess pre-incident matters, respond as a third line of defense (security officer first, law enforcement second) after an incident and help to investigate. They can provide short briefs and recommendations.

Global security

Global security may have a few people on staff who have extensive experience and training in behavioral threat assessments and violence response. They will have the resources to offer the enterprise training programs, create detailed governance, write investigative reports, and complete offender profiles.

Security intelligence (situational awareness, insider threat)
Protective services

Protective services will likely rely on contacts, media, and third-party services to provide them with information. Each member assigned to a geographic region, line of business or specialization (protection, threat assessment, workplace violence, systems, etc.) will have their own sources and needs.

Global security

Global security will usually have a director and a couple of analysts permanently assigned to this. They will act as central recourses for the entire department. They will cover financial, cyber, violence, and intellectual protection, intelligence needs. They will act as a single point of contact to private partners and public agencies. These units will use selective service providers with customized services for intelligence relevant to the enterprise and departments mandate.

Where companies do not have a corporate security department, they can always find a qualified security consultant with experience in regional business units or small to medium businesses to help develop governance, assess their operations, and trouble shoot when needed. Many consultants can adjust their level of engagement to suit the fiscal needs of start-ups, warehousing, small corporate, and small industrial, etc.

Subtle actions with big results

As a new security manager, it was not uncommon for me to go running to emergencies. The problem with this, is when you make yourself a part of the emergency or even victim of it, you may not be able to strategically manage it. If you are the most experienced in emergency response or even helped to write the plan, then having you out of commission is a problem. Picture tomorrows' CSO. Sitting in a meeting room when they get an alert on their tablet. They remain seated, very calm to see the alert messages scrolling to the left. They bring up the cameras in the area and link to the nearest officer or operations center for a situation report. They can instruct, or they themselves can use the tablet to lockdown the area in the push of a button. The CSO can bring the crisis committee into a call, send them a video of the scene, and provide a synopsis without having moved. They can link into the conversation with arriving first responders and the head of the guard response team. Completely calm, cool, and collected. All done from a little handheld device. They could be elsewhere on campus or on another continent. By accepting that you can always improve, learn something new, and by using these tools you will be better prepared and more effective to face the future.

Corporate security tomorrow in conclusion

In the next decade many services that companies have relied on by the public sector for years will become common internal resources. Educated and experienced security professional who are strong in risk and strategy will become must have employees. While we trust so many employers to provide a reasonably secure working environment, companies to protect our data, and expect consistent product and service reliability; security will be an essential corporate service. We will need to focus less on the size of the team, the name, and the level of the leader and duties. We need to become driven, highly skilled professionals. We need to focus on the profession. Engineers, accountants, lawyers, doctors, architects, and other professionals do not suffer these identify crisis. Once we agree on a base line education (degree in security and risk management, organization resiliency, or corporate security), license (CPP), and a general single word title may not be possible. An engineer for example is an engineer. They may be a civil engineer or head of engineering, but they are still an engineer. They work in an assigned industry, or you could say engineering. Security is an industry or function. You cannot easily say, I am Michael, a security. Licensed professional could be a baseline title for a degreed (security specialist, security expert, security risk professional). Alternatively, an industry name, if security is abandoned could be used. If security is used, then we will continue to rely on job levels in corporate security, which may include security analyst, security coordinator, security manager, security director, and CSO. Security consultants can also use variations in title. Somehow, I do not think guardian or protector will catch on. Investigators conduct investigations. There are dozens of security occupation titles. Risk titles now have a whole new meaning. Security can also mean information or cyber today. The title security risk advisor today could cause confusion and therefore you may see physical security risk advisor. As seen throughout this book however I believe that someone performing general cyber security, investigation, and physical security advisory services to their company will be one person in the years to come. The United States has used the title special agent in the public sector in a very broad context. The words criminal, intelligence, and investigator have no literal connection to special agent; however, they are synonymous by reputation, use, and tradition. By using the term protection professional from the CPP designation and adopting that to university programs, written definitions separating security officers and other similar specialties such as executive protection, it may define the role better. Here is how this may look:

- University program—protection services
- License—certified protection professional (ASIS International)
- Baseline industry title—protection professional or protection or protector
- Department, team or unit—corporate security (protection services/global security)

As odd as it first sounds, I think protector could catch on easier than guardian, preventer, or defender ever would. You may still have a director, protection services, or vice president protection services. As discussed earlier this role could be embedded with investigations. The title special investigator could be used. I am not sure if this will ever be settled, however the education, license, and expertise should be standardized globally to align better with the other professionals. I think that protection professional will be the term of the future. Industry titles can vary as they have. The professional term protection professional would be designated for the highest level of accomplished practitioner. An accountant may very well be the head of finance, controller, or auditor. A fraud examiner may be an investigator. Their trade name and employers' title do not have to align. Once we aim to be security experts and nothing more and learn to appreciate what an honor that is, we will focus less on proving ourselves and more on keeping people safe.

Could you imagine an anti-money laundering chief kicking down the doors of organized crime with Interpol? I think not. Future corporate security teams will provide global intelligence, they will be smart efficient and will use a structured approach to roll out a best in class security program globally. By personally going out to every premise, every event and trying to connect with all employees in a global organization are just not possible. By modeling ourselves after calming methodical professionals who think in the reverse that we do, we will see a completely different approach to protection. You can run to every employee who is about to cross the road unsafely, or you can proactively send them a training module on how to cross the road and track their participation in a few keystrokes.

Corporate security departments may be comprised of two or two-hundred personnel in the future. What is for certain is that this career will be highly sought after, professional, and in demand. I believe that the number and size of corporate security departments will grow and where they do not exist, then protection professionals employed elsewhere in some enterprise will be highly regarded subject matter experts within existing departments who add even greater value to the enterprise.

A roadmap for success

7

Making sense of it all

Over the past few chapters, we have been introduced to new concepts and different ways of looking at our day-to-day life in corporate security. I began this book by telling you that it was directed at corporate security, chief security officers (CSO) focused in the physical security space. I hope to this point it has helped to create some new dialogue. With so much information, this may apply to each of you who are at different stages in your careers. By taking things step by step you can organize a plan to see what you will need to be successful as a CSO and in building a successful program. Here we can look at your education, certifications, and career progression. We can also look at your department today. How you are going to apply enterprise security risk management (ESRM) and technology including artificial intelligence to jump into the future.

You may be starting to realize that the lines between the roles of the CSO and chief information security officer (CISO) are blurring. We are entering an era where we will see that the future professional protection officers will be educated, well trained, and a capable response force. These officers will understand what a firewall is. They will know that their building and security systems reside on the network and the importance of data center protection. The information security professionals beginning their careers will be introduced to how a building security system works, how they connect to the network infrastructure and how to protect it. Understanding the why is as just as important as being instructed what to do. To tell a security officer to call you if the temperature in the data center goes up and the alarm sounds seem straightforward. But by telling them that without a cool, dry place the servers will fry, then in an emergency, they may be creative enough to apply a temporary solution while help is on its way.

In some cases, one senior executive will oversee the entire security and investigation programs we know today. If you play a role in prevention, response, and organizational resilience today, you will likely be one entity tomorrow. If you're reading this with uncertainty, then worry not. You will be nearly or completely retired by the time this is complete across the board. It is the CSOs of today, who need to ensure they do not stand in the way of progress, and in fact, help make this happen for our successors.

You do not need to stop everything you're doing to completely modernize your program. You also do not have to keep chasing the next best thing. In this case, you may never achieve any sense of purpose or state of normalcy. There may be no need to change the current structure or reporting lines in your department. Adding some structure and steps to areas of your program that will benefit is a good start. For example, if you have several programs, but only one half have clearly defined job descriptions, roles and responsibilities, and processes, you will need to check to see why? Why is one half of your program so well established and defined while the other not? Why do we create full-scale programs, when we were only asked to consult? Let's take workplace violence for example. This is one of the most value-added situations security can assist their enterprise with. Security may consult for human resources (HR) and legal by advising what steps should be taken, direct premise security to be vigilant and ramp up by providing a heads up, offer security awareness training to at-risk departments and assess the offender.

The future will not be complicated, it will be straight forward. Where financial crimes departments pop up in financial services and banking, the head will not be a CSO. It is more likely you will have a separate protection services department formed that will handle security risk assessment and protection matters, while the security systems operations will go to amalgamated GSOCs or facilities. Certified protection professionals (CPPs) will have the skills to identify key risks to the organization in their domains of expertise. This does not mean that if you are a CSO who has their CPP that you can ignore the changes going on around you. Enterprise will no longer need a dozen CPPs and physical security professionals (PSPs) who still work the way we did in 1995. The department may be 2 or 12 personnel. They will simply be issued a phone and a laptop when they start and with the right software services and applications are able to integrate best in class service to their enterprise on a completely digital platform.

As a CSO you will do very little operational and tactical work. Your role is to be at the table with the other business leaders, hear their strategies and needs, and make sure the security mandate and all your work support this. No more, no less.

Assessing the needs of the enterprise

Often a CSO is hired for their experience. Sometimes what we know, are used to or have come to believe is the only way may not be what your enterprise needs. I myself have often referred to past employers as a point of reference. This may be fine on occasion but can become tiresome to your new colleagues. If you were a leader in an enterprise heavily focused on facilities security and join a core corporate security team who focus more on threat assessment, workplace violence, protection, consulting, investigations, and events, then the team will benefit from your experience. You will, however, need to understand that you are not necessarily there to talk about access control. You need to support the programs in place and gauge, at what level the enterprise needs protection. In reverse, if you have come from a large robust, multifaceted corporate security department as a specialist and are now second in command at a smaller department with facilities security focus, then they may simply not want you to build an executive protection program. When the time is right you may educate them on your experience and the value of these programs. You will need to keep in mind what you were hired for; do that specifically, and a good job of that. If the company does take some interest or engage you later in one of those programs, think. Did they ask me to arrange security for one simple event and I just took that as an invite to try to create a million-dollar task force for a program? Remember some companies do not want the henchmen optics. They do not want or need to spend a small fortune on security. If you are their first CSO, there may be three reasons. The company is new, they are being forced to by regulation or legal problems or they have a need. If they have asked you to tell them what they need, they agree to it all and give you a blank cheque, then build away. If they have reluctantly hired you to solve a problem, do not create another one for them by trying to build an empire from day one. If they did not ask you to try to solve the world's problems and you take them all on, you may be disappointed when you don't get the resources you think you need and may, in fact, find yourself unemployed.

The CSO needs to sit down and compile the data from all recent security reviews or have them conducted and organize the findings, key themes, and recommendations. The CSO needs to review their budget, the program budget, and the total physical security spend for the organization. They will need to write out all the key risk indicators (KRIs) and key performance indicators (KPIs) and create an easy to follow dashboard with data comparing the past 5 years, perhaps broken down quarter by quarter. How many incidents related to premise matters/building emergencies are there that have caused business disruption? How many workplace violence, harassment, bullying, and similar matters have you dealt with? Break them down. Petty office theft of company property and or personal effects are important red flags of other problems and can be considered quality of life investigations. How many requests for service, such as assessments and recommendations on travel and events have you received? There are so many factors to consider. You may have had 45 violence investigations (founded and unfounded) with no losses. You may have had an easily avoidable slip and fall at a premise that cost you a million ($1mil.). Refocusing your efforts, funds, and strategy may be in order. Playing bodyguard may be a lot more fun than designing access controls or facilitating training on hazard reduction; however, if that is what the data is telling you, then this is where you will focus. You may have very busy staff, and believe you need more. Having salaried staff spending hours assessing global risks that do not apply to you or conducting surveillance on petty theft may show executives that you may, in fact, be top heavy or overstaffed. You may not always like what the data tells you but need to do the right thing.

You will need to have an occasional formal and informal meeting with different leaders. This may be the head of operations in the production facility, the general manager of your data center or the C-Suite. Be sure that you separate what they don't like such as not wanting you in their businesses seeing problems, creating expense, and enforcing rules. Listen to what they don't like, such as lack of fair engagement from your team, needs not being addressed, and their budget strains. When you implement costs that truly hurt the bottom line, adjust. When you are told your recommendations are costing too much only to see that they want those funds for im-pratical "nice to haves," address it and ignore it. You may simply have advised them to upgrade the alarm system, and if in that case they complain they are cash strapped then they can ask for more money from corporate.

If you set ego aside, collect, assess, and present honest data, accept helpful criticism and do a good job, you will be happier, more effective, and are ready for this next step.

Providing only what is needed

The CSO should sit down with company leaders. Provide them with a snapshot of where the security program rests in terms of spending, size, scope, mandate, and impact. Then explain what you would recommend today and why. Be prepared to almost always be met with several tough questions on needs, funding, intrusiveness, and to back up everything you say with clear facts, benchmarking, and having considered the big corporate picture, not your personal agenda. If your dream was to be a special agent or have your own police force, it is not the responsibility of your employer to help you create that in their security program. Before you present to them, you will have already conducted a needs assessment, threat, risk, and vulnerability assessment and compiled your key metrics. You will have rehearsed, ran it by your critics, reworked it several times, had to let go of things you really liked, and rehearsed again and again. Ask the leaders where the company is headed, where you can add more value and what they really need from you. Now you can form a business case and security strategy that aligns more with the needs of the organization.

For aspiring CSOs you may have worked in another field or moved your way up from guarding to the top. You may have been a corporate security analyst and progressively made your way level by level over the span of your career. It is often much easier for a new CSO to want to do too much or to overshoot the objective. The company wants a security program and you start to recreate the US Department of Homeland Security, not ideal. If you are well versed at building emergency response plans for security officers that is great. You must, however, learn about crisis management, business continuity, and disaster recovery at the enterprise level. What roles people will play in operations, middle management, and the C-Suite? You need to know where people should be and where they should not be, who should be on the line (phone) and at what table. Where do support and authority come from. Most of all you must know what the expectations of you are and what your role is and isn't.

When you are asked to provide a report, provide the best report possible. That may be a seven slide deck or a 15 page word document. Do not use that opportunity for grievances, say "I told you so" or add erroneous information to get your pet projects in front of executives. Provide what you were asked for when you are asked for it. If this is going to be a problem, be open and transparent with your leader. Before you move from one exciting topic to the next, close the task before you. This may require putting your passions on the back burner, telling someone "no" and a few late nights. Corporate security is not a second career to coast along; the role of CSO is not some wise person on the mountain philosophical role. You will need to work both smart and very hard. Most of my peers who are in larger roles than myself can barely find time for lunch or even unplug for just a minute. There is no sense in adding to that burden (the burden of love we have for our profession and really wouldn't have it any other way), by overpromising and under delivering.

If the enterprise only needs and wants a couple of people facilitating a protection program through service providers, then do a great job at just that.

Finding balance

This section will discuss how not to burn out and the ability to delegate, lead, manage, and not to forget soft skills in the CSOs arsenal of tools running a great program. It will remind CSOs to always leave a professional impression. It is important to understand that image and reputation is just as important as our credentials.

Staying motivated from entry-level security management to becoming a global CSO can be challenging at times. There are a number of factors that cause us to become unmotivated, disengaged and burned out. This can cause us to lose sight of our objectives. I will share some practical exercises I have used to help tackle these.

What are some of the reasons that cause us to lose motivation, become overwhelmed, feel underappreciated, and simply check out?

Perhaps for whatever completely understandable reason you did not get to join your law enforcement counterparts, your career in law enforcement was cut short or you simply miss the respect and camaraderie you had during your career as a law enforcement officer (LEO).

Maybe the job is not what you expected, this is not the slow it down retirement gig you thought it might be. There is not a lot of excitement, you thought you would be in a bunker deep below the earth protecting nuclear codes and yelling "I am almost in the mainframe." Maybe there are five corporate security personnel, 550,000 corporate staff at 30 premises and you are burned out.

The list is never-ending. Now take a minute and ask yourself some questions.

- Am I better suited to investigate frauds instead of managing security guards and systems?
- Do I need to upgrade my writing, business, and security leadership skills to do this job?
- Are the problems I am identifying about the politics, people, and my boss the same ones I complained about at the last three places I have worked? It is me, not them?
- Did I do this to myself? Did I take in too much? Did I say yes to please and forgot to ask for the resources to do it?
- Did my business plan get shot down? Was that plan something I was proud of but not at the pedigree of my peers?

I think you have started to see a trend by now. Do not compare yourself to the royal family (the executive committee). You are the white knight (my knights are whatever they identify as and if you do not accept all forms of diversity; I suggest you find another career). When you're ready to stop being a knight (playing and waging battles) and join the very hard working, educated professionals in the C-Suite who may be under immense pressure all the time (it is lonely at the top) then you and only then can you really complain about wage and status disparity. We as professionals need to elevate ourselves together.

Does this sound familiar? You walk in each morning. You get settled. Sift through a barrage of email, check the calendar and realize that you are moments away from winging it in another meeting, just to look up and see people standing at your door who only need a minute which always means 20?

Keep your ambitions for the program and expectations of your team reasonable. Remain agile, know how to ramp up and ramp down. Move with the ebb and flow of demands. Know when to ask for something and when to stay off the radar. Most departments that seem to be running like clockwork are either in shambles behind the scenes or a faulty deck of cards. Everything is just temporary, both the good times and the bad. I suggest that you take one step at a time and make one-minute decisions. Sometimes the 70% solution is reasonable. As you become more experienced, have greater exposure and become confident in yourself, this will be easier. Not every matter needs to be met with a project. A simple yes, no or decision can suffice. When your leaders get to know you and your capabilities, it will instill a sense of confidence in you to do your job more effectively. Knowing when someone is doing the bare minimum at their own demise and when you need to minimize to bring balance to chaos is something that only a seasoned professional can do.

You need to accept that there are just some things beyond your control that you just can't fix. You quite often do not need to overreact, some things just need tweaking, a nudge a subtle response. Tackle it with logic, not emotion. Passion is good, intense, abrasive or down right unprofessional are not. Finding a balance between the hands on head first or the strategic, calm approach is an art form that will bring you a lot of success as a CSO.

Personal development for the chief security officer

Learning is a lifetime practice; we owe it to ourselves and our employers to continue to grow. As a CSO you will need to keep up with the changes in day to day office technology, the advancements in the industry your employer operates in and the rapidly changing security field. The next generation of CSO will all have a bachelor's degree and most likely their ASIS International, CPP designation. It will be up to these leaders to decide on a range of options. Will your masters in business administration (MBA) or masters in security management (or similar) be the next step? Perhaps your annual continuing education is enough. As most experienced CSOs know, the myth about being strategic and having more time as you become the company's most senior security official is often an incorrect assumption. Trying to tackle graduate school as a CSO is a daunting task. You may find that taking the occasional short college program at night or online, attending a week's long professional development course or even taking a few webinars and classes from your security association to meet your continuing professional education courses is hard enough.

Security practitioners often enjoy training. Some corporate training ironically can become monotonous after the seventh time you have completed it. After that, you will see the irony because as the CSO you will have a hand in producing half of that training. Early career security professionals sometimes need and often want full tactical protection courses. If you're still looking at this as a CSO then you're on the wrong track. Taking finance and accounting program is much more valuable. When taking courses offered by your association, remember that a CSO needs to understand the future, business, leadership, and new ways of doing things. Physical, tactical, and operational courses are not for you. There is an exception when a CSO comes from an academic or business background, they should catch up with some short courses and seminars on the fundamentals.

If embarking on a graduate degree, make sure you are the type of person who is extremely focused and disciplined. Know yourself and be honest with yourself. I have seen many lost professionals having their employer pay for courses up front that they never completed. I will tell you from experience, that taking a university program or designation while working as a CSO is harder than you think. This is something you must discuss with your manager, team, and most importantly your loved ones. You will be carrying textbooks everywhere you go. You will be studying almost every night of the week into the late hours. You will need to keep up with your other obligations. If it will interrupt your employer's needs before exam time, that is not your employer's problem. Use vacation time, cut out social affairs and extracurricular activities for a while so you don't crash or fail.

I suggest trying to limit your designations to one. Know that designation well and keep up with it. If you moved around departments in corporate security and earned different designations according to different roles and then worked your way up designations to an industry gold standard one, then focus on that top certification that is now most relevant to you as an aspiring or new CSO. If you are already a CSO then know your material. Do not walk out of the exam and forget everything. Keep those books on the bookshelves and go through them occasionally, use them as reference material and keep up with new versions.

A CSO must continue to learn formally and informally, it is a privilege and joy. Learning is not a competition; we want everyone else in this industry to be recognized as experts and referred to as professionals. Share, network, and collaborate.

Giving back to the security community

A good way to continuously keep the materials you have learned top of mind is to volunteer and moderate study sessions for those cramming for exams to earn a professional designation. Contact your local chapter and start today. The repetition of creating, reviewing, and teaching the material will benefit you in a few ways. The chance to help inspire and support the next generation of leaders will only benefit everyone involved. There are security meet ups, associations, and similar groups around the world. Getting involved by attending, actively participating, and rotating through board positions are great for your career and more importantly, help the industry.

If you participate on committees to support private and public partnerships, help write a new or to update existing industry standards and guidelines or simply pay your dues and show up, it all counts. During the times I have personally felt frustrated and was not sure what to do with my security program or career when I was younger, attending a meeting with peers who were faced with the same challenges, some behind me on the journey and some ahead, I felt much better. You will occasionally find your next superstar employee or even your next employer. Try to volunteer for the comradery and in the best interest of others. Don't always look for a personal angle. Just doing a great job will help you find some personal satisfaction.

Starting an informal email, telephone, or occasional meeting group (or all the above) with your geographically closest security leaders, creating one for your premise security manager and their peers can go a long way for the local business community.

The power of networking

Security leaders are quite good at formal and informal networking. What was the occasional coffee meet up or association event 20 years ago, morphed into many formal options to connect? Now virtual meet ups, social networking sites, and a greater demand to stay connected and informed have changed the landscape. As a CSO it is not only important to keep connected and benchmark with your local industry peers but to also seek other CSOs from other geographies. Being able to reach out to collaborate, provide information during large-scale crisis, and to leverage practices to keep people safe are just a few good reasons to reach out. Waiting to call your neighbor when you are already in trouble is not a good practice. Asking people for information or help on a cold call may take time. At times security leaders can get caught head down working for a long period of time. Some choose to look inward and work in a vacuum. This often leads to problems. Networking is also about sharing, a two-way street. You cannot always ask or listen and never share back. Networking should happen, appropriately at all levels in your department with their peers.

Connecting with other department heads in your company is also important. You can learn a lot about the organization, support one another, and keep you ear to the ground better. Having contacts outside of the CSO or even security space is also important. It will help to change your perspective, open your mind to new ideas and make you well rounded by talking to academics, professionals, and business leaders.

Is your team assessing the risk of a country you have little experience with? It is not uncommon you have an event planner, investment banker, leader, account executive, or another colleague who has traveled there. Work your internal intelligence network for sources. Many people in the company have great insight and can surprise you. Large organizations have multiple languages, interesting backgrounds, and experiences to leverage. Remember to say thank you.

If you are an accomplished CSO then you are probably familiar with networking. Don't be afraid to speak to your peers or internal peers in like departments. For aspiring and new CSOs, I suggest you start small, reach out, and make it a positive ongoing dialogue. Networking can bring a lot of enjoyment and benefits and is a great tool to use often.

Rethinking your limits

Sometimes we limit ourselves. We allow others to set limits and expectations for us. Occasionally, you are pushed into something new, out of your area of expertise and even your comfort zone, and we not only survive but flourish. Setting reasonable goals, timelines, and expectations are acceptable. To expect that you will become a CSO of a global corporation with little to no education or experience may not be realistic. You need to set a game plan, continuously reevaluate it and charge ahead. Sometimes expecting a company to give you several more full-time employees because that is what the neighbors have or to promote you because you just stayed is not realistic.

If you told me that I would need to grasp basic accounting 20 years ago, I may have turned and ran. Now that I understand the basic principles of managing a responsible budget, finances for security project management or creating a business case, I know that you too can do it. I am not afraid to admit when someone on my team knows more than me presents better than me or is simply more passionate about something. I know when to step back and let someone else do their thing. I also know enough to work hard to improve where I am lacking and close those gaps. There is no cannot, only a someday soon.

It takes a certain type of person to be a lifelong career professional. You may not have set out on this path originally but instead ended up there. I hope that 1 day careers in security leadership or consulting will be a goal right from the time someone is choosing education programs out of high school. If you had another dream but ended up in security, then you may believe you have limits. Limits about learning, specific subjects, and careers. If you are restricted physically perhaps, I believe that this may 1 day be something many will overcome with advancements in medicine. If you had trouble in math, daydreamed in school, and woke up a 25-year-old security manager, fear not. With a positive attitude, hard work, focus, and a good teacher you can accomplish things you never believed. Whatever you got stuck in your head or someone or system told you in grade school is probably wrong. Push yourself to do great things, ask security leaders about their back story. You may meet a CSO who is quite impressive, I can assure you many of them are great people. Most of them probably have not practiced medicine, engineering or went to space. However, they are very smart, hard working, and have what you have. Many security professionals have a distinct way of thinking and personality that give us an interesting view of the world and how things work. Do you notice you may be just a little more street smart, intuitive or have that sixth sense others don't? Do you see risk, hazards, and perils everywhere, in fact, you cannot shut it off? Don't change your way. Embrace it, encourage it, and enhance it with the right training and education. Living a life of protecting people, corporations, and preventing all kinds of loss sounds quite noble indeed.

A healthy lifestyle, a good attitude, and the desire to do something great are what you need to get started. Take one small task, identify or have others share with your areas that you could improve. Ask for help. Take it one step at a time. Complete it; see it all the way through, no quitting. I know you can do it.

Being a great mentor

Throughout your life, you will have many opportunities to be a mentor. This could be for a moment or lifetime. You don't need to put a label on it or make it too formal. There are times when you will be a mentor to your friends and family when you're coaching or teaching. Making yourself available to young security professionals, new security professionals, and aspiring CSOs can really make a difference in someone's life. When I was a young professional I had no family who I could ask about the security field. I entered security management and was a tad lost by some aspect of my role. Often it was a coffee with a seasoned professional after a meeting or a phone call for some advice that turned into a mentoring relationship. I have had the great pleasure of speaking before college students studying to enter this field for several years now. I openly offer all students to connect and reach out to me. Have you ever said to yourself "If I only knew then, what I know now"? Of course, you have. Imagine someone following in your footsteps. They eagerly ask you for direction or advice. On occasion, you tell them about courses and career options they have never heard of. You tell them about different ways of advancing in those careers and where it could lead to, how to steer away from trouble, and how to shine. Just think if some of them follow that advice and can avoid some heartache and take a couple of small short-cuts along the way. Imagine you can see their success.

In every person's life, I believe knowingly or unknowingly they will mentor someone. I think that we all should do this. Have you ever had a mentor, a leader, a real or fictional hero you looked up to? Think of what they did, what they said, and how they behaved that inspired you. What if your mentees had someone to turn to, someone who would encourage them, keep them on the right path, never judge or scold but positively redirect? Imagine you could be that person for them. The last thing any CSO wants to do is to struggle to speak about how professional their career is. If we all gave back to the industry, put our best foot forward and help to mold the generation of security professionals behind us, then they too will inspire others. In that case we would not have to sell anything, our value and reputation would speak for itself.

Mentors are patient, have good moral character, and are willing to share their knowledge and experiences. It does not take hours of sitting down going over all the do's and don'ts of life or how to maneuver the business world in a classroom. If you can take the time to provide sound advice, be a good listener and keep up the positive reinforcement you may change someone's life. We all need someone in our lives we can soundboard off. We need to be inspired by people who have gotten to where we are trying to go. People who stumbled and fell and got back up again persevered and tried again. You must remind them; you will make mistakes, make few, make them small, don't repeat them and learn from each one.

A mentor never takes advantage of the relationship, is always professional and leads by example. A mentor does it for personal satisfaction because it is the right thing to do and nothing else. I hope to see more educational programs, security publications, and associations engaging in mentoring, job shadowing, and pairing up of learners and professionals. I wish you the best of luck with this.

Having great mentors

Many CSOs can reflect on a parent, family member, someone they looked up to when they were growing up, such as coaches, teachers, managers, and many more. When they looked you in the eye and gave you that great advice, acknowledged you, you gained their attention, interest, or respect. If you think about it, from the time you were young to present day you have probably had a dozen great mentors. There are many expressions about the people you surround yourself with. These are often true. I can honestly say that at this stage of my career, I can think of a few accomplished CSOs that I admire and believe that although they have reached the summit of security leadership there is still a great person, athlete, business titan or loved one they look up to, can confide in, and seek answers from. We all need our person; we need our friends, and just as important a mentor.

Some of you will be lucky enough to look at your current manager, past managers or seek one who is also a mentor. You want to go to work each day to learn, be inspired, and share a common interest. If you can find that in your leader then you are quite lucky and should count that as one of the many positives in your role. You will miss it once it changes. As you get older selecting who you want to work for is just as important as all the other things you will consider in that equation. If you have the best job in the world but work for a tyrant, then you won't enjoy it for a moment. You may look up to people in your life and later see a flaw, if they are simply human but still a great role model for you, then that is even better, it makes it more obtainable. You will also realize some people that you looked up to, were not someone to follow and will steer clear of that in the future.

At this stage in my career, I look less for security mentors and find myself gravitating to people who have lived a good life, have conquered things that I have not or may never, but want to learn. I look to people who will help me expand my self-awareness. Some constructive feedback can sting, but welcome it and learn from it, make the change. Let your mentor know you have thick skin and that you want to hear it from them, rather than from someone when it's too late, like when you don't get the job, promoted or simply make an error in judgment.

I look back from time to time and laugh. I wish I could apologize to several of my mentors and leaders, laugh with them at what blunders I may have said or did and thank them for their patience. When I was a young manager I often observed behavior that did not reflect my image for the department. Two things occurred in time. Instead of scolding and handing out penalties, I realized that I too was a young manager and doing a hundred things wrong. Secondly, I look back to times when I was simply lectured by my leaders and realized a younger version of me would have possibly terminated me for less. Therefore, I now know the value of unspoken lessons. Sometimes it is what a mentor does not say is the entire lesson you need. I would like to thank my coaches, my peers, and leaders who simply took the time to encourage me, just have a pep talk, coffee or even left me a friendly piece of advice that has stayed with me forever.

Anyone can be a CSO

If you have a heartbeat, then you have a shot. One thing I love about going to the ASIS International GSX Security Conference is the diversity. There is still a lot of work to be done in every industry and I hope we will all support this. I have met heads of security from many different backgrounds, genders, and other differences. This makes me very proud to be a part of such a diverse global community. There are heads of security with disabilities and those who grew up on each side of the tracks. I see some of the most incredible and professional women taking on more and more senior leadership roles in security and people of every generation working together with common interests. I love sitting in a row of people on one side of me who all served their country and a team of academics to the other side, now all with the same career, similar titles, and the exact same challenges.

If you are determined and willing to give it your very best, then you really do have a good chance of being a head of security. Diversity and inclusion are critical two elements in the future success of any company. CSOs need to make sure their programs, departments, and team reflect this, support this, and are champions and ambassadors for it. We need to be the people that others turn to when they are facing discrimination; we need to set a positive example for everyone. I don't think it stops with saying it or hiring fairly. I think we need to go out on a campaign to attract diverse talent. To make sure everyone knows how great this industry is and that we want the best of the best no matter what differences they may have.

We must speak up about pay equality and help to design workplaces, including security that can accommodate everyone, as a visitor, employee, and even security operator. Don't just send your team for training on first aid or defense classes. Offer them training in sign language or cultural diversity. I believe that with so many security professionals around the world we have a huge opportunity to make a major impact on society and to help effect some real change.

Office engagement

Earlier in this book, I referred to office politics, knowing yourself, and personalities of security managers. These are all important in office politics. Take a good long look in the mirror and if you're not seeing it, ask some people, is it me or them. When I was starting out, my lack of maturity and self-awareness brought on a lot of feedback and quite frankly it stung, and therefore, I argued all the feedback. Now I have listened and been able to tone down my personality to a small degree. Relationships are important. We need to understand that if we want the respect, the role, the title, credentials then we need to adjust to the culture of the office and take it down a notch. Your amazing title and resume all mean nothing if everyone thinks we act like buffoons.

As a security leader, you will often have staff. The people need to be managed, led, and should want to come to work each day and report to you. People leave bad bosses and you can shrug it off as you will, but it will catch up to you. If you must fake nice, perhaps being an individual contributor is better for you. Demonstrate behavior that you want your staff to follow. Play by the rules, treat others with respect and remember to be friendly not friends. If you choose the right people, treat them properly and show them the right path then you know they will represent themselves, you, the department, and company well too. You will be proud of them, be able to stand behind them during challenges and know you have made a difference in their lives.

I have found that my colleagues and peers have had great influence on me. There will always be that one, that person everyone wants to steer clear of including yourself. This is not always possible, if you're the CSO, then you may need to address the person with human resources. My colleagues have taught me a lot, especially those other team leaders who I consider good friends who share what is happening in their part of the company, how things work and what drives them. I know that keeping yourself even, being able to truly listen to what someone is really saying and knowing when and how to read the room is critical to saving yourself some embarrassment. Don't feel the need to speak, just listen. Get involved, go for lunch, join the committee, play in the tournament and remember that everyone will look to you as the CSO as a role model for good manners. If you get involved, make some friends and keep engaged with the company you will really enjoy coming to work each day a lot more.

The boss, most of us have one and I can honestly say that they have made a great impression on me. In the past decade of I have reported to both security experts and great business leaders. They have played a large role in my success and I owe them a lot of thanks. Stay in touch with you leaders, if you had a healthy, professional relationship, then the connect does not have to become lost when one of you moves on. Reporting to a non-security expert is good too. I have been able to learn some incredible things, been exposed to projects and concepts I would have never had the chance to if I only thought about security and wasn't given the opportunity. Keeping an open dialogue with your leader, knowing what their passions and pet peeves are is important to the dynamic. You may have to manage up and must remember that they are much busier and under more pressure than you are.

Office politics sounds like a dirty word, one used by former friends and staff of mine who could not look inward or repeated mistakes daily. Don't be the office jerk. People need to come to security to confide in. They need to know security is there to protect them and to know they will do the right thing. I suggest that you just simply go to work and try to make it a good experience for those around you. It will come back to you with rewards that you may not have yet discovered.

How do I know what we can be doing better?

You are now leading a security program; you have some resources and specialists working diligently. You have established an identity for your department, a clear mandate, and things are moving along. Somehow, you know there is more that can be done, some tweaking and adjusting to make things a little better. You can and should benchmark, conduct an internal review and speak to your leaders. I would also strongly recommend engaging a global risk consultancy. Have them take a holistic look at your entire department and program and come back with some recommendations. You have spent years conducting or facilitating reports and handing recommendations to others. From experience, you know well how that works. Now it is time for us to taste our own medicine. Keep an open mind. You don't have to like what you hear but should take it under consideration.

Governance, oversight, and accountability of corporate security and the CSO are good practices. You may have outside consultants telling you things that save you time and money. They may support ideas you have been saying all along. An independent, unbiased report is worth its weight in platinum. Make sure that they have access to the right people, enough time, and understand your business. I know that this can be a positive experience and expect that you will too.

My team has been restructured

Sometimes you are a part of the change and sometimes you're not. Sometimes you know it is coming or maybe not. You can lead the change or be advised. You leave Friday night as the director of corporate security, reporting to the head of facilities, focused on premises and wake up Monday morning as the global head of protection services reporting to the chief operating officer (CSO), concerned with world issues. First, you must ask is this change good or bad. Was our move in part to us falling behind, becoming irrelevant, and being swept down under a lower level of the organization? Did we fail to adapt to the changing tide for the company who is growing or trimming? Did you not line up with what your former leader kept asking? Perhaps this is a good move, your department profile has been elevated and the company needs a stronger, more focused group to manage crisis and risk. Either way, you need to understand why, course correct, step aside or ramp up, and give it your all.

You have lost bodies, you are in a hiring freeze or you're on hold for the new tools. This is when you must be very creative. We cannot install new systems this year. Then update your decks and offer training on everything to everyone. You had two staff leave and cannot replace them, then speak to your leader, perhaps a weekly report can become a quarterly report. I have seen teams of two or three comprised of well-credentialed, hard-working experts who work smart, efficiently, and do only exactly what is needed, run better programs than some with 20 personnel. Amazingly I had heard those teams of 20 talk about how short they are constantly. As a CSO you must deal with issues. Sometimes you need to put someone on the team in their place, get the person who is not working motivated or move them out. That weak link can be your undoing. It is not the responsibility of your team to put up with it, HR to deal with it or your bosses' problem when it boils over.

If you're a trustworthy, mature, confident, and an all around good CSO, you will be in the loop with restructuring, may help to create it and they will keep you well informed. Lead the change.

Advice for new CSOs

I can say from some experience, listen, and observe. Early wins are great but slow down. Assess, ask why, and take some time to understand. You have a lot to learn. Don't make change for the sake of it, don't make a change just because you think it is wrong. Ask why, think about what they have done about this in the past, what resources they have and what other noncore security work they are expected to do. I admit security does not always get a lot of respect, but they sure are the chore department. You need to be grey, learn all about the company, its leaders, and strategy. Just help, manage the program, and observe. Make hard decisions later; don't overload the team with your vision. They have day jobs. They may not want to move into the 23rd century with you.

Were you hired to make sure that building security is impeccable at every premise? Then stop talking about fraud investigations and executive protection. Do the job you were hired to do very well. I have made every mistake and I have had to admit to it. Don't ostracize yourself with being the teacher's pet or being a security snob. I know that by reading this book you are looking to improve and you need to remember they always need to see the best of you if your best isn't good enough then work on improving. A little humility and civility are important when you're a CSO. Connect with your peers and listen carefully to your leader. You are an advisor and an employee, find that balance.

Advice for retiring CSOs

In the past couple of years, some great CSOs have retired. They continue to be available to their peers, support the industry, and inspire thousands. After 20 years, and even today I still look to the CSOs who have paved the way for us; those who continue to lend an ear and give some advice. After retirement, those who go out and live life remain very engaged and positive are doing a great thing for the industry. I suggest those of you who are nearing the final chapter keep this in mind. We hope you consult, teach, attend events, and become ambassadors for the continued efforts to elevate this as a profession and help us attract top talent.

Stand behind your colleagues

Earlier I spoke about the importance of supporting one another. Personalities aside, every professional, every expert, and security leaders of all levels and places bring value to the field. It is not uncommon to see one of our colleagues speaking on the news about a local crime or a terrorism arrest. I say shame on those of us who choose to start questionings their lack of field experience and law enforcement credentials. If the speaker is not embellishing or outright lying, then they may very well be an expert on that very topic. After spending 20–30 years in the field, earning credentials, attending specialized training, being invited to the table with emergency service leaders to plan major events, having security clearances and spending a thousand hours on crime prevention, I would say that is quite a bit. Unbeknownst to many of us that colleague may have consulted for public services, certified as an expert witness or has a unique passion on that very subject. Perhaps they wrote a book, lecture or belong to a council and are exposed to the best and current information on the subject. It may be impossible for us to know what our colleagues experiences are. They very well may be an expert on the topic. Try not to be judgmental and negative. Instead listen to them with an open mind. Supporting them will in turn elevate our profession. You don't have to agree, but try accept and even embrace one another's differences.

Every time we don't stand behind a fellow professional or worse take them down a notch we are hurting the image others have of us. People should appreciate the thousands of hours each one of us spends learning and working in this field. Everyone will have a guard who makes a tough arrest, a lapse in judgment or gets a raw deal at work. For some of us it will be public, while for many no one will be the wiser. I applaud those with the guts to become a consultant, work hard to earn a living, and are willing to step before the cameras and be judged by armchair juries and #tags.

The next time your colleague is on screen trying to help non-security experts make sense of a senseless crime, say "hey, there is my colleague." Instead of talking about someone's personality flaws or lack of perfection in one of the dozens of expert domains; instead, comment on what they are great at. This will only help to improve how you project yourself and portray people with similar careers, credentials, and interests.

Be a technology innovator

My name is Michael and I have an internet addiction. I have spent countless hours watching innovation videos online. Some of the ideas, concepts, and gadgets for the future home and office amaze me. I want the robot who sorts things for me, just because. When I see someone typing the same two rows of data, scanning for days on end looking for problems, entering data, completing the same templates over and over and over it concerns me. Humans can only do human things. But long monotonous tasks can lead to fatigue and disinterest. If you sit down with some software developers, application suppliers, and people who automate these tasks, have them help you do one simple project, I cannot tell you how life changing that is. The feeling is great. Technology is expensive, well yes new; starting out technology that is being developed can take a lot to get going. Once it has hit the masses, has a large client base, faces global competition and is refined, it can become quite affordable. When we all look carefully at the security technology, office software and new ways of doing things we may be surprised. You really need to take a bold leap. You need to be a pioneer. Encourage your team to embrace these tools, to become experts with them and maximize the potential. Be creative, get uncomfortable.

An ASIS leader, security executive, ambassador of convergence, and colleague of mine once told a story about recognizing he had someone smart in his midst. He gave them an uninterrupted workspace; the right tools and a problem to solve, and low and behold with some ingenuity they solved the problem with a simple technological innovation. This was not just a security matter but a business matter. You never know when you can leverage the company's expertise and tools or when you can use your tools to solve business problems. Hunt for those opportunities. In the next few years things will change rapidly, don't go to your next conference and sit in the same five sessions you have for the past few years. Go to learn about something cutting edge, get excited about it, and become an innovator.

Now what?

I believe that many people reading this are aspiring or current CSOs. I am confident that having higher education, the highest credential or designation offered in your area of expertise and putting a serious effort into moving up progressively in the field are helpful steps and assets for a CSO. If you do not have one of these or are not yet doing this, then get started.

Do you have a program that is doing the status quo? Are you working in the technological dark ages? Take the time to catch up on where you need to get to. Make a game plan; ask your leader for help. Take just one step. Think about how much effort that really took. Write down the benefits. Then repeat this by moving forward again. It won't be easy; it may take some hard work. Do you want to leave a legacy or just show up to work?

Grab every piece of literature, attend every webinar, lecture, and conference and become an expert in ESRM. If you need to ask peers for help, engage a consultant. Make ESRM a part of how you run your operations.

Do you lead a program in a large corporate security department, head up security at a major premise? Do you want to be a CSO in a fortune 500 company? Look for opportunities to work for one, reach out and ask one to be an occasional mentor. Go see them speak, visit with them, get to know their story. Tell everyone that this is your goal, your dream. Make it happen.

Are you a CSO who wants to become that renowned expert? Looking to build the best security program in your industry? In today's world, you must embrace the digital world. You need to gather data, develop metrics, and create dashboards that tell your story. Choose three things and become great at them. Use an intelligence-based risk model to make wise decisions to elevate your department. Do not always look at making a large department, but one that is very efficient and has a high output. Make a list of things your program could do better and another of what you should start doing. Pick one of each list every year and set that goal up on the board for the whole team. See them through.

Running toward the future with confidence

For many years changes in security were slow. Adapting to new laws, techniques or technology was easy. Major changes took several years each. Wearable watches that allow you to take a call, a thousand maps in the palm of your hand and the ability to view your cameras a thousand miles away on a hand-held device have long been here. I don't think you read the manual for most of these things. You received them, played with them, picked up some tips and away you went. Most of what you will be using in your role will be much the same. Natural disasters will occur, the conflict will continue, and crime will happen. You can do something about it. There are millions of public and private sector professionals around the world banned together to prevent, detect, deter, and respond to these matters. You are one of them. This is a very exciting time, a time to be proud of being a security leader. There are so many incredible discoveries about to happen and we can be a part of it. I hope that you will not cautiously peer through the open door but instead burst through it with anticipation.

Team building

Every company, culture, department, and leader will have their own version of team building. We often get caught up in the daily grind, find ourselves running to catch our transit home and deal with our own lives. There are many great things you can do to encourage team building, such as team decorating contests for various holidays, theme days, friendly safe outings, town halls, lunch-ins, and much more. Contact peers, other department heads, and HR. See what you can do, clear it with the boss, and make it a point to remember that you are managing people. Form an office social committee, have them engage the team and plan an event. It could be a picnic at the park, pizza with a guest speaker or movie night. Respect others level of comfort and participation and be sure to know when the staff are having a good time and need time to connect without the boss around.

Maybe you're the only security person? Can you organize a team building event for your boss's other reports? How about for department heads with similar roles?

A night out for CSOs from other companies you know? Inject some positive down-time into your routine that reminds you of the great things about our careers and colleagues.

Don't get caught up in the change cycle

Some of us embrace change, while others avoid it. Some are pushed into it and it is sink or swim. At some point, you will find yourself in a state of change. Sometimes companies begin to cut expenses, jobs, and amenities. A CSO tries to tow the company line may try too hard to please their leaders and forget when to stop. In time you will be working with a skeleton crew, have few resources and have lost your impact. As your service levels to the enterprise degrade, you may become forgotten or drop the ball.

Some CSOs are great at leading change. They can personally adapt to technology very quickly. They can conceptualize a project and then run with it. They are always looking for a better widget, doohickey or method. Even when the 70% solutions must do, they are looking for the next best thing. The team cannot adapt quick enough to the new way, new tool or constant projects. Their day to day responsibilities suffer, because the boss has such grand ideas. A grand idea still takes time to come to life. Know when to embrace the future and change and know when to upgrade and get back to work.

Facing a crisis

CSOs are often great at talking about a potential crisis. They plan for it, practice for it, and use its potential to sell part of their program. Then one hits. You may be thrown into the C-Suite with all eyes on you. You will be faced with very tough, rapid decisions. Shut the entire plant down and evacuate? Call the feds or not? Pay the money or not? These can be career-making or breaking moments. Sometimes the best-laid plans don't work out like you thought they would. A boxer enters the ring with a grand plan and then they get hit and realize the other athlete had a plan of their own. Sometimes the crisis is yours and before you can react you're on the hot seat. When a breach of perimeter, systems or secret occur, you can easily get so caught up on the defensive or "how did this happen" that you forget to close the crisis and do damage control. Focus on doing great damage control for your employer, not your career, that latter should fall in place. If your employer does not want 100 armed guards on site. Perhaps, like many companies, your employer needs to do business on the internet, then it will be hard to blame you when you are faced with a formidable adversary armed with a cell phone and shoestring budget. We all need to stay focused, realistic, and stick together. Solve the problem, don't pass blame. Move on and prepare better for the next one.

Know what is a trend, a fad, and the future

I have seen the security industry try to rebrand everything from our industry name, programs, titles, courses and more. I have see it come back full circle again. I have seen people jump on trends drummed up by salespeople, spend a lot of money and lose large investments. I have seen an isolated case of crime; create a fad that fizzled as quickly as they have come along. Make sure you're not investing in the same thing just repackaged and rebranded. Is this method or technology being used by others? Is it tested, coming from a credible source? Is my company using this application enterprise-wide? Are my peers using this or was it a small one-off moment of excitement? Poor buying decisions can end reputations or careers. The seller does not often sit down concerned about the potential risks for you. You may not always want to be the first to invest, but also don't want to be last to make the change. It will take some research, experience, and time to make these decisions better. Knowing what the future way or product is and knowing how to take hold at the right time is an art form. Make simple, informed decisions and keep your program prepared for the future.

Being a leader, not a proverb

In today's world, many great leaders really inspire us. They have a dream, a vision, and give great speeches. They speak publicly much more than in the past and have many ways to connect with us. Most of us gravitate to someone who is positive, motivating, and exciting. As a future CSO, you will have likely grown up in a time when many leaders have had to win popularity contests and received a million likes online. There is nothing necessarily wrong with this.

As a CSO you may look to these great business titans, read their books, follow their mantra, and study their videos. Maybe you follow them online and subscribe to their quote of the day. Having roles models is great. We must make sure that while we are actively working as global heads of security, what we say makes sense. Inspiring people with motivational speeches is great. Trying too hard to make the history books not so much. A longtime well accomplished CSO who has been there, done that is almost expected to pass along words of wisdom. But a mid-level career manager who speaks to their company or team in slogans may begin to lose the audience and end up sounding like a fortune cookie. Try to be original, keep it to a minimum and keep it relevant.

Small acts of heroism

Nearly a decade ago I was walking back to the hotel in Calgary, Alberta with my manager Dave Sulston and Tim O'Neil who was with the RCMP at the time. We were walking toward the rush hour crowd on a busy sidewalk. Distracted and lost in thought, as usual, I stepped off the curb to avoid people (a bad habit of mine) and right in front of a city bus coming from behind me. Tim grabbed me in a split-second, and yanked me back onto the sidewalk as the bus whizzed by. I honestly tribute Tim with saving my life that day.

Many people believe to credit someone with saving our life they must be a brain surgeon or a soldier who saved you from a hail of bullets, in the heat of battle. In fact, security offers steer people away from near misses every day. Everyday heroes like software engineers and other similar experts will find ways to help stop distracted driving accidents. Soon we will need to train security personnel about distracted deaths, such as people taking selfies near cliffsides, people walking toward escalators with augmented reality, heading toward train tracks playing scavenger hunt video games, walking across the street or parking lot looking at phones and wearables.

Losing a child in public is an absolute nightmare. Sometimes children think hiding in a rack of clothes is hilarious. You can catch all the shoplifters in the world but finding one missing child is worth all the cameras in the world when setting up in your local department store. Security guards chasing skateboarding kids away seems silly until that kid is suffering a concussion on the concrete, then someone will ask where security was at the time, the youth was injured. Executive protection specialists are sometimes party poopers when they deny a trip, night venture, etc. They know what dangers lay out there and don't want you to be another statistic. If I ever have an accident while working I am very happy there are tens of thousands of first aid trained security personnel, and one is almost never more than 100 yards away.

You're on your way

Ultimately, I hope that by now you want to be a great CSO who is ready to lead into the future. I encourage you to seek expert material on some of the topics highlighted here. Get the conversation started, do a little critical thinking, and see what others think about these topics. Remember when you first looked at that name on your degree, designation, offer letter or desk? Keep that as a great memory and something that drives you. Go back to that day one feeling, that day one ambition and enthusiasm. Have you joined an association, attended an event or read a trade magazine? If not, I suggest you get started. If you have, then get involved, write, speak, volunteer. Have you done all of this? Are you already a CSO? Try leaving the notebook for a week. Enter everything into the calendar, make a note or put it into a spreadsheet immediately. On the fly? Use your phone to make a note, send an email to yourself or even make a quick voice note.

You know what to do, where to find the information and most of all you know what you want. The future is exciting, and you are well on your way to doing great things. Best of luck, I will see you in the future.

Helpful checklists

This section is focused on people working to be subject matter experts, other department heads (business continuity, investigations cybersecurity, information security (CISOs) and or CSOs of protection services, corporate security and global security). It provides some suggestions to help them throughout their career. You can choose to ignore them, try them all or modify them to fit your needs.

As mentioned earlier in this book there are many entities that have formed associations or groups solely focused on providing professional designations, certifications, fellowships, and chartered standings. There are multiple levels for hotel professionals, hospital, marine, college and university, and protection officers. You can choose to work your way up all the certifications in your industry, you may do this and then do a chartered or other designation which may be the highest standard in your region. Perhaps you want to work your way up the four ASIS International designations and be a quadruple crown. Perhaps at this stage in your busy career, it may be wise to simply achieve the highest one designation available. Here are some tips to not only earning a designation but also get a higher test score, feeling very confident before the exam, and remaining strong in knowing the materials afterward.

Earning a professional designation

- Explore what designation path or single designation is best for you.
- Consider (in some cases this is required) joining the association who offer this program.
- Reach out and speak to a couple of people who hold those or that certification.
- Read the materials offered online to understand the outline of the materials, topics, and exam(s). Make sure this is right for you.
- Use official, privately made or local chapter produced practice exams to see where you stand in your current knowledge base.
- Enroll in a local study group, join a discussion group online, seek videos, and other methods of learning. If these are not available in your area, seek a mentor in person or online.
- Do not set out just to earn letters attached to your name. Set out to learn something that interests you, to do great on your test(s) and to become a true lifetime expert.
- Get the materials and start to familiarize yourself with them.
- Apply for the designation and set an exam date. Do not set it too soon or you may see that life gets in the way. If you have other designations, are savvy at multiple choice tests, and are very disciplined at self-learning and self-study then you may be ready to write earlier. If you book too far out, you may procrastinate until the last minute.
- Take a book with you on your portable device or on hand everywhere. On the way to and from work on public transit, on vacation, and even have a copy just in case in the trunk. You never know when you can grab a few minutes to read.
- Read alone, out loud, slowly. Absorb the material. Make some notes, highlight sections.
- Record yourself reading it, play it back in the car, etc. Actively listen, don't zone out.
- Once you have read through the material thoroughly twice, obtain or make yourself PowerPoint slides. Condense the sections or domains into 3–4 small decks each. Extract the most critical points. In the last month read these continuously.

- Pick up material on how to master multiple choice exams. Immediately eliminate the answer that is obviously wrong. Look for the best choice. Then read the second and third a couple of times. Eliminate the least likely from that one. Then take the best two and reread the question and those options again. Make the right choice.
- Before the exam, there are two types of people. Those who need to pull all-night study drills for a couple of weeks, take a couple of days off work and cram. Then stop a day or two before. Then there are those like me. Study to the last-minute walking into the exam room and then unload it as quickly as you can onto the system.
- Once you pass, continue to refer to this material and the updated versions of it regularly.

This next list which is also only a guideline is for core corporate, physical, cyber or information security specialists. There are many ways to go about this.

Becoming a security specialist

- Find, enroll and complete a short beginner's course in that field and specialization.
- Seek entry-level employment with the intent to commit to that role as a learning opportunity.
- Complete all the required training and seek opportunities to do more, get rounded experience, and find a niche you enjoy.
- If possible, make a progressive move from analyst to a coordinator or individual contributor to team lead or supervisor etc.
- Complete an entry-level designation when you have the qualifying period of employment completed.
- Join the relevant association, network, and read the trade papers and journals.

Within the 5–6 year period, you will be a specialist.

After having become a specialist, you may want to work on a specific practice area such as system design, protection, threat assessment, etc. You may or may not at this time pursue larger leadership responsibility. To become an expert, you will need to be able to demonstrate the right level of education, experience, and exposure. There is no formula. You will know when you get there.

Becoming a security expert

- Complete a variation, if not more of the checklist covered in the list of considering in becoming a security specialist.
- Complete a full time consecutive 8–10 years in the field.
- Earn the highest level of credential you can.
- Add relevant, higher education to your resume. (Earn a diploma or degree, go to graduate school).

- Choose between physical, information, and cyber security and or one of the like disciplines and focus deeper in those areas.
- Consider helping to write standards or guidelines, a white paper, book, articles, or speak.

We often get to a point where we are so busy that we miss the deadline, objective or get lost in the day to day and forget about our strategy. Here are some tips to keep on track.

Staying on target and keeping motivated

- Keep a calendar and task list. Keep them on your phone and computer. Forget the notebook, scraps of paper, stickies, newspapers, and napkins. That is not where you organize your work.
- Keep goals and objectives manageable.
- Open no more than two tabs at a time. Do not have four applications, several browsers, and ten videos on the go.
- Take notes, keep minutes, and agendas.
- Know when to say no.
- Close something small or easy before you add something else to the list.
- Complete the most important thing for the boss and the item that is due before the end of the week.
- Keep your desk spotless.
- Don't lug piles of work back and forth each day. Keep your bag, case, etc., clean and clutter free. Take one small item home to complete, or just keep your inbox well managed while you are out of the office.
- Speak up and ask for help.
- Delegate appropriately.
- Do what needs to be done, not what someone else feels is urgent.
- Keep time between meetings. Block time to work quietly.
- Work is for work, not shopping, surfing, or watching shows.
- If your phone is distracting, lock it in a drawer.
- Classical or instrumental music is easier to concentrate on than videos or talk radio.
- Do not write a novel when a paragraph will do.
- Hand in good reports, not large reports. Quality, then quantity.
- Tell yourself how great it is to be a security professional and avoid daydreaming.
- Get engaged with the industry and work, it will keep you motivated.
- Work hard, do not procrastinate, tackle the thing you least want to deal with first.

Some of us do not delegate enough, while some delegate everything. Some delegate to the superstar only and some delegate by reward (give the best jobs to favorite staff). Keeping the team engaged at just the right level can be challenging.

Motivating the team

- Assign a team member to share a word of the day.
- Start a team quarterly newsletter.
- Encourage people to join workplace committees and to attend workplace teams, clubs, outings, and functions.
- Treat them well, like adults, like professionals.
- Thank them by saying thank you.
- Acknowledge their feelings and or efforts even when you have to say no or not great.
- Don't ignore them and try not to micromanage. Teach or share information.
- Hold team meetings, save time to talk about the big picture, for questions and answers and listen sincerely. Being dismissive is a track for a poor relationship or worse.
- Deal with problem staff head on, up front, and on time.
- Go for a meal, host pot luck, have a picnic.
- Suddenly break up the mid-week monotony and have a stretch break, play some music, and pass out refreshments and treats. Say thank you to everyone.
- Let them present on something interesting they are working on.

Conclusion

Being a CSO, is a privilege. It takes a long time and a lot of dedication to your career no matter what path you took to get there. Sometimes a little personal sacrifice and some smart decisions pay off. We cannot forget the family, friends, staff, and leaders who help us get there and gave us a shot. By being the very best you can be, you are paying them back as they share in the rewards. If you are working in the security field today, I am quite certain that you have an incredible career ahead of you. You will make lifelong friendships, have the honor of seeing and doing some cool things, and will be placed with a lot of trust and responsibility.

One day you may be wearing a guard uniform and several years later you may be helping secure matters of national security. You may find yourself halfway through your career as a new CSO still wondering how you ended up there. The earlier on in your career you realize, then accept, and in time embrace your role in security the happier and more rewarding your career will be. The next generation of leaders will have set out to go to school to become security professionals. These people will have the best careers of all. They will have known what they wanted to do and have realized their dream. So much trust is placed in us and we have an opportunity today as CSOs to help create a profession that everyone is proud of. I know that by working together, with a common interest that serves this industry we can bring some further uniformity to our career path, education, certifications, and jobs.

I am committed to meeting as many of you as possible, to learn from you, collaborate and share. I know that many people in this industry have taken the time to help me grow professionally and to become better at protecting people, information, and assets. I want to pay this forward. I hope to look back on a career spanning more than 40 years and be proud to have known many of you, to celebrate your successes, and to mark milestones in our efforts to elevate the security profession.

Appendices

I have provided the following three example organizational charts focused on Corporate Security.

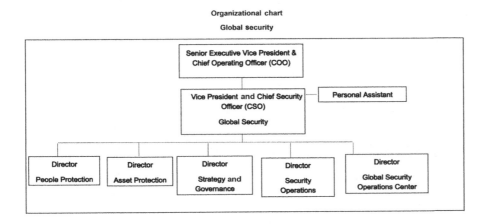

Organizational chart

Global security

- Senior Executive Vice President & Chief Operating Officer (COO)
  - Vice President and Chief Security Officer (CSO) Global Security — Personal Assistant
    - Director — People Protection
    - Director — Asset Protection
    - Director — Strategy and Governance
    - Director — Security Operations
    - Director — Global Security Operations Center

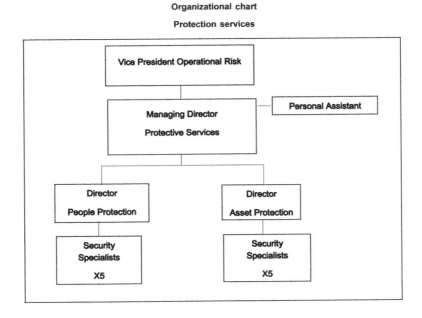

Organizational chart

Protection services

- Vice President Operational Risk
  - Managing Director Protective Services — Personal Assistant
    - Director People Protection
      - Security Specialists X5
    - Director Asset Protection
      - Security Specialists X5

227

Organizational chart

Security

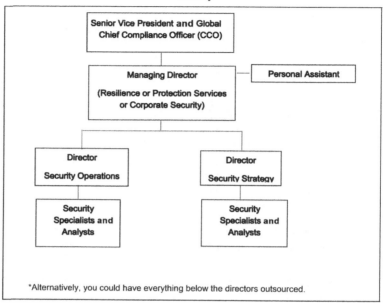

Senior Vice President and Global
Chief Compliance Officer (CCO)

Managing Director
(Resilience or Protection Services
or Corporate Security)

Personal Assistant

Director
Security Operations

Director
Security Strategy

Security
Specialists and
Analysts

Security
Specialists and
Analysts

*Alternatively, you could have everything below the directors outsourced.

Suggested reading

Books

Allen, B., Loyear, R., & Noakes-Fry, K. (Eds.), (2017a). *Enterprise security risk management.* Rothstein Publishing.

Allen, B., Loyear, R., & Noakes-Fry, K. (Eds.), (2017b). *The manager's guide to enterprise security risk management: Essentials of risk-based security.* Rothstein Publishing.

Baillie, C., & Sennewald, C. A. (2016). *Effective security management* (6th ed.). Oxford, UK: Butterworth-Heinemann an imprint of Elsevier.

Cabric, M. (2015). *Corporate security management; challenges, risks, and strategies.* Oxford, UK: Butterworth-Heinemann an imprint of Elsevier.

Cloutier, R. (2016). *Becoming a global chief security executive officer.* Oxford, UK: Butterworth-Heinemann an imprint of Elsevier.

Fennelly, L. J., Beaudry, M., & Marianna, P. (2017). *Security in 2025.* Alexandria, VA: ASIS International.

Goodman, M. (2016). *Future crimes: How our radical dependence on technology threatens us all.* Anchor Canada.

Hayes, B., Kane, G., & Kotwica, K. (2013). *Corporate security organizational structure, cost of services and staffing benchmark (research report).* Elsevier's Security Executive Council Risk Management Portfolio.

Hyacinth, B. T. (2017). *The future of leadership: Rise of automation, robotics, and artificial intelligence.* MBA Caribbean Organisation.

Peterson, D. (2018). *Enterprise security risk management: Building a world-class asset protection program.* Oxford, UK: Butterworth-Heinemann an imprint of Elsevier.

Smola, A., & Vishwanathan, S. V. N. (2008). *Introduction to machine learning.* Yahoo! Labs Santa Clara, Departments of Statistics and Computer Science, Purdue University, College of Engineering and Computer Science, Australian National University, Cambridge University Press.

Sorrelles, E. (2016). *Security litigation, best practices for managing and preventing security-related lawsuits.* Oxford, UK: Butterworth-Heinemann an imprint of Elsevier.

Tyson, D. (2007). *Security convergence, managing enterprise risk.* Oxford, UK: Butterworth-Heinemann an imprint of Elsevier.

White papers

Johnson. (2018). *Tomorrow's Chief Information Security Officer.* johnson.partners.

The CSO Roundtable of ASIS International. (2010). *Enterprise security risk management: How great risks lead to great deeds.* Alexandria, VA: The CSO Roundtable of ASIS International.

Articles

Dataversity. (2016). *The "Shape Shifting" role of the chief security officer.* https://www.expertsystem.com.

Elbeheri, A. (2015). *Enterprise security risk management: A holistic approach to security.* LinkedIn.

Fitzgerald, M. (2003). *All over the map: Security org charts: Where does security fit into the organizational chart? CSOs offer plenty of opinions, but consensus is hard to come by.* CSO From IDG.

Fruhlinger, J. (2018). *What is a chief security officer (CSO)? Understanding this critical role.* CSO From IDG.

Harris, J. (2018). *ESRM in action.* Alexandria, VA.: Security Management, ASIS International.

Qualtrough, E. (2016). *Barclays CSO and CISO roles merge—Chief Security Officer Troels Oerting on future threats and board support: Barclays security chiefs Troels Oerting and Elena Kvochko discuss cyber strategy and merging the CISO and CSO roles.* CIO From IDG.

Schlein, T. (2015). The rise of the chief security officer: What it means for corporations and customers. *Forbes.*

Security Management Staff. (2018). *Career pathways in security. Security Management.* A Publication of ASIS International.

Wackrow, J. (2017). *The evolving role of the chief security officer: Rethinking effective risk management for 2017.* CSO From IDG.

Wiessman Guthrie, C. (2016). *Chief security officer may be the job of the future that no one wants: The gold rush for top security leadership is anything but stable.* www.fastcompany.com.

Index

Note: Page numbers followed by *f* indicate figures and *b* indicate boxes.

Made in the USA
Middletown, DE
21 November 2019